# THE GREENPEACE BOOK OF CORAL REEFS

# THE GREENPEACE BOOK OF
# CORAL REEFS

## Sue Wells
## Nick Hanna

 Sterling Publishing Co., Inc.   New York

Library of Congress Cataloging-in-Publication Data Available

10  9  8  7  6  5  4  3  2  1

Published 1992 by Sterling Publishing Company, Inc.
387 Park Avenue South, New York, N.Y. 10016

Produced by Cameron Books, PO Box 1, Moffat
Dumfriesshire DG10 9SU, Scotland

© 1992 by Cameron Books and Greenpeace Communications

Distributed in Canada by Sterling Publishing
c/o Canadian Manda Group, PO Box 920, Station U
Toronto, Ontario, Canada M8Z 5P9
Distributed in Australia by Capricorn Link Ltd.
PO Box 665, Lane Cove, NSW 2066

Edited by Jill Hollis
Designed by Ian Cameron
Picture research by Jill Hollis

Greenpeace editorial adviser: Jeanne Kirby

Filmset by Cameron Books, Moffat
Reproduced by Brian Gregory Associates, St Albans
Chlorine-free paper made by Hannover Papier, Germany
Printed by Royal Smeets Offset, Weert, The Netherlands

Cameron Books gratefully acknowledges the help and support of
Jeanne Kirby and Sebia Hawkins of the Greenpeace Pacific
Campaign.

Sterling ISBN 0-8069-87952

*Picture Credits*

The illustrations in this book are reproduced by permission of the following
photographers and organisations. (Where two or more pictures appear on the
same page, they have been identified by letters in clockwise order from the top
left of the page.)

Ardea 96a (Jean-Paul Ferrero); 8b, 9, 12a, 22a, 23a, 47b, 48, 68 (Ron and Valerie
    Taylor); 63a, 78 (Valerie Taylor)
Barbara Brown 57a, 57b, 75a
Cameron Books 43
Coral Cay Conservation 26b, 149, 154
Nigel Downing 66, 84b, 84c
FLPA 51 (M. Newman)
Florida Institute of Oceanography 64a
Florida Marine Research Institute 90
Footprints back jacket, 17b, 34, 35b, 37, 45, 46, 71a, 94b, 100b, 106b, 107a, 107b,
    108b, 117, 131a, 133a, 134b, 147b (Andy Dalton), 21, 83, 91a, 109b, 110, 118a,
    118b, 119c, 127a, 130, 133b, 135a, 136, 139 (Nick Hanna); 93a (Cecil Ingham); 33a
    (Carlos Lima); 17a, 123 (Connie Rus); 97a, 103b, 103c, 104, 118c (Barry C. Russell)
Greenpeace 80, 137; 18a, 28, 70a, 103a, 115 (Robert Aston); 36 (Julie Brooks); 49
    (Kathleen Bryan); 27a, 69 (Michael Dean); 16a, 41a, 41b, 67b, 73, 74, 91b, 95b,
    106a, 143 (Lorette Dorreboom); 96b, 111a, 111b (Bob Edwards); 72 (Douglas
    Faulkner); 24 (John Goldblatt); 29, 108a (Roger Grace); 150b (Brian Lapointe);
    25a, 88a (Fernando Pereira) 84a (Elizabeth Salter)
Julie Hawkins 23c, 112
Martin Le Tissier 44, 81b
E. Lovell 22b
Angus Macfarlane 16c, 19b, 53a, 53b, 121

James Maragos 153
NHPA 97b (Bruce Barnetson); 129 (James H. Carmichael); 86b, 116a (Trevor
    McDonald); 10a, 38 (Ashod Papazian); 58a (Karl Switak); 10b, 14a, 47a, 77b
    (Bill Wood; 62 (Leon Zann)
Pitcairn Islands Scientific Expedition 27b (G. and M. Moss)
Linda Pitkin 1, 2, 3, 4/5, 12b, 13b, 14b, 30b, 32, 33b, 33c, 33d, 40a, 42/43, 59,
    60/61, 64b, 67a, 77a, 79, 82, 87, 89, 99, 100a, 102, 105b, 109a, 113a, 114, 116b,
    125, 135b, 148, 154/155
Planet Earth 128 (Pete Atkinson); 15 (Leo Collier); 85 (Georgette Douwma);
    145 (Nicholas Penn); 50, 152a (Doug Perrine); 141 (Flip Schulke); front jacket,
    120a (Peter Scoones); 140 (Herwarth Voigtmann); 134c (Bill Wood)
Oxford Scientific Films 11a, 81a; 35a (Jeff Foote/Okapia); 120b (Howard Hall);
    113b (Laurence Gould); 95a (Pam and Willy Kemp); 10c, 142 (Rudie H.
    Kuiter); 31b (Aldo Brando Leon); 31a (Zig Leszczynski); 54, 63b (Peter Parks);
    150a (James H. Robinson); 11b, 151 (Norbert Wu)
RIDA 25b (David Bayliss)
Saba Marine Park 146
Anne and Charles Sheppard endpapers, 13a, 16b, 18b, 19a, 30a, 55, 70b, 70c,
    126, 131b, 144, 147a
Smithsonian Tropical Research Institute 86a (Charles Hanson)
US Department of Energy 88b
Tom van't Hof 65, 75b, 86c, 127b, 138a, 138b
Sue Wells 23b, 26a, 39a, 39b, 40b, 58b, 71b, 76, 93b, 94a, 95c, 98, 101a, 101b,
    119a, 119b, 122a, 122b, 134a, 152b
Alan White 8a, 52, 105a, 132
Map (p.20) by Andras Bereznay

*Authors' Acknowledgements*

A book like this, compiled from information from diverse sources,
would not have been possible without the assistance and support of
numerous people. It is impossible to list them all by name, but our
thanks go to all those who responded so promptly and helpfully to
our requests for assistance.

We would like to thank all those in the Greenpeace Pacific
Campaign who provided information, and special thanks go to
Jeanne Kirby for her tireless efforts and support. We are also
particularly grateful to Dr Callum Roberts and Julie Hawkins for
their invaluable assistance in the final stages of the book.

In addition, Sue Wells would like to thank the numerous
colleagues and friends throughout the world who have shared their
conservation projects and data so openly over many years in the
hope that it will contribute to the wise management of coral reefs.
Thanks also to the World Conservation Monitoring Centre and
IUCN-The World Conservation Union, who supported early
information-gathering efforts for coral reefs, without which this book
would have been very much more difficult.

It is important to mention that some of the topics in the book are
controversial in the sense that there are contradictory theories and
different perspectives on their significance, but we have tried to
present a balanced view as far as possible. With a subject as topical as
coral reefs, research is providing new information daily. We have
tried to keep abreast of new developments and apologise for any
omissions. Any mistakes are, of course, the authors' responsibility.

# CONTENTS

# Introduction

A thriving coral reef is one of the most glorious sights on our planet. For sheer colour and exuberance, reefs can arguably outdo any other natural habitat, and in the huge diversity and number of plants and animals they support, they are second only to rainforests. And yet, paradoxically, these 'rainforests of the ocean' are found only in shallow tropical seas where the nutrients essential to growth are practically non-existent.

Coral reefs have existed for 450 million years, making them probably the oldest ecosystems on the planet. Coral animals, the remarkable little creatures that build reefs, are responsible for creating the largest structures made by life on earth – big enough, in some cases, to dwarf even the most ambitious edifices constructed by humankind. But this extraordinary ability is no defence against the assaults suffered by reefs as a direct result of human activities. Sewage and toxic chemicals are pumped over them, silt from construction sites chokes them, soil run-off smothers them, and boat and cruise ship anchors smash into them. They are even bombed with explosives by fishermen desperate for increased fishing yields where over-fishing has decimated the populations of fish. A survey in the 1980s found that reef damage had occurred in 93 of the 109 countries with reefs and coral communities.

Ironically, as reefs have become ever more stressed, their value to humanity has been thrown into sharp focus. Since the dawn of humanity, the biological abundance of coral reefs has provided sustenance for coastal communities in the tropics, yielding a bountiful harvest of food as well as many other products as diverse as building materials, medicines and jewellery. The possible yield from properly managed reef fisheries worldwide is enormous, and the range of medicines for which reef animals and plants may be a source is only just beginning to be explored.

Reefs also have an invaluable function as natural breakwaters, protecting the land and coastal settlements from the violence of the ocean and providing natural harbours. They are an essential defence against rising sea levels, and if they disappear artificial replacements would cost billions of dollars. The very existence of coral islands and many of the sandy beaches so beloved by tourists in the tropics is heavily dependent on healthy reefs, which are, of course, an important attraction in their own right.

Reefs have always been at risk from natural catastrophes, notably, ferocious hurricanes. In normal circumstances, they have a remarkable capacity for regeneration, but the continuous onslaught from human interference is now diminishing their ability to recover from natural impacts. And although we can only speculate at present, it is possible that humanity has unleashed the greatest threat to reefs yet in the form of increased sea temperatures caused by global warming.

The world community is now well aware of the plight of the rainforests and the threats posed by deforestation and global warming, but the dangers that face marine ecosystems are not so well known. Over the last decade, though, enormous advances have been made in our understanding of the problems facing reefs and in seeking solutions to safeguard their future. Many of these solutions have been there all along, embodied in the wisdom and traditional knowledge of the communities whose lives have been intricately connected to reefs for centuries. Other responses involve a creative partnership between local communities, conservationists and government, sometimes coupling modern management techniques with ancient customs, and, most importantly, taking a holistic approach to managing the land and the sea with all their interlinked habitats.

If you are lucky enough to visit a coral reef, treasure the moment and be aware of the fragility of this colourful and exuberant wilderness. This book aims to show that even if you live far away from coral reefs with no prospect of actually going to one, it is now time to act in their defence. They may be out of sight beneath the waves, but they should never be out of mind.

*Reef with several colonies of* Acropora *corals at Sipadan, Malaysia – south-east Asia has some of the most diverse reefs in the world.*

# CHAPTER ONE

# THE LIFE OF THE REEFS

Anyone snorkelling or diving over a coral reef for the first time is likely to find it a bewildering, mysterious place, teeming with life of every description in what appears to be a random explosion of exuberance and colour. But beneath the apparent chaos are complex processes and patterns of behaviour that allow vast numbers of reef creatures to share this habitat, creating an ecosystem of dazzling intricacy. Life on the reef is an endless cycle, always in flux, changing as constantly as predators chase prey and as night follows day.

The day dawns swiftly in the tropics, and within moments of the light spreading suddenly across the reef, the nocturnal inhabitants disappear into their chosen retreats. Soon the pace becomes hectic as other creatures emerge to take over areas just vacated by night-feeders. At first light, the daytime predators arrive in search of an early morning meal: sharks, barracuda and other ocean-going species move in to cruise and hunt along the reef wall and surge channels. In the early morning sunlight the fish seem to multiply, shoaling together for protection or darting from the cover of one coral to the next in their search for food.

Each creature, from the smallest shrimp to the biggest grouper, begins to work the reef to its advantage, exploiting the particular niche to which it is adapted. Flamboyant butterflyfish glide gracefully within the shelter of the reef, pausing from time to time to nip away at corals; unusually, these fish feed on coral, extracting the live tissue from the skeleton with their elongated snouts. Dark spots on their tails look like eyes (confusing predators who will attack the wrong end of the fish), and their flat, thin bodies allow them to hide in the narrowest of crevices. Butterflyfish often swim in pairs, creating a paintbox of colour against the deep blue beyond. Other daytime grazers seen on many reefs are gaudy parrotfish, so named both for their bright, parrot-like colourings and for their beak-like mouths, which are specially adapted so that they can

*Opposite:* Chromis, *members of the damselfish family, characteristically using staghorn coral* (Acropora *sp.*) *for protection.*

*Below left: long-nosed butterflyfish* (Chelmon rostratus) *on the Great Barrier Reef, and, right, another species of butterflyfish* (Forcipiger longirostris) *in the Philippines showing the effectiveness of a confusing eyespot.*

scrape at and eat the extremely fine sea-weed growth that coats much of the reef's surface.

Foraging in the same areas as parrotfish are territorial damselfish, many of which 'farm' the seaweed in their territories, aggressively keeping out other hungry herbivores and creating little patches of green seaweed 'lawn' on the reef. Some damselfish remove the larger seaweeds that they do not feed on, producing a fine, even turf of filamentous algae; others even go so far as to remove sea urchins that have come to feed on it. Surgeonfish keep competitors at bay with the threat of a swipe from the scalpel-sharp spines on the sides of their tails; also known as doctor-fish or tangs, they are one of the commonest reef herbivores all around the world.

While grazers like these keep seaweeds in check on the reef, other species feed on the plankton that sweeps past on ocean currents – minute plants and ani-mals often invisible to the human eye and including the larvae of numerous marine creatures, among them corals and other reef animals. During the day, huge schools of fusiliers patrol the reef feeding on plankton, relying on a swift turn of speed to escape when threatened by predatory fish. In channels between the lagoon and the open sea, manta rays hover effortlessly in the tidal currents, scooping up plankton in their gaping mouths as it flows towards them. Other plankton-feeders are the glittering, jewel-like *Chromis*, members of the large dam-selfish family, but they are less daring than bigger fish and will dart back to the protection of branching corals at the first hint of trouble. Some fish, like triggerfish and pufferfish, specialise in eating sea urchins, and hawksbill turtles graze on sponges on the reef, disappearing into the murky depths at the first sign of any human visitor.

In the shallow, sunlit waters of the reef lagoon, sea cucumbers proliferate, and conchs move slowly aross the bottom, grazing on seaweeds. The sand and coral rubble on the lagoon floor presents many fewer hiding places than the reef itself, and creatures that spend their lives there must adopt different tactics to escape preda-tion. They include flatfish such as flounders, which bury themselves in the sand leaving only their eyes exposed, lizardfish, sting-rays and the tilefish, which builds a system of burrows like a rabbit warren, pulling coral rubble over its many entrances to hide them. Another diligent engineer is the little jawfish, which builds burrows by using its mouth to shovel bits of sand and coral.

Other creatures go about their daily business with less fear of being eaten, like the remarkable pufferfish which, when threatened, sucks water into its abdomen and blows itself up to over twice its normal size, making too much of a mouthful for most predators. Spiny puffers and porcupinefish rely on a similar trick but with the addition of sharp spikes which project outwards when they inflate themselves, creating a significant deterrent. Many fish escape being eaten either by sporting bright colours, which warn predators that they are poisonous, or by having a camouflaged appearance that allows them to melt into the background and escape detection.

Mutually beneficial (or symbiotic) partnerships abound on a reef and show that there are more complicated patterns of survival than eat or be eaten. Several species of damselfish, called clownfish (*Amphiprion*) avoid predators by living among the stinging tentacles of sea anemones from which they are protected by a coating of mucus. During the spawning season the male defends the clutch of eggs deposited near the anenome with great tenacity, surprising even divers with its fierce determination in driving away intruders.

Another intriguing symbiotic partnership exists between cleaner fish and their 'clients'. Over fifty reef species live by cleaning detritus and parasites off larger fish, sometimes even entering their mouths

and gills to remove material. This grooming or valet service is habitually carried out at special locations known as cleaning stations; fish in need of a clean will visit a particular spot on the reef in the expectation of finding an appropriate cleaner species there. The routine is so established that fish may actually queue up for the service. This is an essential function: it has been suggested that if all the cleaner fish are removed from a reef, overall fish populations would decline and the health of those that remain would deteriorate.

Hermit crabs live in the cast-off shells of molluscs and sometimes camouflage themselves by attaching a sea anemone or sponge to the shell; the extent to which the anemone or sponge benefits from the free transport provided is not so clear.

Perhaps the most important symbiotic relationship on a reef is the one between a number of animals, notably corals, giant clams and some of the sponges, and the tiny, single-celled plants called zooxanthellae (*Symbiodinium microadriaticum*) that live actually within their tissues and use sunlight to photosynthesise, producing food not only for themselves but also for their hosts. During the day, giant clams expand their brilliantly coloured 'mantles' – the part of the animal that protrudes from the shell to catch as much sunlight as possible.

*Yellow-spotted burrfish* (Chilomycterus spilostylus) *inflated to an impressive degree as a strong disincentive to would-be predators in the Red Sea.*

*Above: a clownfish* (Amphiprion percleraion) *nestled among the stinging tentacles of its sea anemone host, safe from predators, and right, a steephead parrotfish* (Scarus microrhinus) *tries to ensure that it gets an undisturbed night's sleep by forming a web of mucus to prevent any predator from picking up its scent.*

*Opposite: two symbiotic relationships. Left, a moray eel* (Gymnothorax javanicus) *being attended to by a pair of cleaner shrimps* (Lysmata amboinensis). *Right, a cleaner wrasse is providing an efficient service for a coral trout. Cleanerfish eat shrimps and worms that live among coral, but a large part of their diet is composed of the dead scales and tissues, fungal growths and parasites that they remove from larger fish.*

As the light begins to fade from the tropical sky and dusk falls over the reef, predators such as grouper become more active. Lurking beneath overhangs or in caves, groupers cannily change colour to match their surroundings, preparing for ambush: in one swift onslaught from its lair, a grouper will devour its hapless prey, returning to hang motionless again, ready for the next surprise attack. With the onset of night, butterflyfish, parrotfish, wrasse, angelfish and other daytime animals begin to retreat into their chosen hiding places, nestling into the branches of soft corals or squeezing themselves into the smallest of spaces to escape detection. Angelfish and surgeonfish seek deep cracks in the reef; some wrasse bury themselves in the sand. Several species of parrotfish and some wrasse form a cocoon of mucus around themselves at night which acts as a protective envelope, trapping their scent so that they remain undetected by predators.

Diving by night is an unearthly experience as you float in the vast darkness surrounded by unseen eyes. But turn your flashlight on the reef and you will witness

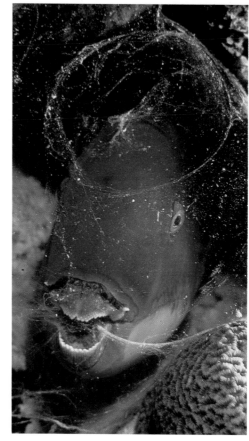

a scene which is as busy as it is during the day, although with different participants playing the leading roles. The characteristically large eyes of squirrelfish, soldierfish and cardinalfish help their night vision as they come out of hiding to feed on the plankton that rises up through the water as night falls. Perhaps the most extraordinary of nocturnal fish is the flashlight fish, which has bioluminescent pouches beneath its eyes that 'light up' at night, when flaps of skin are retracted from them, attracting the plankton on which it feeds; the fish can even blink its lights on and off, apparently at will, perhaps as a signal to others of the same species.

Many animals – prey and predators alike – change colour as night falls. Reddish colours are the first to alter, making some fish that look brilliantly coloured during the day appear black and virtually invisible. Pink and red squirrelfish and soldierfish, for example, hide practically motionless under coral overhangs or ledges during the day, emerging only at night to feed.

Fish such as jacks, snappers, porgies and grunts hide in the reef during the day,

moving away at night to feed in nearby seagrass beds. Many of the snail-like molluscs (called gastropods) are nocturnal and remain hidden on the reef during the day. *Trochus*, green snail, conch and scorpion shells move slowly around grazing on seaweeds. Others are carnivorous, among them the beautiful murexes, triton and trumpet shells, helmet shells and cowries. Many sea slugs or nudibranchs, including the flamboyant Spanish dancer (*Hexabranchus sanguineus*), hide from sunlight and venture out at night to feed on sponges, corals and anemones; their gaudy coloration clearly indicates to daytime predators that they are highly poisonous.

At night, the reef takes on an even more garden-like appearance. The corals themselves stretch out their tentacles to catch food from the plankton. Sharp-spined *Diadema* sea urchins, normally motionless by day, can be seen moving up the reef in an armada of bristling, waving spines, to feed on algae. Feather stars (which belong to an ancient group of animals called crinoids, related to starfish and sea urchins) make their way up the reef by dark

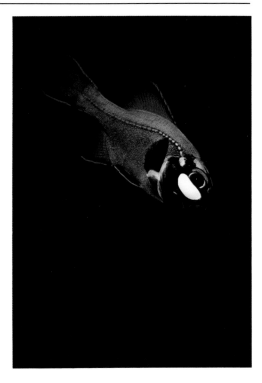

*The strange flashlight fish* (Photobletheron palpebratus) *with its bioluminescent pouches exposed – the light is produced by luminous bacteria to which the fish plays host.*

*Once thought to be plants, featherstars or crinoids can be extremely numerous in parts of reefs where there are good, food-bearing currents. The one pictured opposite (top) is characteristically perched on top of a section of reef where its frond-like arms can feed most easily on the plankton. Opposite, below: wonderfully colourful sea slugs in the Red Sea, their smart livery almost certainly a warning to would-be predators of their poisonous nature. The tufts of tentacles on their backs are gills.*

*Left: double-tooth soldierfish* (Myripristis hexagona) *venture wide-eyed into the dark, having hung motionless under an overhang in the reef during the hours of daylight.*

from their daytime crevices to perch high up, clinging to seafans or corals, unfurling their brightly coloured, feathery fronds and making the most of the food-bearing currents. Even more spectacular are their relatives the basket stars, whose delicate, multibranching arms also trap plankton.

Some of the larger animals associated with the reef are also more active at night. During the breeding season, green turtles labour up the beach and may spend several hours under cover of darkness digging holes in the sand in which to lay their eggs. The nightly rhythms of the reef continue until daybreak, when the whole process is again thrown into reverse. The nocturnal feeders retreat into their chosen hiding places and the daytime shift takes over; the crinoids curl themselves up and the corals, sensing the light, withdraw their tentacles into their stony skeletons. The cycle begins again.

## The Nature of Corals

The word 'coral' is applied to a range of different animals in the group (or phylum) known as Coelenterata. The name derives from the Greek 'coelenteron', meaning 'hollow gut', and refers to the central tube through which the animal feeds, breathes and removes waste.

Corals can be broadly divided into two groups: those that build reefs (hermatypes) and those that do not (ahermatypes). The crucial difference between these is that the hermatypic corals (sometimes called hard or stony) contain zooxanthellae within their tissues and ahermatypic corals do not.

The coral animals or polyps that are the architects of the reefs look like tiny sea anemones, another of the animals in this important and diverse phylum, which also includes seafans and jellyfish. Each polyp is like a short, hollow tube with the base sitting on or in its limestone skeleton and a mouth at the top surrounded by tentacles. Coral polyps range in size from less than a millimetre to several centimetres in diameter. The tentacles are armed with small stinging cells called nematocysts which fire out barbed darts to paralyse and capture plankton drifting by in the currents. But this satisfies only a small proportion of the polyp's needs, and most of its food comes from another source altogether: the tiny zooxanthellae, which are invisible to the human eye and live within the coral tissue. The coral polyp supplies the zooxanthellae with carbon dioxide, and the zooxanthellae use sunlight to convert this, together with carbon dioxide from seawater and their own waste products, into oxygen and carbohydrates. The excess carbohydrates are taken up by the coral polyp and used to good advantage: the carbon is used to make limestone or calcium carbonate – a process known as calcification – so building the stony skeleton in which the polyp lives. Most of the polyp's food comes from these captive plants and the partnership is the key to the building of the impressive and fantastic structures that are coral reefs. This symbiotic relationship explains why reefs grow where they do: in shallow clear seas, and rarely below a depth of forty metres, for without sunlight, the zooxanthellae cannot perform.

## Types of Coral

'The corals constitute a chaotic collection of individuals, and the uncertainty as to what may be considered a species is the first problem that must confront anyone who happens to study corals . . .' so wrote Fredric Wood-Jones rather desperately in 1907. Like other early reef scientists, he was baffled by the difficulties of categorising different corals. A great deal more is now known about them, but the classification of corals is a problem that continues to dog modern marine biologists.

Most reef-building or hermatypic corals are in the group of coelenterates called the Scleractinia which have stony, limestone skeletons. A few are found in other related groups, such as the fire corals (*Millepora*) in the family Milleporidae, organ-pipe coral (*Tubipora musica*) in the family Tubiporidae, and blue coral (*Heliopora coerulea*) which is in the group Coenothecalia.

There are numerous non-reef-building or ahermatypic corals. These feed on plankton alone and are able to grow in locations such as dark caves and overhangs, and in deep, cool waters where reef-building corals cannot survive. Although many are often found on the reef, ahermatypic corals cannot secrete enough limestone to create the large structures that form it. They comprise a very wide range of species, some

*This hardyhead (*Pranesus *sp.) would normally be part of a large shoal whisking round the reef, but appears to have been stunned by the stinging cells (or nematocysts) of these* Tubastrea *polyps. (Corals usually use their stinging cells to catch tiny animals in the plankton.)*

*Opposite: coral reef scene in the Bahamas including the spectacular pillar coral (*Dendrogyra cylindrus*).*

*Below: soft corals (*Dendronephthya *sp.) in the South China Sea.*

## Precious coral

Most commercially valuable precious coral comes from the Mediterranean or from deep seamounts in the Pacific. Valued since prehistoric times, precious coral has long been carved into masterpieces of statuary and jewellery. Mediterranean precious coral (*Corallium rubrum*) has been exploited for centuries, and Torre del Greco, just south of Naples in Italy, is the centre of a flourishing coral-carving industry. As the traditional coral grounds off Spain, Italy, Greece and North Africa became increasingly over-exploited, the trade turned to the rich stocks of the Pacific which are currently extracted by the Japanese and Taiwanese. Many of these beds are now also over-exploited. Efforts to introduce sustainable management are underway in the Mediterranean, but are hampered by the secretive, competitive and family-based nature of the industry.

One of the most damaging aspects of precious coral harvesting is the frequent use of dredging devices such as the Italian bar and the St Andrew's Cross, which have widely replaced the traditional, more selective method in which divers harvest individual coral colonies, choosing them according to size and quality. The Italian bar is a cylinder up to six metres long with nets attached to chains on the bar and weighs over a tonne. Like other types of fishing using dredges, it strips large areas of seabed of marine life, damaging far more coral being than is actually harvested; in some instances the coral beds have been completely destroyed. In 1986, Greenpeace campaigned against the use of the Italian bar in Spanish waters. An encounter between the Greenpeace boat Sirius and a coral fishing boat using this method generated a great deal of publicity, and, soon after, the Italian bar was made illegal in Spanish waters as it is in several other countries.

rather distantly related. Soft corals are common inhabitants on reefs, tending to thrive where strong currents bring plentiful supplies of plankton, and extending their vividly coloured tentacles to feed: as their name implies, they lack a rigid skeleton. Bushy forests of black coral and the long trailing whip corals (both in the group Antipatharia and known commercially as semi-precious corals) often grow on reefs and in deep caves. They have horny, flexible skeletons which in some species can be polished and used to make jewellery.

The beautiful pink, red, gold and other precious corals of the jewellery trade occur in cooler or deeper waters and are not found on tropical reefs, although colonies may occur in large beds on the sea floor or attached to rocks. They are more closely related to the coelenterates called seafans than to reef-building corals, and their internal, jointed calcareous skeleton can be polished to gem-like quality.

## Coral Reproduction

Corals reproduce in two ways. Asexual reproduction occurs when the parent polyp buds or divides to form a daughter polyp, an exact genetic copy of the parent, to which it remains attached, linked through the living tissue. By this method, new polyps are gradually added and a coral colony is built. Only the outside of the colony has living polyps; the inside is made up of the accumulated dead skeletons of earlier polyps. New colonies can grow from broken fragments of larger colonies if the conditions are right; this is one way in which reefs recover from damage inflicted by storms and hurricanes. A few corals, both reef builders, such as the mushroom coral (*Fungia*), and non-reef-builders, are solitary and do not form colonies – their polyps grow to a large size but remain alone.

Corals can also reproduce sexually by spawning: releasing eggs and sperm into the sea. The sperm then fertilises the eggs in the water, and a new individual, called a planula larva, develops.

As recently as 1982, it was discovered that corals often spawn en masse on the same night once a year. On the Great Barrier Reef over 130 species of coral spawn

*Some black corals are long and whip-like; others, like this colony, are bushy. These non-reef-building corals usually grow at depths below twenty metres.*

*Opposite, left: star coral (Montastrea sp.), with clearly separate individual polyps, and, right, an aptly named brain coral (shown here with tube sponges), in which the polyps and their skeletons are fused to form complex wavy-lined patterns.*

*Remarkably, many corals on the Great Barrier Reef, like this Acropora, spawn on the same night of the year.*

in a single night, releasing countless millions of eggs and sperm into the water in a synchronised event without parallel in the animal world. This takes place more or less predictably after dark in the week following the full moon in the late spring or early summer. (In other places where coral spawning has been observed, however, species spawn within a fairly short time of each other but are less well-synchronised, or, sometimes, do so at completely different times.)

No-one is exactly sure why or how this extraordinary mass spawning takes place. Temperature, tides, day length and the moon may all play a part in triggering the event. The swirling mass of eggs and sperm may confuse predators such as fish and so give the fertilised eggs a greater chance of surviving, and the slight tides that occur at the equinoxes when spawning usually take place may give eggs and sperm a better chance of mixing before being swept away. Some species of starfish, marine worms and other reef invertebrates also synchronise their spawning.

The coral larvae, which float up towards the light and join the plankton, can be up to a millimetre in length and variable in shape, depending on the species. They already have zooxanthellae (passed on by the parent polyp) in their tissues. If they survive, they will float for several days or weeks, according to the species. Eventually, the larva swims down and settles on a hard, rocky surface, such as a dead coral skeleton or piece of bare rock. It then changes into a polyp and begins to form its limestone skeleton and to reproduce asexually to create a new colony.

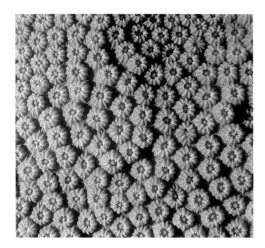

## The Growth of Reefs

Close examination of the surface of corals reveals as many patterns as there are species. These complex and intricate living sculptures are created by multiples of the cup-shaped limestone depression which each polyp builds and in which it lives, and the shape of the colony is influenced by the way in which the polyps bud to form identical copies of themselves. In many species, such as the massive boulder-like *Porites* corals, star corals (*Montastrea*) and the branching *Acropora* corals, a polyp gradually takes on an oval shape and forms a second mouth, eventually splitting in half to form two distinct polyps. In other species, the polyps never completely separate, and long lines of partially budded polyps are formed that create wavy patterns across the surface of the colony, as in various species of brain corals.

The bewildering variety of shapes and sizes of coral colonies depends not only on the species, but also on where the coral is growing. On a reef front, for example, where there are strong waves, corals tend to grow into robust, mound-like or flattened shapes. In sheltered, more gentle environments such as the reef lagoon, delicate branching forms proliferate.

The amount of light available also affects the shape of a colony and some species are highly adaptable, able to grow differently depending on whether they are close to the surface or in deeper,

more sheltered parts of the reef. The branching *Montipora* corals are particularly variable: in shallow water they form thickets of bushy growth whereas in deeper water, they spread themselves more thinly, taking on the shape of enormous plates. In some cases this may be so that the zooxanthellae can catch the maximum amount of light, although some species grow in this form even in shallow water. Some corals can adapt to different conditions on the reef while others can grow only in conditions which suit their requirements fairly exactly in terms of available light, strength of currents and water clarity.

The final result of the accumulation of coral colonies, new ones overlying the dead skeletons of old ones, is the creation of a reef. As the colonies grow and eventually die, they leave behind hard skeletons for other corals to settle on, or other creatures to colonise. The dead corals at the base of the reef slowly break down to form sediment and coral sand, which in time become compacted into coral rock.

Many corals grow very gradually, and the creation of a reef can take centuries. Among the slowest-growing are the massive corals, which increase at the rate of between five and twenty-five millimetres a year, and reach great ages, with some colonies living for hundreds of years. In the 1970s, scientists discovered that if they passed an X-ray through a section of a coral, annual growth rings (like those found in trees) would show up. Some corals on the Great Barrier Reef have been discovered by this method to be 800 to 1000 years old. A three-metre high coral in Florida probably started growing

*Above: a luxuriant growth of 'table' or 'plate' coral, Papua New Guinea, and, opposite page, bottom, a colony of staghorn coral (Acropora sp.) on the Great Barrier Reef. Two kinds of algae also play important parts in building and strengthening reefs: Halimeda (below) of which some species are so vigorous that the stalks grow a new pad every day, and (opposite page, top), red calcareous algae.*

at about the time the Pilgrim Fathers landed in America in 1620.

Branching species of coral grow much faster, especially Caribbean staghorn (*Acropora cervicornis*), which can increase by up to ten or twenty centimetres a year, about ten times the rate of growth for massive corals, but their branches are very fragile and easily broken by waves and storms.

Other organisms apart from corals contribute to the structure of the reef. Red calcareous (or coralline) algae may form heavy encrustations, helping to bind the framework together. These are common on Pacific atoll reefs where they form hard ridges in the breaker zone, helping the reef to withstand strong waves. Often, much of the sediment and sand that fills the gaps in coral reefs is formed by the breakdown of an unusual seaweed, *Halimeda*, which has tiny, plate-like leaves containing calcium carbonate. Large solid sponges

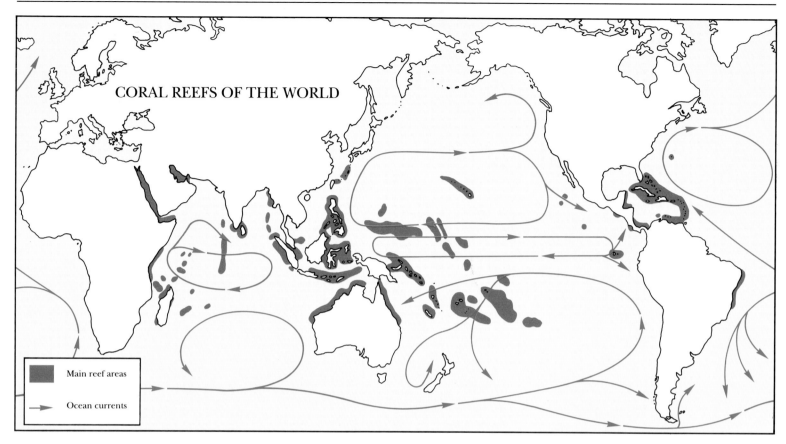

CORAL REEFS OF THE WORLD

Main reef areas

Ocean currents

also play their part, particularly in deeper waters, and on some reefs, molluscs such as giant clams, oysters and the vermetids (which live in shells strangely shaped like worm casts) strengthen and increase the amount of calcium carbonate on the reef. Patch reefs in the lagoon of Takapoto, one of the atolls in French Polynesia in the Pacific, have been estimated to be made of some 70 million bivalves (clams, pearl oyster and other species) which almost swamp the corals.

Reefs do not, of course, grow as fast as the individual coral colonies, since corals are constantly being broken by storms and waves or eroded by predatory and grazing animals. When a coral dies, its skeleton is quickly overgrown by seaweeds and then attacked by a variety of animals that bore into the skeleton: dead staghorn branches have been known to disappear within a year in this way. Boring and eroding animals often operate in succession. Worms are often the first in, boring tubes and creating a habitat for the other animals that follow. Amazingly, it is the innocuous-looking sponges which can have the biggest impact: some species bore into corals by

releasing chemicals which break down coral skeleton into tiny coral chips. These fragments then filter down and form part of the structure of the reef, in some cases accounting for as much as forty per cent of the sediments on a reef.

Grazing animals also affect reef growth. Surgeonfish, parrotfish and sea urchins all eat algae that lives on both live and dead coral as well as on encrusting algae. Parrotfish crush up the limestone skeleton that they scrape away with the algae, and excrete it as a fine sediment in their faeces; sea urchins tend to remove large quantities of dead coral while browsing on filamentous seaweeds. All these activities slow down the growth of a coral reef, making it extremely difficult to measure the actual growth rate of a whole reef. One way of doing the calculation is to work out how much calcium carbonate is produced, and biologists measuring this have estimated that reefs grow upwards at between one and fifteen millimetres a year. The rate varies according to the type of reef and its location (atolls seem to grow more slowly than fringing and barrier reefs) and an average is about seven to ten millimetres a year.

## Where Reefs Are Found

Coral reefs grow only in warm, shallow, tropical seas. Seawater temperature is a very important factor – the optimum is around 26 to 27°C. Most lie between the tropics of Cancer and Capricorn, and the majority are found in the Caribbean, around the Indian Ocean islands, in the Red Sea and Arabian (Persian) Gulf, around the island nations of south-east Asia, and in the South Pacific. They are also found where warm currents flow out of the tropics; the Gulf Stream allows reefs to grow in Florida and Bermuda, for instance, and in the Indo-Pacific warm currents permit their growth as far north as southern Japan and in the southern part of the Great Barrier Reef region. Cold currents prevent reef growth, so there are no reefs on the west coast of Africa and most of western America.

Some corals, however, do manage to grow, albeit more slowly and less luxuriantly, at both higher and lower temperatures. Reefs in the Arabian (Persian) Gulf, for example, can survive enormous fluctuations in temperature from as low as 13°C in cold winters to up to 38°C in the summer. Corals used to more stable climates would die if subjected to such extremes.

Ocean currents and the length of time that coral larvae can survive are other factors that influence where coral reefs are found. The larvae of some corals settle within a few hours of forming, and these species tend to have narrow distributions; others drift for days, weeks or months and are likely to be found on reefs distributed across the oceans. Some, for example, are found from the east coast of Africa all the way across the Indian and Pacific Oceans. Coral larvae sometimes settle and grow into small colonies on floating objects such as volcanic pumice stone, coconuts and logs and may be dispersed to new reefs by 'rafting' on ocean currents. At the end of the last century, corals were found on the Cocos-Keeling Islands in the Indian Ocean attached to small pieces of pumice that had originated from the 1883 Krakatau eruption in Indonesia. And more recently small pieces of pumice with corals attached have been found in Hawaii; these pumice fragments almost certainly came from the eruption of Volcan Barcena on San Benedicto Island off the eastern coast of Mexico in 1952.

In both the Atlantic and Pacific Oceans, warm, eastward-flowing currents are either absent or weak, and this, combined with the cool currents found on the eastern sides of these oceans, explains the lack of reefs on the west coasts of Africa and the Americas. But in the Pacific Ocean, the easterly current increases every ten to fifteen years during the phenomenon of changed weather patterns called El Niño and at this time coral larvae may travel much further, as did the early Polynesians who were able to use El Niño periods to pursue their eastward migrations across the Pacific. Reefs are found on both sides of the Indian Ocean because the monsoons cause a complete reversal of currents each year, so that larvae are distributed around the ocean.

As well as temperature and ocean currents, a number of other factors affect coral growth and thus reef distribution. Although corals in shallow waters, as on reef flats, may be able to tolerate temporary flooding with fresh water, they can be damaged or killed by prolonged heavy rainfall or soil run-off from the land. Reef growth tends to be poor or non-existent near river mouths, which explains why there are no reefs on the coasts around the Amazon, the Mississippi, the Ganges and the Indus.

Dark, deep waters, muddy habitats and strong wave action all provide poor conditions for coral growth, and true reefs rarely form under such conditions. Sometimes, however, 'communities' of corals grow that may look like reefs but lack the ability to actually build up on themselves.

Some volcanic islands, like Niihau in Hawaii, are subsiding too fast for true reefs to form, but thriving, non-reef-building coral communities grow on the underwater slopes of limestone and basalt. In the deep and sometimes turbid waters of the Gulf of Mexico, flourishing coral communities are found on some of the limestone knolls that rise from the sandy sea floor. The Florida Middleground, for example, has a rich community, dominated by sea fans and coral with horny skeletons, but including a number of stony corals. Like true reefs, these attract large populations of fish, and the Middleground is the site of an important commercial snapper and grouper fishery.

## The Parts of the Reef

Different communities of animals and plants live in different parts of the reef system, reflecting varying environmental conditions in several fairly clearly defined zones.

Lagoons – the areas of water that are separated from the open sea by the reefs – are an important part of most reef ecosystems. They vary enormously in size and depth, but generally have a sandy floor and, except in closed atolls, good tidal circulation. Lagoons often support a rich community of plants and animals that thrive in sandy habitats such as seagrasses, sea cucumbers and burrowing animals. Sometimes corals are entirely absent, but often they are scattered over the lagoon floor, becoming more abundant towards the reef itself. The sheltered waters of deeper lagoons provide ideal conditions for the growth of large colonies of branching corals, as well as coral-covered outcrops, bommies or pinnacles.

Where the water is deep enough, on the lagoon side of the reef, there is often an area of rich coral growth called the back reef, with corals that thrive among gentle water currents.

The reef flat can be a gentle slope running from the beach to the reef front or the flat area between the lagoon and the reef front. It is made of sand, mud, rocks, seagrass, seaweed and scattered corals. This reef flat is regularly exposed to the air by very low tides and may be covered by only a metre or so of water at normal

*Uninhabited island, the Maldives. The pale strip of water immediately in front of the island is the lagoon and reef, far shallower than the surrounding ocean.*

*Above: this enormous coral colony or bommie in Kiribati has formed a miniature reef system, providing a home for other corals and reef animals. Left: a coral colony growing in shallow intertidal waters has been forced to grow outwards rather than upwards, as a result of being exposed to the air regularly at low tide; the central part has died and the living colony forms a ring-shaped structure, called a micro-atoll.*

low tide, so it is only the most resistant corals that can survive here. As they are unable to grow vertically upwards after a certain height, the coral colonies are forced to grow horizontally outwards, sometimes leaving a dead, flat and eroded centre, forming a 'micro-atoll'.

Coral abundance and diversity gradually increase seaward across the reef flat to the reef crest, the highest part of the reef where the waves break. On windward oceanic reefs and those exposed to heavy surf, there may be an algal crest of coral-line algae which forms the highest and most resistant point of the reef. From the reef crest, the fore-reef (or reef front or reef slope) descends into deep water; it can sometimes be divided into an upper and a lower fore-reef, which have different species of coral living on them according to the amount of light available and the force of wave action. The upper fore-reef is often the richest part of the reef, as it is at the optimal depth for coral growth and receives plenty of light and a steady supply of food and oxygen in the waves and currents that cross it. Sometimes, buttress-like projections of coral grow out from the reef at these depths and what are known as 'spur and groove' formations develop. The spurs are covered with a dense and diverse growth of corals, and the grooves become deep, sandy channels, swept clean by waves and tidal currents. Coral diversity gradually decreases down the lower fore-reef, until it is dominated by flat and encrusting colonies of corals like *Turbinaria*, *Leptoseris* and *Porites* that are tolerant of low light intensities.

The reef itself is often inextricably linked to other habitats. In the open oceans, these may simply be the tiny coral cays or sandy islets found on atolls. Elsewhere, reefs tend to lie adjacent to seagrass beds and mangrove swamps, and complex relationships evolve between the various habitats.

The clarity of unpolluted tropical seas and the excellent visibility which so delights divers on reefs is due to the fact that the water contains very little organic matter or sediment. Much of the tropical ocean is a vast aquatic wasteland, a 'nutrient desert', and yet, paradoxically, it is home to coral reefs, which are one of the richest ecosystems in the world. What makes this

possible is a complex system of recycling nutrients via the food webs that link all the inhabitants of the reefs and sometimes adjacent habitats such as mangroves and seagrasses. Like other animals and plants, corals need nutrients such as nitrogen, phosphorus and trace elements in order to grow. Nitrogen is extracted from the water by microscopic blue-green algae on reef flats, other seaweeds on the reef and bacteria in reef sediments and seagrass beds. Blue-green algae and seaweed fragments are then swept onto the reef in currents and are eaten by animals there. Bacteria can also remove dissolved phosphates from reef waters, and in turn become food for reef invertebrates. Fish play a major role in the recycling of nutrients on the reef, which are returned to circulation through their faeces.

Mangroves, of which there are over fifty species, are an important part of coastal ecosystems in the tropics: they fringe about twenty-five per cent of the coastline, particularly along estuaries and muddy coastlines where plenty of fresh water runs into the sea from the land. Mangrove forests are dark, swampy places and are frequently the first victims of coastal developers, who see them as nothing more than a breeding ground for mosquitoes. But they are, in fact, crucial breeding grounds for many other creatures and home to numerous invertebrates, fish and birds. The extensive aerial root systems of mangroves provide a firm base for the attachment of oysters and mussels, and supply oxygen to the below-ground roots of the plants. Many juvenile fish, including reef species, shelter and feed among the mangrove roots, at a relatively safe distance from the many predators on the reef. This nursery habitat can be of great importance; in some areas, certain species of juvenile reef fish have been found to be twenty times more abundant on reefs that are near mangroves and seagrass beds than on those that are isolated.

There are only about fifty species of seagrass (which is the only marine plant to produce flowers), but it is widespread in all seas, often forming dense beds in shallow sandy areas adjacent to inner reef flats; in clear water seagrass may grow as deeply as twenty metres down. These beds of

vegetation slow down currents and so probably encourage the settlement of larvae; they also provide a nursery habitat for numerous species including reef fish and spiny lobsters. The leaves offer a place of attachment for eggcases, small invertebrates and seaweeds. Some sea urchins, surgeonfish and parrotfish eat seagrass, tending to graze the areas closest to the reef (to which they retreat for shelter) and so creating 'haloes' of bare sand in the beds around patch reefs. Seagrass is also a major part of the diets of turtles and dugong, and dead seagrass is eaten

*Top: lettuce coral (*Turbinaria *sp.) is often found in deeper parts of the reef where it grows in large, plate-like formations to catch every available bit of the rather limited amount of light filtering down through the water. Above: mangroves, showing their characteristic aerial roots, in Honda Bay, Palawan, the Philippines.*

*Left: seagrass (*Thalassia testudinum*) in the Hol Chan Marine Reserve, Ambergris Caye, Belize, Caribbean Sea.*

by detritus feeders such as crabs and sea cucumbers, often after being carried by currents far from where it originally grew.

Just as mangroves and seagrass beds make an important contribution to life on a reef, so coral reefs help to protect them from erosion by waves, provide some of the sediment for the muddy habitats of mangroves and form the sandy seabeds needed by the roots of seagrasses. In their turn, seagrass beds and mangroves trap sediment from the land – soil run-off and silt suspended in river water – so protecting the reef from the harmful effects this could have. Dead plant and animal remains containing nitrogen and other nutrients are swept over the reef from seagrass beds and mangroves, providing food for reef creatures. Mangroves and seagrasses themselves provide valuable food for many organisms, from bacteria up to fish, that are eaten by larger fish commuting from neighbouring reefs.

Rich reefs can, of course, be found away from such habitats, as in the case of remote oceanic atolls, but where they do exist side by side, the complex relationships that have developed between them are critical to the maintenance of each ecosystem and the disturbance of any one can have profound impacts on the others.

Sandy beaches and those small, sandy islands so often depicted as the archetypal 'desert island' (known as cays or keys in the Caribbean, and *motus* on Pacific atolls) are an integral part of the reef ecosystem. They consist of sand and rubble from the skeletons of corals and other reef animals that have broken down and have then been washed onto the reef flat by waves and currents; gradually, as the sand and rubble accumulates, the deeper layers become cemented into a solid mass called beachrock. At least in their early stages, beaches and cays are very vulnerable to erosion by wind and waves, often changing shape or even washing away completely. Some coral islets remain as mere slivers of sand, but others eventually become stable enough for vegetation to take hold, although they rarely get more than two to three metres high. The plants which survive on coral cays are generally those that can tolerate salt water and have seeds which can travel long distances in the sea – such as coconut palms and pandanus.

Uninhabited coral cays and atoll islets are often important nesting sites for marine turtles and seabirds such as pelicans, frigatebirds, boobies, gulls and terns. On undisturbed cays where there are no predators, sea bird colonies can be enormous: Rose Atoll in American Samoa, for example, sometimes accommodates over 310,000 birds of twenty different species. On Bird Island, a coral cay in the Seychelles, over two million sooty terns visit during the breeding season. Many seabirds depend partly on coral reefs for food; for example, half the diet of the crested tern (*Sterna bergi*) on the Great Barrier Reef is made up of reef fish.

Coral islets are also the last remaining stronghold of the coconut crab (*Birgus latro*), whose populations elsewhere have been decimated by people killing them for food. The largest terrestrial invertebrate in the world, the coconut crab can measure up to a metre across from leg tip to leg tip.

## A Turbulent History – Reefs of the Past

Fossil reefs can be found far inland today, for example in the centre of the Australian sub-continent, or remote from tropical seas, as in the cold, windswept fells of the Lake District in the north of England. Their presence indicates the enormous forces of nature that created the oceans and continents as they are known today. The first reef-like structures appeared about 2000 million years ago, well before the evolution of animals, when life consisted of simple plants and bacteria. They were built by plants, called blue-green algae; these formed mounds known as stromatolites which trapped limestone sediment. Fossil stromatolites can still be seen in several places across the world, and colonies of living stromatolites still retain a precarious hold on existence in Shark Bay in Western Australia.

Communities more like modern reefs, with algae, sponges and early forms of coral, started to dominate warm shallow seas about 450 to 500 million years ago. Symbiosis between plants and corals may have evolved on these reefs, enabling them to benefit from the sun's energy through photosynthesis, as reefs do today. These 'reefs' covered huge areas 350 million years ago, but were wiped out in the first wave of mass extinctions of marine life 245 million years ago. The reef-building corals of today began to appear about 10 million years later, developing first around the shores of the western Tethys Sea, in the area that is now southern Europe and the Mediterranean. By 150 million years ago, many coral species had evolved and had become widely distributed.

A second and even larger wave of mass extinctions took place 65 million years ago when about one third of all animal groups disappeared, including the dinosaurs and many corals. Once again

*Uninhabited coral cays, like this one in the Pacific which has been formed by the accumulation of sediment on top of a reef, often provide safe breeding sites for sea birds such as red-footed boobies (Sula sula); a juvenile is shown opposite.*

*Fossil coral (Isastrea) dating from the Middle Jurassic period and found in Gloucestershire, in the west of England.*

new coral species evolved and by about 50 to 20 million years ago reef distribution in the Caribbean and Indo-Pacific had pretty much taken the form it has today.

During the Ice Ages (1.8 million years ago), seawater was frozen into the expanding polar ice caps, and sea levels fell, leaving most coral reefs high and dry. As the climate has warmed over the last 20,000 years, the sea has risen by about 100 metres, but not at an even rate. About 10,000 to 15,000 years ago it was rising at the rate of 10 to 20 mm per year and many atoll reefs probably drowned. Fringing reefs also drowned but new ones were able to develop at higher levels on high islands and continents. For the last 6,000 years, sea level has risen at an overall average of about 10 mm per year, although over shorter time periods the rate has varied. Sometimes it has been higher, but for the last hundred years, for example, it has slowed to a rise of only 1.2 to 1.4 mm per year.

## Types of Reef

Taken in the context of geological time, reefs have undergone remarkable changes. They have survived continental drift, land subsidence, sea level change, and the consequences of the Ice Ages: repeated, dramatic temperature fluctuations, rapid changes in rainfall and soil run-off, among other environmental factors. All this means that the shape, structure and distribution of modern reefs probably have less to do with the particular species that built them than with geological history: the depth and shape of the ocean floor, the geology of the area and past sea level changes.

A fundamental distinction can be made between shelf reefs, which form on continental shelves, as in the Caribbean, and oceanic reefs which develop in deep waters, such as most of those in the Pacific. Within these two broad divisions there are a number of different reef types.

*Fringing reefs* grow along the edges of continents and around islands, close to shore but sometimes separated from it by a shallow lagoon. Fringing reefs are common in the Caribbean, in south-east Asia, in the Red Sea and around the Indian Ocean. Where there is murky water

caused by soil run-off (washed into the sea as silt), fringing reefs rarely grow to any substantial depth.

*Barrier reefs* develop along the edges of continental shelves or around islands that have become partially submerged (see description of atolls below), and are separated from the mainland or island by a wide, deep lagoon. More fragile corals grow on the lagoon side of the barrier than on the open ocean side where they would have to withstand the force of large, more violent waves.

The best-known example is the Great Barrier Reef which extends for nearly 2,000 kilometres along the east coast of Australia and represents about three per cent of the total of the world's reefs. Although it has evolved like a barrier, it is in fact not a true, continuous barrier reef but comprises a string of individual reefs known as ribbon reefs. Other important barrier reefs are in Belize and the Bahamas in the Caribbean, and Papua New Guinea, New Caledonia and Fiji in the Pacific.

*Atoll reefs* generally begin as fringing reefs around volcanic islands. As the island subsides, because of the sea floor sinking or the sea level rising, the fringing reef forms a circular barrier reef separated

*Left: fringing reef, surrounding the high volcanic island of Moorea, French Polynesia, in the Pacific. Above: Laughing Bird Cay, one of the islets on the Belize Barrier Reef. Opposite, top, part of a large atoll, Tarawa, one of many that make up Kiribati in the Pacific Ocean, and, bottom, a complete atoll, Ducie Island in the South Pacific.*

from the island by a lagoon. When the island finally disappears, the circle of reefs is left, sometimes capped with small coral islands, enclosing the lagoon. The whole structure is called an atoll.

Atolls vary in size from tiny Rose Atoll in American Samoa at only 640 hectares in area including its lagoon, one of the smallest in the world – to Kwajalein in the Marshall Islands, which covers over 2,000 square kilometres and has a lagoon which reaches depths of over 60 metres. Atolls are often found in chains, indicating the presence of former mountain ranges. Most atolls are in the Pacific, but there is a long chain in the Indian Ocean stretching from the Chagos Archipelago in the south, through the Maldives to the eleven atolls of the Lakshadweep (Laccadive) Islands (which belong to India) in the north. The word atoll comes from the Maldivian word *atolu*.

There are no true atolls in the Caribbean, although some reefs on submerged rises or mountains have circular atoll-like shapes, such as Glovers Reef that lies just outside the Belize Barrier Reef.

Reefs grow in many other shapes and forms; as with much of the natural world, it is difficult to put them all into carefully defined categories. Many are intermediate between two of the main forms. Chuuk (Truk) Lagoon in the Federated States of Micronesia and Bora-Bora in French Polynesia, for example, are known as 'almost-atolls', as they are halfway to becoming true atolls – the central islands have not entirely disappeared yet. On continental shelves and in deep lagoons, patch or platform reefs develop on hard rocky outcrops on the sea bed in shallow areas, and in similar, but deeper waters, larger so-called bank reefs form.

## Inhabitants of the Reefs

Reefs are home to more species than any other ecosystem in the sea. The total number of reef species in the world is still unknown, but up to 3,000 species can be found together on a single reef in south-east Asia, and over 1,000 on a single Caribbean reef. Only tropical rainforests, estimated by some to be home to a staggering 30 million insects, have a greater number of species, although due to the vast number of fish that inhabit them, reefs contain a larger number of vertebrates (animals with backbones) than rainforests. Reefs also have many more major animal groups (or phyla) than any other ecosystem on land or in the sea.

How do so many creatures live together in such crowded conditions? The key lies in the extraordinarily complex web of inter-related but different patterns of behaviour and specialisations among reef species. At One Tree Reef in Australia, nearly 150 species of fish have been recorded in an area of less than fifty square metres. Such high diversities are made possible by specialisation. Some fish, like butterflyfish and territorial damselfish, spend their entire lives on the reef; others, such as some sharks and schools of pelagic (open sea) jacks, use it only for feeding. Some fish are active only at certain times of day or night: the parrotfish sleeps at night and feeds during the day; squirrelfish do the reverse.

The richest reefs, with the greatest diversity of plants and animals, are in the region bounded by Indonesia, Malaysia, the Philippines and southern Japan. Of the 700 or so reef corals that are known in the world, 600 are found in this region; over 400 are found in the Philippines and Japan, and about 350 in Indonesia, although there are probably many more to be discovered here. Up to 200 corals may occur on a single reef in south-east Asia. This high diversity extends equally to other reef animals and plants (for example, about 2,000 fish are known from the region), and is partly due to the fact that the greatest area of reefs is found here (giving more opportunities for new species to evolve) and partly because of its geological history. When the sea level was lower, the region comprised three separate basins, within each of which numerous species evolved.

The variety of species on a reef decreases eastwards across the Pacific. On the Pacific coasts of Costa Rica, Colombia and Panama, reefs are built by just eleven corals, and the Hawaiian Archipelago, on the north-eastern edge of reef growth, has about forty-five coral species. Fish diversity drops from the 1,000 species known in Belau (Palau) to about 600 in the Hawaiian Archipelago, and 300 in the Eastern Pacific. This decline is due partly to the fact that conditions for reef growth become less good towards the east; islands and shallow waters for reef growth become increasingly sparse, and the water currents are un-favourable for the transport of larvae. In the Indian Ocean, conditions are more favourable and fairly high diversities of reef species are found all the way across to East Africa and the Red Sea. The Atlantic and Caribbean also have low diversities, with a total of only 70 to 75 coral species, none of which are found in the Indian and Pacific oceans, and about 520 fish species. This region separated many thousands of years ago from the Indo-Pacific, and at that time had a relatively poor reef flora and fauna. Although the environmental conditions in the Caribbean are now appropriate for reef growth, the area has still not caught up with the long history of the Indo-Pacific region, in terms of numbers and diversity of species.

Unlike terrestrial animals, few marine animals are endemic or restricted to a small area – the result of their larvae floating freely in the oceans. The exceptions are species that do not have floating larvae or have larvae that float in the currents for a very short time around isolated reefs or in semi-enclosed seas. Although most coral species are very wide-ranging, ten corals are unique or endemic to Brazil, several are endemic to the Red Sea, and at least one species is known only from the Chagos Archipelago in the middle of the Indian ocean. Up to twenty per cent of corals and thirty per cent of fish in Hawaii are thought to be endemic, although further work on the many remote and unstudied reefs in the Pacific may show that they have wider distributions. Some corals, even if wide-

spread, occur in very small populations. In Indonesia about 150 corals are rare or very rare, and about a third of all corals found in Japan are rare or have restricted distributions.

*Fish.* Reefs have a spectacular variety of fish: over 4,000 to 5,000 species have so far been described, and there are almost certainly more to be discovered. Their prodigious array of colours, patterns and body shapes reflect the innumerable habitats available: the surging waves on the

*A blenny (*Cirripectes *sp.), one of the smallest fish on the reef, lurking in a dead barnacle shell, surrounded by an encrusting sponge. This is the kind of crevice in the reef where the female will lay her eggs, deserting them immediately afterwards and leaving the male to defend them.*

*Opposite: A school of gold-lined sea bream (*Gnathodentex aurolineatus*) and a couple of snapper (*Lutjanus *sp.) on a reef in Belau, Micronesia.*

reef crest, the relative calm of a pool on the reef flat, the sandy bottom of the lagoon, or the darkness of deep caves on the outer reefs. Reef fish include some of the smallest known fish, such as tiny gobies, some of which are less than a centimetre long, and some of the largest: the sharks.

*Echinoderms.* Starfish, brittle stars, sea cucumbers, sea urchins and feather stars all belong to the group known as echinoderms or 'spiny-skinned' animals. All echinoderms have a unique radial structure and tend to be easily visible, since they are comparatively large and live on the surface of the reef and on sandy lagoon bottoms. They too show an immense diversity: there are, for example, known to be up to 100 species of sea cucumber in the Pacific waters of Chuuk Lagoon alone. Sea urchins play a very important role in creating reef sediments

and keeping seaward growth on the reef at bay, but in large numbers they can damage reefs. Perhaps the most infamous echinoderm is the crown-of-thorns star-fish (*Acanthaster planci*) which can devastate reefs in the course of its coral-eating.

*Crustaceans*, among them large spiny lobsters, prawns and crabs and the tiny, delicate coral shrimps, are protected by a hard external skeleton like a jointed suit of armour. They too are numerous on reefs, often spending much of their time hidden in crevices. There is still much to learn about the ecology and behaviour of crustaceans and about how many there are on reefs. Many, like cleaner shrimps, have symbiotic relationships with other reef animals, in the same way that cleaner fish obtain food by removing external par-asites living on fish.

*Molluscs* are even more abundant on reefs than fish, and display a similar vast range of form and function: about 4,000

*Opposite, top: nurse shark (*Nebrius ferrugineus*), which, despite its size (it can grow up to 3.2 metres long), is a docile creature, unlikely to harm divers; bottom: a brittle star, a close relative of starfish on a*

*sponge. Above: the pretty little golden coral shrimp (*Stenopus sp.*), which often goes unnoticed by all but the most observant divers. Below: spider or arrow crab (*Stenorhynchus seticornis*) with the giant Caribbean anemone*

species live on the Great Barrier Reef alone. They include giant clams, sea slugs, snails, octopuses and many other varied forms and are an essential part of the reef food web, providing up to twenty per cent of the diet of many fish.

*Sponges* are among the simplest of marine creatures in terms of their structure. Their bodies are simple aggregations of cells that enclose a system of canals through which water is pumped, bringing food and oxygen and removing waste. The name of the phylum, Porifera, means 'pore-bearer' and describes the surface of the animal which is covered in tiny holes. Like many reef invertebrates they are sedentary, that is they stay in one place, and filter minute organic particles from the sea water; some, like corals and giant clams, have symbiotic zooxanthellae. Their bodies are strengthened by spicules, which according to the species, are made of calcium carbonate, silica or other compounds. Ancient reefs of 420 million years ago consisted mainly of sponges and although modern reefs are formed largely by corals, sponges are still an important component. Many sponges are poisonous to most other reef creatures, but others provide food for fishes, turtles and molluscs.

*Marine Worms.* Perhaps surprisingly, coral reefs teem with marine worms. Many live in coral heads and dead coral rock: in a single dead coral (weighing a mere three kilogrammes) from the Great Barrier Reef, a staggering 1441 worms, belonging to 103 species, were found. The most attractive and conspicuous marine worms are the tube-dwelling fan worms and Christmas tree worms, both of which have brightly coloured and patterned crowns of tentacles which they use for filtering food.

Numerous other lesser known and smaller groups of animals inhabit reefs. Jewel-like anemones are found scattered over the rocky surfaces of drop-offs (the steep, ocean-facing side of the reef where it falls away from the reef crest) or buried in lagoon sediments with only their petal-like tentacles visible. Sea fans wave their feathery fronds in the currents to catch plankton. Sea squirts – strange, leathery, sac-like animals that live up to their name by squirting jets of water when disturbed – are found in colourful clusters.

*Above: a most decorative sea slug (Chromodoris sp.) from Borneo. Opposite, top left: rough file clam ( Lima sp.), which like many clams has an uninteresting shell, is a delightful sight when the soft part of the living creature is exposed; bottom left,  pink vase sponge (Dasychalina cyathina), gorgonians and fairy basslet (Gramma loreto) in the Caribbean; top right, colony of fan or tube worms (serpulids) in the South China Sea; bottom right, sea squirts (Didemnum molle), so-called because, after taking in water through one opening, they 'squirt' it out of another, removing food and oxygen from the water as it passes through them. These are colonial sea squirts which have individual inhalant syphons, but share the communal exhalant syphon at the top of each colony.*

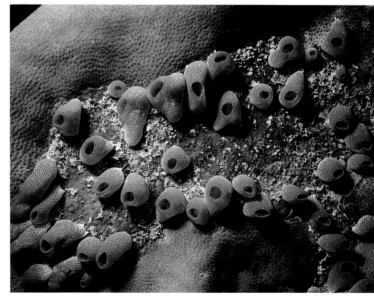

Although animals are often the most obvious inhabitants of the reef, the reef community as a whole would not survive without plants, which capture the sun's light to produce energy and form the basis of all the reef food webs. The zooxanthellae play an essential role, but numerous larger seaweeds are also important, forming – as they do – the main food for many fishes and invertebrates. Many, like red coralline algae and the green *Halimeda,* have calcium carbonate in their tissues, and when they break down, they form an important part of the reef sediments.

*Mammals and Reptiles.* Few marine mammals and reptiles can be described as true reef animals but several species are often spotted near reefs and may visit them to feed. Up to ninety per cent of the diet of the Hawaiian monk seal (*Monachus schauinslandi*), for instance, consists of reef fish. Sea snakes are still fairly common and are often encountered streaking over reefs of the Indo-Pacific, but most large marine vertebrates are now comparatively rare, their populations heavily reduced by human exploitation.

Caribbean monk seals (*Monachus tropicalis*) are now probably extinct, and the Hawaiian monk seal has a precarious hold on existence, with remaining populations now found only in the remote and now protected North West Hawaiian Islands. The dugong (*Dugong dugon*) of the Indian and Pacific Oceans, and the manatees (*Trichechus* sp.) of the Atlantic and Caribbean feed entirely on seagrass and other rich vegetation, and so are often found near reefs, though rarely on them, as they prefer the better protection and more plentiful food afforded by silty waters. Dugongs and manatees are both now endangered: they have been hunted extensively in the past, and are now threatened both by the disappearance of their shallow-water habitats, and by human activities such as power-boating. Dolphins and some of the whales that live or breed in tropical waters, such as humpbacks (*Megaptera novaeangliae*) are occasionally seen near reefs.

Turtles are often seen on reefs. The hawksbill (*Eretmochelys imbricata*) is most closely associated with coral reefs, and is found all round the world in the tropics,

nesting on small beaches and coral cays and feeding on sponges and invertebrates on nearby reefs. Green turtles (*Chelonia mydas*) are also found in the whole of the tropical belt, and are often seen swimming near reefs, but they feed mainly in shallow-water areas on seaweeds and seagrasses. The loggerhead (*Caretta caretta*) is also a circumtropical turtle and may be found in the same general areas as reefs, feeding on a variety of bottom-living invertebrates; with its powerful jaws it can easily crush the shells of clams and conchs. Its main nesting populations are in Oman and Florida. The Olive Ridley (*Lepidochelys olivacea*) is an Indo-Pacific turtle and nests on mainland rather than island beaches. The Leatherback (*Dermochelys coriacea*) is unique in spending most of its life in the open seas around the world, foraging mainly in temperate waters for jellyfish. But it nests on tropical sandy beaches and so may occasionally be encountered in coral reef environments. Marine turtles are all now threatened, the result of being continually hunted by humans for their eggs, meat, shell and skin.

Above: manatees (Trichechus manatus) are seen only occasionally on reefs, preferring the protection of the more turbid waters of sea-grass beds.

Opposite: bottlenose dolphin (Tursiops truncatus) exploring a reef crest in the Caribbean in search of a meal.

Right: green sea turtle (Chelonia mydas) asleep under a coral colony.

# CHAPTER TWO

# PEOPLE & REEFS

There have been people living near coral reefs since prehistoric times, making use of the rich source of food they provide as well as depending upon them for other common necessities such as tools (made from shells) and building materials (coral rock) for their houses.

Little is known about the earliest communities that subsisted on or near reefs, but archaeological sites where coastal people lived often reveal middens – prehistoric rubbish dumps – with large numbers of shells of reef species and fish bones. Some of the early Aboriginal people who arrived in Australia from south east Asia around 15,000 BC lived by harvesting fish, crustaceans and molluscs from coastal waters, though archaeological evidence is scant, as the Barrier Reef of today is several metres higher than the original reefs, and the sites where the Aboriginals lived are now deep below the ocean surface, covered when sea levels rose at the end of the Ice Age. Perhaps, one day, exploration of caves deep under the outer Barrier Reef may reveal more about the Aboriginals'

early existence. Middens 2000 years old on the south coast of Papua New Guinea have shown that the local people used to eat a far greater range of species than are harvested today, particularly of molluscs.

Archaeological excavations in 1991 on remote Henderson Island in the eastern Pacific have shown that Polynesians lived there between the 13th and 15th centuries, and a rock shelter has been discovered which contains thousands of well-preserved bird, fish and turtle bones, coral grinding tools and adzes made out of giant clam shells. Food remains showed that large quantities of reef products were eaten, including the meat of turban shells, turtles, crabs, lobsters and a variety of reef fish such as surgeonfish, jacks, porcupinefish, wrasse and groupers. The Polynesians abandoned the island around the seventeenth century for reasons that are as yet unknown, and Henderson is now uninhabited.

Reefs are still a crucial source of food for coastal people in the tropics all over the world, yielding a huge number of edible creatures, among them lobsters, limpets,

giant clams, octopuses, sea urchins, parrotfish, surgeonfish, goatfish and snappers. Different people develop tastes for different species. In Japan, pufferfish are considered a great delicacy, in spite of the fact that without highly skilled preparation they can (and do) cause fatal poisoning. The Palolo worm, which leaves the reef and comes to the surface in huge numbers to reproduce, is regarded by the Samoans as a special treat. The spawning is triggered by the moon at the autumn equinox and harvesting of the worms at this time is a major social event. In many cultures, turtles, sea snakes, dugongs and manatees have in the past been killed for subsistence use, and the practice continues where abundance and legislation allow, though large marine animals and reptiles are now much less plentiful than they used to be and many species are endangered. Seaweeds, which contain essential vitamins and minerals, are also eaten.

A wide range of non-food products for everyday use derive from reefs. Shells have long been used for decoration, either as

*Opposite: school of horse-eye jacks* (Caranx latus). *Jacks have been eaten by humans since prehistoric times, and are usually caught by hook and line as they patrol the edges of reefs in search of food.*

*Puffer fish* (Arothron mappa). *Several species of puffer fish are referred to as 'fugu' by the Japanese and eaten as a great delicacy; specially trained cooks have the difficult task of avoiding the various highly poisonous parts of the fish (which can include the blood) to prepare this sought-after food.*

*Above: yellow goatfish (*Mulloides vanicolensis) *in the Red Sea – another common food fish that congregates in large schools and makes trips out from the reef to feed in the lagoon and other sandy-bottomed areas.*

*Opposite, top: coral on the south-west coast of Sri Lanka, where it is collected in huge quantities from the reefs and, as rubble, from*

*the beaches, and burnt in simple kilns to make lime. On some Pacific islands, fine lime made from coral is chewed with betel nuts, which are popular in some parts of the tropics and seem to act as an appetite suppressant; bottom: a wall constructed of coral in the Maldive Islands, where coral is a commonly used building material because of the shortage of any alternative.*

jewellery or simply to adorn the walls of houses. Throughout countries in the Indian and Pacific Oceans, cowries (particularly *Cypraea moneta*, the money cowrie, and *Cypraea annulus*, the ring cowrie) were collected in huge quantities and the shells used in their natural state as currency. In Papua New Guinea, money cowries and other marine shells have been used for barter between coastal and highland peoples for over nine thousand years. In Kenya, money cowries are still collected and strung into necklaces, which are used in bartering for basic food stuffs, paraffin and matches in some coastal communities.

Coral blocks provide a readily available source of building materials and have long been used in house construction in many parts of the tropics. On small islands and atolls such as the Maldives, where there is little stone or rock on land, coral was and still is the only local source of building material. Building blocks are cut as whole chunks from the coral rock, and cement and road aggregate are made by grinding up coral. Another reef resource, queen conch shells, has been used for construction in the Caribbean, crushed up and added to cement to provide additional strength.

Both coral skeletons and shells can be burnt to make lime, which has a variety of uses. In the Caribbean, lime made from queen conch shells has been used for whitewashing houses. In many Asian and Pacific cultures, chewing betel nut is a widespread habit, and in the Pacific, the lime which is commonly chewed with the betel is made from stony corals; lime made from live coral is said to taste better than that made from dead coral. (This seemingly insignificant use of coral in fact accounts for a surprisingly large quantity being harvested: on the island of Yap, the 5,000 or so betel chewers consume around half a kilo of lime each a week, amounting to about 130 tonnes per year.)

Traditional, pre-industrial use of reefs for food, decoration and building in small, coastal communities has probably had relatively little impact on reef ecosystems. Not only has the level of exploitation usually been slight in terms, for example, of the quantity of any one species taken, but the very fact that the people of these societies have until recently depended on the

health of the natural world for their own survival has given them a detailed knowledge of their environment and a keen awareness of the finiteness of its resources. Systems of using the reefs have often been developed to ensure that these resources were not over-exploited.

Many subsistence fishermen in the tropics clearly understand the need for the conservation of fish stocks, a fact that has been only belatedly recognised in temperate-zone fisheries. Some of the conservation measures now being taken tragically late in the day by westernised countries (such as closed seasons and closed areas) were being used by reef fishermen centuries ago.

In some cases, such conservation measures may have been intentional; in others, local customs and beliefs have served the same purpose inadvertently. Laws and decrees (or taboos) which prevented certain foods being eaten, helped to avoid resource depletion. On some islands in the south Pacific, for instance, eating turtle and octopus was the exclusive privilege of local rulers, and these foods were forbidden to the common people. Sophisticated systems of taboos combined with a rich storehouse of ecological knowledge acquired over the generations has meant that for the most part traditional communities have lived without damaging the long-term future of their environments.

## Reefs in the Twentieth Century

The development of global trade, the steady westernisation of economic systems and population growth have all contributed to a radical alteration of the exploitation patterns of the past in many tropical countries. It used to be the case that only those people living near the reefs made use of them; commerce with outsiders was limited to what changed hands through a small amount of trade and barter.

Nowadays, reefs provide food and materials for consumption and use all over the world. Improved methods of transport and dramatically expanding populations have led to more intensive harvesting of reef species and subsequent overfishing. With the erosion of the knowledge and beliefs that formed the cornerstone of these communities and ensured sensitive use of reef resources, exploitation in many cases has escalated beyond the capacity of the reef to support it.

Another significant factor has been the development of export markets for species that fetch high prices overseas. Traditional fisheries harvest an enormous variety of animals, but commercial markets switch the focus to particular species: mother-of-pearl shells have a high cash value in the luxury goods market, lobsters and fish such as grouper (which can be processed or frozen for export) also command high prices. This selectivity depletes certain species and erodes traditional fishing customs. An early example was the demand for mother-of-pearl in Asia and Europe at the end of the l9th century. By the beginning of this century, reef molluscs such as pearl oysters, green snail and *Trochus* were being traded in huge quantities. Around 35,000 fishermen were involved in this trade in the Arabian (Persian) Gulf, and a similarly large fishery was operational in the Gulf of Mannar between India and Sri Lanka. Pearl oysters can still be found in both areas, but no longer support commercial fisheries – the industry's attentions have now been transferred to Australia and the Pacific.

With every new use that is found for reef species in commerce and industry, reef depletion has escalated rapidly. Giant clams, for instance, are collected mainly as food, but their shells have become increasingly popular as curios; there is also an industry in Indonesia that crushes them up to make high-quality flooring tiles – up to 650 tons of giant clams per month were being brought into the capital of Jakarta for processing during the 1980s. As supplies have dwindled and live clams have become increasingly rare, the industry has turned to fossil clams dug out of reefs and beaches.

*During the day, giant clams expand their coloured mantles (the part of the animal that protrudes from the shell), to catch as much sunlight as possible, which is then used by the zooxanthellae living in symbiosis with the giant clam, in the same way as the relationship works for coral polyps. Some of the eight giant clam species are quite small. The burrowing giant clam which lives half-buried in dead coral is only five to seven centimetres long, but the largest species are the giants of the bivalve (two-shelled mollusc) world. The largest can live for fifty years or more growing up to a metre in length and weighing over two hundred kilogrammes. Their fleshy meat is popular throughout much of the Pacific and is greatly sought after in Asia.*

*Floor tile, manufactured in Indonesia, whose main component is crushed giant clam shells.*

These are just some of the better-known examples of pressures that far exceed any impact subsistence use has generally had on reefs; but the general development of coastal areas (including the growth of tourism) has also taken its toll on reef ecosystems around the world.

The process has been well illustrated in American Samoa, where for many centuries the Samoans had lived in harmony with their reefs, relying on them for subsistence. A complex system of traditional rights, with ownership of reefs vested in the village chiefs, used to ensure that the reefs were protected from generation to generation. At the beginning of this century, when the country became an American dependency, many of the 5,000 or so inhabitants of the main island of Tutuila still relied on the reefs for food. In one of the earliest detailed reef surveys, carried out between 1917 and 1920, the American biologist Alfred Mayor described the extensive reefs in Pago Pago harbour as 'luxurious'.

The first major change came with World War II, when Pago Pago Bay became an important US military base and was subjected to dredging and land reclamation. By the 1950s, a commercial tuna fishery had been introduced, with American-owned canneries being built in the harbour and the development of a modern fleet of 250 tuna fishing boats. The area became increasingly industrialised, necessitating further dredging for harbour space. By the 1970s, the bay was busy with freighters and fishing boats. To cope with the growth in air travel, the airport was extended out into the lagoon, and reefs were dredged to supply material for building roads.

As a result of these outside influences, Samoans began to eat more canned and processed food. Their immediate dependency on the reef decreased, and with it, inevitably, their sense of responsibility for reef resources. It takes only one generation for knowledge that is passed from parent to child by example to begin to be lost. Now, the emphasis has shifted from using the reef to feed one's own community to taking much larger quantities of food for sale and ultimately export. The downward spiral continued: destructive fishing methods such as poisoning and dynamiting began to be used, and littering and dumping of rubbish on reefs and lagoons became common. By 1960, the total population of American Samoa had reached 20,000; it now numbers nearly 50,000, with some 35,000 people living in the vicinity of Pago Pago harbour.

In the late 1970s, marine biologists resurveyed the same reefs that had so delighted Mayor in Pago Pago Bay in the early years of the century. Only two sites still had healthy living reef; fifty years of abuse meant that the rest had disappeared or suffered grave damage.

It is difficult to put a precise figure on the area of reef that has been damaged worldwide as a direct result of human exploitation and neglect, but it is clear from examples such as American Samoa that the impact can be devastating. The scale of the problem has given added impetus to reef research, and biologists are now studying the health of reefs and setting up monitoring programmes to follow reefs over time so that these changes can be better understood and appropriate conservation measures implemented.

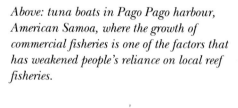

*Above: tuna boats in Pago Pago harbour, American Samoa, where the growth of commercial fisheries is one of the factors that has weakened people's reliance on local reef fisheries.*

*The health of reefs in American Samoa has worsened as human pressures on them have increased. This damaged reef in Fagatele Bay is now in a marine sanctuary, which will, it is hoped, give it a chance to recover.*

## Reef research

The study of coral reefs got off to a late start compared to the study of many other aspects of the natural world. This was not surprising: reefs lay a long way from the early European centres of science and biological study, and, like all marine ecosystems, could be investigated only by observation from the surface or the scrutiny of samples brought up from the seabed.

Until the 16th century, it was generally thought that corals were plants (particularly colourful and luxuriant areas of reef are still referred to as 'coral gardens'). But early naturalists realised that corals were not typical plants and coined the name 'zoophytes' or 'animal plants' for them. It was not until 1752 that French biologist Jean André Peysonnel described corals as animals: he had realised this some ten years earlier, but it was considered such an outrageous idea at the time that he had published anonymously in order to preserve his reputation. Unfortunately, this did not immediately clarify matters, as the honeycomb appearance of coral skeletons led others to think that reefs were built by industrious insects.

*Left: coral reef scene with colourful soft corals and glassfish (Anthias sp.) in the Red Sea. An early reef biologist called William Beebe gives some idea of the excitement felt by early biologists on seeing reefs close up for the first time in his book* Beneath Tropic Seas *(1928): 'The general impression of hours and days spent at the bottom of the sea is its fairy-like unreality. It is an Alice's Wonderland, where our terrestrial experiences and terms are set at naught. The flowers are worms, and the boulders living creatures; here we weigh but a fraction of what we do on land; here distance is sheer color and the sky is a glory of rippling light . . . Until we have found our way to the surface of some other planet, the bottom of the sea will remain the loveliest and strangest place we can imagine.'*

*An improbable juxtaposition, not least because of the disparity in sizes: flamingo and gorgonian looking like a tree from Mark Catesby's* Natural History of Carolina, Florida and the Bahama Islands *(1731-43).*

With the expansion of maritime trade to the tropics during the l9th century, the coral reefs of the world finally became more easily accessible to western scientists. Naturalists and scientists were soon fascinated and enthralled by the complexities of reefs and the intricacies of their geological history, biological processes, evolution and community structure.

For early scientists, one of the great mysteries about coral reefs was how atolls and barrier reefs originated. The development of fringing reefs seemed to be easy enough to understand, but how did barrier reefs and atolls grow in the middle of the oceans, thousands of feet above the sea bed?

The answer was supplied by Charles Darwin, whose pioneering book on the natural history of coral reefs, published in 1842, could be considered to mark the beginning of reef science. While on his five-year voyage around the world in HMS Beagle, Darwin formulated the theory that as volcanic islands slowly subside beneath the sea, the reefs surrounding them grow upwards at the same rate. Eventually just a ring of coral, the atoll, is left, with the island completely submerged. The only atoll that Darwin actually visited was Cocos (Keeling)

in the Indian Ocean, where he landed in April 1836, towards the end of the Beagle's voyage. The only way to prove his theory, however, would have been to drill through the limestone of the atoll to show that it lay on volcanic rock. Aware of the lack of proof and the doubt surrounding his explanation, Darwin wrote towards the end of his life: 'I wish some doubly rich millionaire would take it into his head to have borings made in some of the Pacific atolls and bring home cores for slicing from a depth of 500 to 600 feet.'

In the 1920s, efforts were made to test the idea by boring through the atoll of Funafuti in Tuvalu, but the scientists were unable to drill deep enough and failed to hit the underlying volcanic rock. Finally in 1952, just over a hundred years after Darwin had proposed his theory, he was proved correct when two holes were drilled in Enewetak Atoll in the Pacific, which showed that the limestone was over 1,500 metres deep and that beneath it, as predicted, was volcanic rock. The fossils found at the bottom of the drill cores were all of shallow-water species, showing that these strata had once been at sea level. Only four years after Darwin's voyage, an American geologist, James D. Dana, visited many Pacific atolls and reefs on several expeditions dedicated to reef research, and by 1881, Alexander Agassiz was mapping the reefs off Florida from a steam launch in an effort to understand their geology.

The greatest advances were made once scientists ventured under the water and on to the reef. Humans have been lured underwater since prehistoric times, in search of food, pearls, sponges and other valuable products, but they have always been restricted by having to come to the surface frequently for air. Greek sponge divers and the pearl divers of the Orient performed fantastic feats in staying underwater longer than any ordinary swimmer would expect, but it was not until the invention of diving suits in the 19th century that it became possible to stay beneath the surface for any meaningful length of time.

The earliest diving studies on reefs were carried out in 1914 when William H. Longley and Alfred Mayor, clad only in overalls and sneakers for protection, became the first biologists to wear diving helmets in the Caribbean. Mayor also pioneered the world's first reef laboratory on behalf of the Carnegie Institute of Washington, which was established in 1904 at Dry Tortugas, an island at the end of the Florida Keys.

By the 1930s, underwater studies on reefs were being carried out in many parts of the Caribbean using primitive methods such as the system developed by biologist William Beebe, who dived using air provided by a car tyre pump connected via a hose to his helmet.

The invention of scuba gear (the name means Self-Contained Underwater Breathing Apparatus) by Jacques Cousteau and Emile Gagnan less than fifty years ago revolutionised reef research, allowing detailed studies to be carried out for the first time. Despite the advances achieved using scuba equipment, most reef research is still restricted to fairly shallow water (down to depths of around sixty metres) but the development of underwater photographic and video equipment has been enormously valuable in adding to our knowledge of reef processes.

Study of the deep reef became possible in the 1960s and 1970s with the development of submersibles and so-called underwater habitats, again pioneered by Cousteau who, in 1963, spent a week in his 'underwater house' in the Red Sea. Today, marine biologists can live on the seabed for extended periods of time in environments such as this, so gaining access to far deeper reefs than they could explore by other means for such long periods, only having to decompress once on the final ascent to the surface.

New laboratory techniques have also meant that reef research has made enormous strides over the last decade. The annual growth rings, similar to those found in trees, that show up in X-rays of coral skeletons, have not only been found to reflect growth rates, but can also give information about the composition of the water that surrounded the coral at different times, reflecting freshwater run-off, nutrient concentrations, and the presence of metals and chemicals in the water. This effectively makes corals a historical database, and it is now possible to compile detailed pictures of weather patterns in reef areas over hundreds of years: coral skeletons show that when Captain Cook was sailing along the Great Barrier Reef in 1770, a nineteen-year period of drought had just come to an end. Changing patterns of land use are similarly mirrored in the bands.

The discovery and interpretation of annual growth rings make corals a potentially invaluable source of information for meteorologists (in forecasting the weather), for engineers (in calculating the possible impacts of dams), for farmers (in the prediction of droughts and floods) and for archaeologists, who could add climate to their data relating to ancient societies.

Satellite imagery is also being used in reef research. Sophisticated computer-mapping technology and satellite pictures allow detailed descriptions to be built up of coastal and marine environments, even in locations thousands of miles from where the information is processed. In the Turks and Caicos Islands a project is underway to map the whole of the South Caicos Bank, a vast triangular limestone platform covering 7,500 square kilometres in the middle

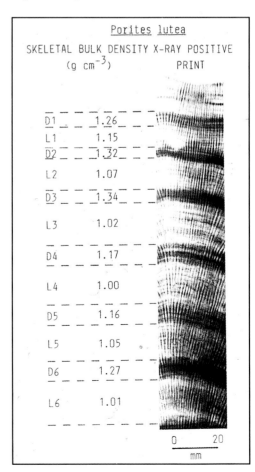

_Porites lutea_

SKELETAL BULK DENSITY X-RAY POSITIVE
$(g\ cm^{-3})$ PRINT

| D1 | 1.26 |
| L1 | 1.15 |
| D2 | 1.32 |
| L2 | 1.07 |
| D3 | 1.34 |
| L3 | 1.02 |
| D4 | 1.17 |
| L4 | 1.00 |
| D5 | 1.16 |
| L5 | 1.05 |
| D6 | 1.27 |
| L6 | 1.01 |

0    20
mm

*Opposite: X-ray photograph of a slice of* Porites lutea *coral showing growth rings indicating variations in skeletal density; a light band plus a dark band is generally held to represent a year's growth.*

*Above: shoal of silversides (Atherinidae family) over seagrass beds in the Turks and Caicos, one of the habitats that will be susceptible to more effective management once mapping and monitoring of the area have taken place.*

of the islands, which contains important reef and seagrass habitats. This information, which will be regularly updated on a computer database, will be invaluable in planning the management of the fisheries in the area. A similar project in the British Virgin Islands is using aerial photographs to produce a computerised coastal atlas for the Department of Conservation and Fisheries. This will allow reefs and other vulnerable coastal resources to be identified and should lead to more sensitive planning of potentially damaging activities such as land reclamation or sand mining.

A great deal still remains unknown about reefs and how they function; new species are continually being discovered as more remote reefs come under the scrutiny of marine biologists. But despite the potential for discoveries of this nature, reef biologists are becoming increasingly preoccupied with various aspects of the most urgent, single topic concerning reef environments worldwide: that they are no longer the rich, productive ecosystems they once were. As early as the 1930s, coral reef scientist J. Stanley Gardiner observed that reefs on inhabited islands in the Indian Ocean had declined in quality since his earlier work in 1905. As the cumulative and complex pressures from both human and natural sources subject reefs to ever greater stress, and the threat looms of potential damage from global warming and sea level rise, a detailed understanding of the problems surrounding reefs and the causes underlying them is a high priority in reef research.

Reef scientists worldwide are now trying to understand the extent to which changes for the worse are due to human impact or to natural environmental variation, in order to provide the data needed by conservationists and people managing reefs. The more information there is available, the fuller and more effective an appraisal can be and the better targeted any subsequent action. One handicap is the lack of long-term studies on reefs. Because the appropriate technology has only recently become available, there are very few cases where a single reef has been studied for a long enough period of time to show natural variations in diversity, structure and ecology.

Although some might suggest that action is being taken rather late in the day, major efforts are now underway to set up long-term studies of reefs. These monitoring projects will provide a way of following the health of reefs over time. Equally importantly, they should give early warning of any problems developing on reefs, and thus allow an opportunity for intervention before damage has become severe.

Numerous tropical countries have now instigated reef-monitoring projects. In some countries, schemes have been developed to teach local people and amateur divers the skills of working underwater so that they can participate in long-term studies. Elsewhere local scientists are developing their work programmes to ensure that standardised information on corals, fish, characteristics of the waters around the reef, the weather and other factors that effect reef health, is gathered at regular intervals.

As well as monitoring at a national level, it is important to look at reefs on a much broader scale. This means that research institutes and those involved in reef management need to collaborate on regional and global initiatives. In the Caribbean, twenty-six marine laboratories have started a co-operative project with the support of UNESCO to monitor reefs, mangroves and seagrass beds using a standardised method to produce information that will be collated and analysed at the University of the West Indies in Jamaica. In southeast Asia, a similar cooperative project is also underway. More difficult to organise, but nevertheless important, is a genuinely global investigation of what is happening to reefs. Several international agencies are in the process of developing such a project, which will involve a large network of cooperating marine laboratories and will build on the work being carried out at regional and national levels.

Monitoring is clearly not a substitute for reef management and conservation, and it is important that waiting for the result of these studies should not be used as a reason for delaying action – a tactic that has been employed in other contexts where there are vested commercial or political interests which would prefer to maintain the status quo. It will be many years before

all the information required to understand the complex processes that take place on a reef is available and perhaps even longer before conclusive scientific proof of what is causing damage to coral reefs can be produced. In the meantime, while this information is collected, action must be taken immediately to bring to an end or at the very least to alter the practices that are already heavily implicated in deteriorating reef health.

*Above: brain coral with sea fans and another gorgonian. The toxic compounds that sea fans use to repel other reef animals (including corals) that might otherwise prevent their growth and survival are important in both traditional and modern medecine. Opposite, top: slate pencil urchin (*Heterocentratus mammillatus*), another reef animal used in traditional medecine; bottom: a hydroid, one of many poisonous reef creatures which can deliver a nasty sting.*

## Medicinal Uses of Reef Species

Just as forest plants have been used for hundreds of years by local people for medicinal purposes, so some reef plants and animals are known in traditional coastal communities to have curative properties. In the Philippines, the meat of giant clams is eaten to treat malaria, and *Trochus* meat is thought to ease childbirth; spines of the pencil sea urchin were once ground up with vinegar and used to treat ear problems. In China, a traditional remedy was made up from boiled seafans to stop children feeling scared, and the same concoction was also believed to cure tuberculosis. Black coral was mixed with other ingredients by the early Hawaiians to help lung problems, and red organ-pipe coral is still used in India to alleviate coughs and bronchitis. In Asia, certain seaweeds have been gathered to treat a variety of ailments, such as stomach and lung problems, and in the Caribbean, some species are used as tonics.

As with medicinal forest plants, there is no magic about the use of such substances in human medicine. Plants and animals living in 'crowded' conditions, as on reefs and in rainforests, often produce poisons to fight off competitors and defend themselves against predators. About half the sea fans, horny corals and related coelenterates on the Great Barrier Reef, for example, are toxic to fish. Some substances produced by reef animals and plants also have other functions, such as acting as anti-foulants to prevent other plants and animals settling on them. Anyone who has dived or snorkelled on a reef will be well aware of the danger of touching certain animals like fire corals, stonefish, crown-of-thorns starfish, bristle worms and cone shells, all of which can be toxic.

Some of these poisonous substances can have beneficial properties in other contexts, and in recent years there has been growing interest in their potential for use in modern medicine, as many reef species have been found to have pharmacological and microbiological properties. Chemicals from sponges have provided a model for a new drug, Ara-C, which is used against herpes and some cancers. Prostaglandins, used to treat cardiovascular disease, asthma

and gastric ulcers, occur abundantly in some sea fans; concentrations in one Caribbean species (*Plexaura homomalla*) are some ten million times higher than in any other organism and experiments are underway to try to find methods of extraction. The related sea whips contain pseudopterosins that are potentially of value as pain-killers, although a marketable drug is still many years away.

Coral skeletons, however, are already in regular use. The skeletons of many reef-building corals are similar in structure to human bone, and French researchers have discovered that they can be used in place of bone grafts. Carefully sculpted pieces are inserted into fractures and bones damaged by cancer, or used in bone-lengthening operations. Blood penetrates the tiny channels in the coral skeleton which then dissolves, allowing new bone to form in its place, often in as little as three weeks; since 1982, over 5,000 people have had coral implants of this sort. The advantage of this method is a curious one: coral is not recognised as foreign material by the human immune system, as bone grafts donated by other people are, and so the coral is rarely rejected.

Research is also being done into the pigments that protect shallow-water reef corals from damage by ultraviolet light, with a view to using these as models for synthetic compounds that will make more effective sunscreen creams and oils.

The potential use of reef species in drugs and medicine is, for some, a powerful argument for reef conservation, although these applications are as yet minimal since most pharmaceutical research is still concentrated on forest species. But the possibility that the medical use of reef species could become yet another source of over-exploitation were it to take off must be kept in mind. Some uses are already causing concern, particularly the large quantities of sea fans currently being exported from India to Europe and the United States for pharmaceutical research. The amount of coral taken for bone grafting has worried some Pacific islanders, but the overall quantities required are small and it should be possible to find a sustainable method of collection. Controls should certainly be put in position and enforced.

One of the first discoveries by modern scientists relating to the medicinal use of reef species derived from a practice developed many centuries before by coastal people in Maui: the deadly poison used by the ancient Hawaiians on the tips of their spears came from an anthozoan (a relative of coral that resembles seaweed). This *limu make-o-Hana* or 'deadly seaweed of Hana' was found only in one particular tide-pool on the lava coast of Maui, and, according to legend, disaster would strike if the animal was touched. Local people were reluctant to reveal the whereabouts of the pool, but the researchers managed to locate the anthozoan and subsequently isolated the poison and named it palytoxin. A derivative of this has now been synthesised and is used in an anti-cancer drug. While the researchers were discovering the pool, part of their laboratory burnt down, as if in fulfilment of the legend. Some might wonder whether this in any way reflected a feeling that ancient cultural traditions were being intruded upon and the natural resources of the island plundered by foreigners. Certainly it is almost

*Pharmaceutical companies are looking at many species such as the sea whips shown opposite as potential sources of new drugs.*

without exception large corporations that profit from the drugs produced from reef species, and at present there is no requirement for them to make any sort of payment to the local communities or countries where these substances are found. Multinationals and research institutions are already filing patents for and buying rights to compounds from some reef species.

As with forest species, this raises yet again the spectre of the rich nations of the North plundering the resources of the South with very little benefit to the people from whose lands – or reefs – the materials have been extracted. Until recently, it has not been possible to patent plants or other natural life forms but now the huge agro-chemical and biotechnology companies are pushing for this to be changed. If successful, they will achieve a monopoly on patented life forms which will spirit away the rights to use these precious reserves from the third-world nations and the people who have acted as custodians of these resources and, in many cases, whose traditional knowledge has led to these 'discoveries' by western science.

*Below: Hana Coast, Maui, Hawaii, where traditional knowledge of the properties of a reef animal called an anthozoan has led to the development of a modern drug.*

# CHAPTER THREE

# VULNERABILITY & RESISTANCE

Most coral reefs lie in the hurricane belt and from time to time suffer devastation when struck by tropical storms. And these are not the only violent natural disturbances to which reefs are subject. Other events that may have a profound impact on reefs are: abnormal weather patterns, fluctuations in sea-water temperatures (making the water suddenly too hot or too cold for corals to withstand), unusually heavy rain (causing shallow reefs to be inundated with fresh water), or extreme low tides (that expose the coral polyps to the risk of drying out), disease, and population explosions of predators. Volcanic eruptions

may deluge reefs with molten rock, and earthquakes can plunge them far too deep in the sea to survive or hoist them high and dry out of the water. Despite the violence of these assaults, it is now known that in the long term they can actually have a beneficial effect on reefs, as long as recovery between events is not disturbed by additional stresses. Just as, in a rainforest, a fallen tree may allow the space and shaft of light that enable new seedlings to grow, so the clearing away of corals on a reef exposes new areas for coral larvae to settle on, and contributes to maintaining the balance between species.

*Volcanic eruptions can cause immense damage to reefs or prevent their formation. In Hawaii, there is little reef growth around the most volcanically active islands, like this one (opposite), but rich reefs develop around older, dormant volcanoes.*

*Hardly a building on the Yucatan coast of Mexico was unaffected when Hurricane Gilbert struck in 1988; this scene near the marine laboratory at Puerto Morelos was typical. Much less visible, but very serious damage was also sustained by reefs in the area.*

## Hurricanes

Tropical storms are called hurricanes, cyclones or typhoons according to their intensity and the geographical region where they occur; the huge damage they can cause to coral reefs is now well documented.

Discovery Bay is a bite-shaped indentation on Jamaica's north coast where Columbus is said to have landed in 1494. Beneath the sea, a fringing reef extends across the mouth of the bay, broken only by a channel created to let shipping through. Apart from the dredging of the channel in 1966, the reef flourished undisturbed for several decades, building up a dense covering of different corals, seaweeds and sponges. As the site of one of the first tropical marine laboratories, founded in the 1940s, where some of the earliest detailed underwater studies of reefs were carried out by Dr Thomas Goreau, the bay attracted coral reef scientists from all over the world. Goreau's descriptions of the Discovery Bay

reefs became classics and form the basis of much of the reef work carried out today.

But he would barely recognise the reefs as they are now. In August 1980, Hurricane Allen hit Jamaica's north coast. Although the eye of the hurricane was sixty-five kilometres away, it still had catastrophic results, smashing branching corals, toppling some of the massive corals, ripping up sea fans and sponges and scouring the reef with suspended sand. Little was left on the shallow reefs, apart from a few massive colonies of rugged star coral. The extensive thickets of elkhorn coral that had dominated the reef were reduced to mounds of rubble. Slightly deeper on the reef, its relative the staghorn coral had almost completely disappeared. In effect, practically everything on the reef had been obliterated.

Slowly, over the years, the fringing reef started to grow again and replenish itself, with the corals, sea fans and other reef inhabitants patiently building the reef in the same way that they had been doing

since long before Columbus made landfall. Then, eight years later, in 1988, disaster struck again when Hurricane Gilbert unleashed its destructive power across the Caribbean. In Discovery Bay the reefs had still not recovered their former luxuriance when powerful waves smashed through them once again, stripping off many of the reef plants and animals and filling the water with sediment that took weeks to clear. This hurricane had effectively set back the clock of reef recovery to the beginning of the decade, and in 1989, the reefs received yet another battering from Hurricane Hugo.

Hugo passed directly over the island of St Croix in the US Virgin Islands where the West Indies Laboratory is situated and extensive information on the reefs had been collected, providing a prime opportunity for detailed before-and-after comparisons of the impact of a hurricane on a reef. Winds during the hurricane reached an estimated 220 to 272 kilometres per hour, probably with even stronger gusts. A bicycle that had been stored hanging in a cupboard in the research station kept a record of events on its battery-operated speedometer after the cupboard door had blown off – when the wind had died down it had clocked up a stationary journey of over 2,400 kilometres at some 144 kilometres an hour. Waves over six metres high battered the southern coast all night.

The hurricane had a very variable impact on the reef, depending on the type of coral colony, the depth at which it was growing, and the orientation of the reef to the wind and the waves. In general, wind speeds of 120 to 150 kilometres an hour cause fairly limited damage to reefs, from which they recover in a decade or so, but once the wind is blowing at over 200 kilometres an hour, a reef is likely to be so badly affected that it will be half a century before it has fully recovered. On St Croix, while some reefs appeared practically untouched, others, notably those facing south, had suffered badly. Worst hit were the south-facing reefs on Buck Island, designated a marine park in 1948 and of great importance to the tourist industry, where coral destruction was virtually total to a depth of twelve metres.

It is not just corals themselves that are badly hit by hurricanes. After Hugo, dead fish and invertebrates were washed up in quantity on the beaches. In circumstances of this sort, fish populations, after an initial decline, usually recover within a year or so, although there may be more herbivorous fish, which profit from the increased abundance of seaweed that grows on dead coral.

Reefs in the Caribbean and Pacific are regularly damaged by tropical storms. For local people, hurricanes cause massive disruption. On St Croix, for example, well over three-quarters of the buildings were destroyed, there were serious food and drinking water shortages in the immediate aftermath, and electrical and telephone services were interrupted for about three months. Today, disaster relief programmes are generally initiated rapidly, with airlifts of food and the provision of temporary housing. In the past such aid was not available and people had to take natural catastrophes in their stride.

Although it is no consolation to the visiting diver or local fisherman who sees a favourite reef reduced to nothing but rubble or buried under sand in the space of a few hours, it is now known that these apparently destructive natural forces play a key role in maintaining the richness and diversity of reef life. The faster-growing species (such as elkhorn and staghorn corals) suffer the most damage, giving the slower species, like the more robust massive corals, a chance to catch up. The massive corals never take over completely because the branching corals start to recover and recolonise the reef comparatively rapidly.

Tropical storms also play a role in building coral islands and sandy coastlines: powerful winds and waves roll coral rubble up to islands and whip sand away from their beaches. On uninhabited islands and coasts, these natural processes are of little concern to humans, but where erosion and flooding strike heavily populated areas, the human cost can be high.

Although there are usually several hurricanes in the Caribbean each year, the frequency with which individual reefs are struck by them has been on average (over the last 120 years) once every seven years – a relatively short interval, but enough to allow a reasonable opportunity for corals to regrow. In Jamaica, a virtually storm-free period of forty years, from 1944 to 1980, allowed the reefs in Discovery Bay to flourish and to be studied undisturbed – but this was exceptional. In the Pacific, Fiji had an average of three storms a decade from 1940 to 1980, but eleven have struck over the last ten years. Six cyclones hit French Polynesia during 1982 and 1983, causing huge coral boulders to break off and provoking an avalanche effect in some areas that resulted in one hundred per cent coral damage to a depth of thirty-five metres.

Some climatologists now believe that tropical storms may be happening more

*Left: in 1989, this reef at Sombrero in the Philippines (an area hit by several typhoons a year), was devastated by a violent storm, which left broken coral rubble strewn across the reef and piled up on the beaches.*

*Opposite, top: staghorn coral (Acropora sp.), which is easily broken by hurricanes; fragments are capable of regenerating quite quickly if the reef suffers no other stresses; bottom: massive corals, like this one, are more resistant to heavy waves and stand a better chance of surviving violent storms than branching corals.*

going back over a meaningful period of time, it is difficult to be sure whether the remarkably high number of tropical storms in the Pacific in recent years can be put down to global warming or natural variations in weather patterns (see box). Many climatologists, however, now suspect that these may indeed be alarming signs of the effects of global warming.

The idea that human-induced global warming could result in more intense and more frequent tropical storms with which coral reefs simply cannot keep up is tragic enough, but there are also many other pressures on reefs that could slow down their recovery and stress them even further. The fringing reef of Discovery Bay, for example, has suffered not only a succession of hurricanes, but over the last twelve years has seen mass mortality of sea urchins, heavy overfishing and increasing pollution from sewage. The result is a virtual monoculture of brown seaweed. Hurricanes can wreak havoc on a reef, and if the recovery processes are interrupted, as seems increasingly to be the case, the balance between destruction and regeneration may shift to an extent that they no longer play a useful role in maintaining the richness and variety of reef life, but serve only to hasten its demise.

## The Greenhouse Effect and Global Warming

As greenhouse gases – mainly carbon dioxide, methane, nitrous oxide and chlorofluoro-carbons (CFCs) – accumulate in the atmosphere, they trap the sun's radiant heat and the atmosphere warms up. Output of carbon dioxide, the main greenhouse gas, has increased by twenty-five per cent since the mid-nineteenth century, as a result of the growth in energy consumption, the burning of fossil fuels and the destruction of forests that absorb carbon dioxide. The broad consensus among the world's climate scientists is that unprecedented global warming awaits us (the only doubt being the speed and the types of impact it will have) unless we cut our greenhouse gas emissions immediately. Predictions as to the rate of temperature change vary widely, but the world's climate modelling centres estimate that unless we cut emissions, the atmosphere will warm up by something between 1.5 and 5°C by the end of the next century. This will have a variety of effects on the marine environment: sea temperatures can be expected to increase, sea levels to rise, and storms may become more intense and frequent.

often and increasing in intensity. We know that there has been enormous variability in climate over past centuries, but as there is practically no climatic data available

## Turning up the Heat: Coral Bleaching

It comes as a shock to snorkellers or divers if, as they are swimming along above a reef, they suddenly encounter an area of corals with absolutely no colour at all. The customarily vibrant hues are completely missing, and patches of reef appear as startling white blotches, looking rather as if they have been soaked in household bleach; indeed this phenomenon has been given the name 'bleaching'.

The sudden whitening of the corals is a result either of the pigment in the zooxanthellae, chlorophyll, becoming much less concentrated or, more often, of the zooxanthellae themselves actually being expelled from the polyps. If a coral loses all its zooxanthellae, and thus its strong brown-green colours, it turns totally white or reveals the pale colours of the skeleton that are normally masked. If some zooxanthellae survive, the coral may recover after a few months, but if bleaching is severe, the colony will die. Many of the other reef inhabitants that have zooxanthellae, such as sponges, gorgonians and sea anemones, also bleach in a similar way.

Various environmental changes seem to be able to trigger bleaching, but the majority of bleaching events in recent years have taken place in areas where the sea-water temperature has been unusually high for the time of year. Other causes include: a drop in temperature (as when cold winter fronts strike northerly reefs), prolonged exposure to air (as during a very low tide), freshwater dilution (as after heavy rainstorms), intense sunlight (causing increased ultraviolet radiation) and even some forms of pollution.

Although it was first noticed over sixty years ago on the Great Barrier Reef, coral bleaching only came to widespread attention in the early 1980s. In 1982/1983, a phenomenon called El Niño struck the Pacific with particular force. El Niño is a set of disruptive weather patterns that occurs in the Pacific at approximately three- to five-year intervals, often at Christmas – hence its name, 'The Child'. In normal years, winds are from the east and a tongue of cool water extends westwards into the Pacific from the coast of South America. During an El Niño year, winds in the tropical Pacific blow predominantly from the west, reversing current directions and replacing the normally cool water with warm water.

The 1982/1983 El Niño was the strongest on record this century and had a dramatic effect. The surface temperatures of the ocean in parts of the Pacific rose by as much as 5°C and in many areas stayed for four to five months as high as 30-31°C, to depths of as much as thirty metres. Marine organisms often live in water which is near the top limit of temperatures they can tolerate, so that an increase of just a few degrees can prove fatal. In summer months, when the sea is at its warmest, corals may be precariously close to, and within perhaps one or two degrees of their upper limit. When sea temperatures rise as much as they do during El Niño, this stress causes bleaching in corals and other reef animals.

Over the winter of 1982/1983, vast areas of coral bleached in the eastern Pacific. In Costa Rica, half the corals on the Pacific coast reefs died, and up to eighty per cent of the corals on the Panama reefs and ninety-five to a hundred per cent of reefs in the Galapagos Islands perished. Many others, as far apart as French Polynesia and Indonesia, were affected.

Bleaching following El Niño appears to be part of a natural cycle of events. On some reefs, a sufficient number of corals survive with at least some of their zooxanthellae for recovery to take place, albeit slowly. In the last decade, however, bleaching has been reported from numerous locations worldwide, many of them outside the area of influence of El Niño. Major coral bleaching took place in Florida, Puerto Rico and Jamaica in 1987, 1989 and 1990. Large numbers of other reefs in the Caribbean have been affected, as well as reefs in Australia, Japan, Indonesia, Vanuatu, Oman, Hawaii, the Maldives, Fiji, the Red Sea, Bermuda and the Gulf of California, and with them (although to a lesser extent) sponges, gorgonians and sea anemones. In almost all cases, these bleaching events have coincided with an increase in the surface temperature of the ocean. In 1988, the Caribbean did not suffer any significant bleaching, but this may

*Acropora and other branching corals are usually the first to bleach when sea temperatures rise, turning pallid versions of their original colours if some of the zooxanthellae are lost and completely white if all the zooxanthellae die.*

*Opposite: coral polyps (Pocillopora sp.) showing the symbiotic algae, the zooxanthellae, that live within them and die when subjected to high water temperatures.*

have been because Hurricane Gilbert cooled the waters in its wake.

In 1991, about half the corals on the reefs at Phuket in Thailand bleached, over a period when water temperatures in the Andaman Sea were 2°C higher than normal. In French Polynesia, sea temperatures in March 1991 were 1° higher than normal, and bleaching took place on many of the reefs around the Society Islands. The outer slopes of barrier reefs and the fringing reefs seem to have been worst hit (although the reasons for this are still not known), but reefs in lagoons were also damaged. As in many bleaching incidents, the branching corals were worst affected with up to ninety-five per cent damaged at some sites. By July 1991, many of the Society Island reefs were showing some signs of recovery; whether they will continue to do so remains to be seen. It

is possible that these recent bleachings are connected with the El Niño of 1991/1992, but it is difficult to see how this could account for the incidences in the Caribbean.

There may, however, be another more disquieting explanation for the higher water temperatures recorded in some areas, and this is global warming. The difficulty in finding out whether or not increased sea temperatures and apparently associated cases of bleaching are definitely due to global warming is lack of information. There are very few sites in the world where sea temperature records have been kept over long periods of time, so it is hard to know whether recent changes are natural fluctuations or part of some more long-term trend due to the greenhouse effect.

Exactly how global warming of the atmosphere will be reflected in the oceans is not yet known. It is unlikely that sea temperatures will increase in a uniform manner, or that in the immediate future they will rise above the critical point for corals (29.5 to 30°C) throughout reef areas. But it is quite possible that there could be greater seasonal and annual variation, with, for example, more violent El Niños. In the early stages of global warming, ocean temperatures might increase slowly enough for both corals and their zooxanthellae to adapt. But this would be a slow process, involving gradual selection of different genetic make-ups. Different corals have different tolerances to high temperatures, both within species (corals in the Persian Gulf are able to withstand higher temperatures than the same corals in waters that do not experience such high summer temperatures, for example) and between species.

If the rate of warming, or the length of time that the high temperature lasts in any particular locality, is the trigger for bleaching, the consequences of even intermittent and localised increases in sea-water temperature could be serious. A temperature rise lasting for a matter of weeks could be enough to kill a whole reef. If there is widespread, serious bleaching, with little recovery, coral species that are rare and have small populations could be put at risk; the 1982/1983 El Niño appears to have caused extinction, through bleaching, of a species of fire coral (*Millepora*) that was found only in the eastern Pacific, and seriously reduced populations of two other fairly rare species.

Since the faster growing branching species are often bleached first, this could result in slower growing massive corals becoming dominant, which would in its turn mean that overall reef growth would slow down considerably. If a bleached reef then suffers further damage from either a natural or a human-induced disturbance, it will take longer than usual to recover because the faster growing species on it have already been hit.

There are many unanswered questions about bleaching. Why, for instance, do some species, such as branching corals, succumb more quickly than others? Why are some parts of the reef affected and not others? How far are causes other than higher temperatures, such as ultraviolet radiation or increased pollution, to blame? To try and answer some of these ques-

tions, major research programmes are being set up and there is now much greater emphasis on monitoring reefs on a regular basis. Reef biologists are starting to record not only what is happening to corals, but also all the external factors that might affect their health, including sea temperature, cloud cover (which affects the amount of light they receive), water quality and wave strength.

It will be some time before we know for certain whether or not coral bleaching is an early signal of global warming, but the mere possibility that it could be is a powerful reason for increased action to curb emissions of greenhouse gases and to understand the functioning of the reef ecosystem. Given that a rise in sea temperature of 1° or 2°C above the normal summer maximum over a few weeks or months could cause widespread coral fatalities, there must be no question of waiting for the results of monitoring – important as they are – before action is taken.

## *Reefs and the Rising Seas*

President Maumoon Abdul Gayoom of the Maldives is a worried man. All 1,190 islands in this atoll nation are less than two or three metres high, and, if projections of rising sea levels due to the greenhouse effect are correct, this tiny country, with a total land area of only about 300 square kilometres, could be significantly smaller and suffering major deterioration of its freshwater supply by the end of the next century.

Higher temperatures will cause the water in the oceans to expand and mountain glaciers to melt, both of which will make sea levels rise. The polar ice caps will also be affected, but due to the complexity of predicted climate change, it is not known how this will be reflected in changing sea levels. How quickly sea levels will rise is a matter of debate: the latest calculations suggest an increase of about twenty centimetres by the year 2030, forty centimetres by the year 2050 and just over half a metre by the end of the next century, but this is nevertheless a rate up to five or six times faster than anything the world has experienced in the recent past.

The Maldives is only one of several atoll nations threatened by sea level rise due to global warming. 'We are an endangered nation', said President Gayoom in 1987, when he spoke at the United Nations, adding his voice to those of leaders from other low-lying atoll nations like Tuvalu, Kiribati, Tokelau and the Marshall Islands. In the Maldives, the airport at Hulule, which is crucial to the tourist industry, would be regularly flooded at high tide if the sea rises by only half a metre. If sea levels were to rise by as much as one metre, a fifth of the land on Majuro, the most densely inhabited island in the Marshall Islands, would be lost. While other nations that will be affected have at least some high ground or islands, the impact for those dependent on the land in areas that would be inundated would still, obviously, be catastrophic.

Many low-lying islands may still become uninhabitable, even if they are not entirely submerged by the sea. Rain falling on an atoll island accumulates in the limestone rock that is the base of the island, forming a freshwater reservoir or lens. Wells

## *Ozone Depletion*

Depletion of the ozone layer through the widespread use of CFCs (chlorofluorocarbons) in coolants, aerosols, air-conditioning and numerous materials such as plastics, is now an issue of global concern. The importance of the ozone layer is that it reduces the amount of ultraviolet radiation that reaches the earth; over recent decades it has become clear that high intensities of ultraviolet light can have serious effects on human health. Skin cancer is one consequence and there is already evidence of increased incidence in some parts of the world, as well as growing concern about the link between ultraviolet radiation and cataracts and damage to the human immune system.

Much less well known is the fact that ultraviolet light damages marine life. The huge community of plants and animals that live in the upper two to three metres of the oceans are particularly at risk; phytoplankton and the larvae of numerous animals can be killed or damaged by it, affecting the complex food webs of which they are the basis. High-intensity ultraviolet radiation also has a direct impact on corals, by killing the zooxanthellae and increasing the impact of bleaching from high temperatures. At present, the greatest ozone depletion is occurring in both northern and southern

temperate regions, and if this extends to the tropics, the consequences could be extremely serious for coral reefs, particularly as ultraviolet radiation penetrates sea water much more easily than was previously thought. Corals are therefore very vulnerable, despite the presence in the zooxanthellae of a protective pigment.

In 1987, the Montreal Protocol was drawn up as an inter-governmental response to the problems of ozone depletion and hailed as a landmark treaty, a model for future environmental protection. Under this international agreement, most nations agreed to cut by half their production of CFCs by the year 2,000. Sadly, this was very much too little action far too late, and six months after it had been signed, the treaty was declared inadequate by the very parties that had crafted it. Since then the Protocol has been strengthened to include a wider range of harmful emissions and faster reductions in their use. It is clear to many people, however, that the treaty, which allows for the continued production of ozone-destroying chemicals, is currently failing to protect the ozone layer successfully. Greenpeace, among other environmental organisations, is calling for an immediate ban on all ozone-destroying chemicals and their replacement with safe alternatives to save the earth's protective ozone layer.

sunk into the lens provide the only regular source of water for drinking and agriculture, and if the sea rises, salt water will gradually penetrate this freshwater source. In any case, if storms become more frequent as a result of climate change, islands will be flooded with salt water more often.

Reef geologists studying the origins of coral reefs sometimes informally describe three types of reef according to their ability to keep pace with changing sea levels: 'keep-up' reefs are those that keep pace with sea level rise, 'catch-up' reefs lag behind and then catch up as sea level rise slows down, and 'give-up' reefs drown. According to this scenario, many reefs are now in a catch-up phase as their growth has lagged behind sea level rise caused by the warming of climate over the last 20,000 years since the Ice Ages.

If reefs continue to grow at their current average rate of seven to ten millimetres a year, they should be able to keep pace with sea level rise at least until the year 2030, particularly those that have sheltered reef flats with fast-growing corals that will benefit from slightly deeper water. After that, as the sea level starts to rise more rapidly, most reefs will probably lag behind (even if growing at the maximum rate) and might then eventually drown. Reefs seem to 'give up' when the sea level

*Above: flooding in Male (capital of the Maldives), following a tropical storm, illustrating the vulnerability of low atolls to sea level rise.*

*Below: a demonstration in Male in 1989 during a governmental meeting of 'Small Island States' on global warming and sea level*

consistently rises more than about twenty millimetres a year.

There are likely, however, to be significant variations in different parts of the world. Reefs in the Caribbean, for instance, may not be able to keep pace with even a slow rise; much of the staghorn and elkhorn coral which dominated these reefs has already fallen victim to disease and pollution (among other impacts) and although the reefs might be able to keep up for a short time, storms will probably accelerate shore erosion, increasing sedimentation, which will kill corals. In contrast, corals on reef flats on the Great Barrier Reef might grow faster, as the deeper water (at least to about five metres) will provide slightly better conditions for colonies that would otherwise have been exposed to the air at low tide. All the same, faster growth would probably occur only on fairly sheltered reef flats with minimal wave damage. More importantly, no reefs will be able to maintain even normal growth rates if the corals themselves are unhealthy. If pollution and other forms of stress caused by humans become more widespread, the ability of reefs to withstand even a moderate increase in sea level will be very much in doubt.

Changes in sea level in fact take place in many parts of the world as a result of movements of the earth's crust. Sea level on

some Hawaiian islands, for example, is rising by over three millimetres a year because the land is sinking, and there are islands off Papua New Guinea where the sea level is falling because land is being uplifted.

When earthquakes and other tectonic events affect the coastline, the effects can be dramatic where reefs are concerned. Earthquake activity in the Galapagos killed three patch reefs in the 1970s: in Urvina Bay a reef was suddenly lifted right out of the water, while at Punta Espinosa, another gradually rose above sea level, and at Pinzon Island, a third was completely buried by sand. Reefs around some Hawaiian islands are frequently disrupted by lava flows and eruptions.

Countries such as the Maldives long ago came to terms with living in a changeable and unpredictable environment. As Darwin wrote in his study of coral atolls, 'The inhabitants of the Maldiva Archipelago, as long ago as 1605, declared that "the high tides and violent currents were diminishing the number of islands", and I have already shown . . . that the work of destruction is still in progress.' Despite these dire predictions, the Maldives are still here, not least thanks to the coral reefs that encircle and protect them.

Healthy coral reefs act as natural breakwaters, deflecting and absorbing the force of the waves and thereby saving lives and property. Between seventy and ninety per

## Reefs as Carbon Dioxide Sink?

Corals, sponges and other reef organisms all remove carbon dioxide from the ocean surface as they build their limestone skeletons, possibly accounting for as much as half of the calcium carbonate deposited in the oceans. It has been suggested by some that this could mean that coral reefs might act as a sink, soaking up or removing excess carbon dioxide from the atmosphere. Attractive though this idea is, it is highly unlikely that reefs could lower carbon dioxide levels, partly because it rests on one highly optimistic assumption: that reefs will burst into renewed and faster growth. The reality is that if rates of sea level rise overtake those of reef growth, coral growth will ultimately slow down. Furthermore, calcium carbonate in the sea eventually breaks down once it has reached a certain level of concentration, and carbon dioxide is re-released into the atmosphere; this would offset any positive advantages the reefs might have as a carbon dioxide sink.

cent of wave energy is dissipated when a wave breaks on a reef. The people of the Maldives recently discovered too late the high value of this protection. When land was reclaimed on Male, the capital, in the 1980s, a breakwater was built to protect it using 905,000 cubic metres of rubble and coral taken from the adjacent reef. High waves during a tropical storm in 1987 damaged the breakwater badly, and a new one-and-a-half kilometre breakwater had to be built using concrete blocks. Had the original reef been left in place, it might well have provided the protection that proved to be necessary. The new breakwater cost US$12 million (paid for with foreign aid money), putting the original value of the reef at about US$8,000 a metre. Most countries where this problem might arise through insensitive development could not possibly find the money themselves, and there is no guarantee that foreign aid would be available if it were needed.

Keeping reefs healthy could well be one of the best ways to protect land from rising sea levels, but clearly a more far-reaching and long-term solution to this problem would be to halt global warming.

*Above: low-level sandy islands like this one in the Maldives are naturally subject to erosion. This scene, with the sea fast advancing on a settlement, is likely to become increasingly common if sea levels rise. Left: in the 1970s, an earthquake lifted this reef at Urvina Bay in the Galapagos Islands right out of the water.*

*Flourishing reefs like those shown opposite and over the page probably represent the best protection from the effects of sea level rise for low-lying atoll nations in the Indian and Pacific Oceans.*

## Coral Reefs and a Changing Climate

Over the millennia, reefs have adapted during numerous warming periods, and they may well survive the next fifty to a hundred years, albeit in an impoverished form, and flourish once again in the future. Existing corals and zooxanthellae might be replaced by strains adapted to higher temperatures. Reef animals dependent on seasonal temperature changes to trigger their breeding cycles may find that these are altered. As equatorial zones become too hot, perhaps reefs will simply start growing elsewhere; they may even return to the Mediterranean, where they existed over 150 million years ago. But all this is hopeful conjecture and of little benefit to existing coral reefs now bearing the brunt of the damage or to the people whose lives are bound up with the health of the reefs.

In the opinion of many of the world's climate scientists, global warming will have a variety of consequences, one of which will be to intensify the natural climatic disturbances. Coral growth could be slowed by increased cloud cover (causing decreased sunlight for the zooxanthellae), higher rainfall (diluting the salinity of shallow waters) and changes in ocean currents that might bring nutrient-rich waters on to the reefs. Increasing frequency of storms and rising sea levels will leave their mark, but rising sea temperatures are likely to have the most profound impact. And the combination of all these factors is likely to decrease coral reefs' capacity to regenerate.

Healthy coral reefs will inevitably cope better with global climate change than will damaged reefs: the arguments have never been stronger for their protection and sustainable use. In the near future, sea level rise and ocean warming will probably happen fairly slowly and irregularly and will appear as a gradual increase in sea level, storm frequency and intensity, flooding, sedimentation and bleaching.

*Striped sweetlips (*Plectorhincus sp.*) over* Acropora, *the fastest growing coral on the reef, here forming impressive table-like structures.*

Healthy coral reefs will continue to provide sediment for beaches and islands which will in turn help to counteract the effects of erosion.

It is to be hoped that the potential threat to reefs from global warming will now give added impetus to efforts to slow and halt greenhouse gas emissions and curb energy consumption. In the United States, there was sufficient concern about coral bleaching by 1990 for the US Senate to arrange a hearing at which a number of scientists testified and called for further action and research. Disappointingly, as with most issues of this nature, the appeals at that time produced scant results. The burning of fossil fuels is responsible for sixty per cent of that part of the greenhouse effect that is due to human factors; where we need to use energy, changing to renewable technologies such as solar power must be a high priority. Some countries are taking action by passing legislation that will penalise those who waste energy, but others are reluctant to do anything and are using the uncertainties that surround the evidence of global warming to delay action. The wealthy nations of the world are responsible for a large proportion of greenhouse gas emissions, but it is the developing countries that will suffer most, as they have less money, expertise and technology to cope with its potential consequences. The planned Global Climate Change Convention, currently being negotiated by 100 nations, is an encouraging sign that the international community is beginning to address the problem. But international agreements of this kind are only a first step, which must be followed up by effective legislation in individual countries if any real reduction in carbon dioxide emissions is to be achieved.

## Crown-of-thorns Starfish

'Starving millions eat up the Barrier Reef' and 'Australia declares war on starfish army attacking Barrier Reef', ran the headlines. It is not often that starfish make the front page, but the Great Barrier Reef is so crucial to the tourist industry in Australia that newspapers had a field day

during a population outbreak of crown-of-thorns starfish a few years ago. As a result, the crown-of-thorns starfish (*Acanthaster planci*) turned into the best-known coral predator on the reef.

Most people are aware of the crown-of-thorns because of its activities on the Great Barrier Reef, but it is found from the Red Sea across the Indian Ocean and south east Asia to the Pacific, and is known as *taramea* in the Solomon Islands, *alamea* in Western Samoa and *nikarem* in the Torres Straits Islands. It does not occur in the Caribbean or the Atlantic. A formidable and impressive-looking creature, it can reach up to thirty centimetres or more in diameter and as it progresses inexorably across the reef, it devours a large area of coral every day. It eats coral by pushing its stomach out through its mouth (the feeding method used by most starfish) and secreting digestive juices on to the polyps, breaking down the coral into a sort of 'polyp soup', which it absorbs through the stomach wall. It then pulls its stomach back into its body, leaving nothing behind except the white limestone skeleton of the coral.

Starfish populations have always fluctuated in cycles, low densities alternating with dramatic outbreaks which can cause massive reef damage. When present in large numbers, crown-of-thorns starfish often eat together in groups, and whilst eating they secrete a chemical which attracts other starfish to the area. As the number of starfish in the feeding site increases, the 'smell' of digested coral increases still further, pulling even more starfish into the 'aggregation' (as feeding groups are known). This is why they seem to congregate in such fearsome numbers and destroy reefs so quickly.

Damage seems to have been most serious in Australia, which has experienced two series of outbreaks in the past twenty-five years. A survey of 228 reefs in the central section of the Great Barrier Reef showed that about a third of these have been damaged in the last five or six years. However, outbreaks have also occurred elsewhere in the Pacific and Indian Oceans over the last two decades. About ninety per cent of the corals in Fagatele Bay in American Samoa were affected by an outbreak in 1978, for example, and extensive damage was caused by an outbreak on the reefs of Moorea in French Polynesia between 1979 and 1982. There have been outbreaks in parts of North Male and Ari Atolls in the Maldives since 1990, although it appears that at least some affected reefs are being recolonised by corals already. It can take a minimum of ten to twenty years for a reef to recover from major damage by the crown-of-thorns, and much longer if the reef becomes re-infested with starfish or over-run with seaweed or soft corals before recovery is complete.

The discovery of crown-of-thorns starfish spines in sediments from fossil reefs shows that they have been an important part of reef life since modern reefs first formed. Like hurricanes, starfish outbreaks play a role in maintaining high species diversity, by killing some corals and allowing others to become established. In recent years, however, outbreaks seem to have been happening more often, causing longer lasting damage and hindering recovery rather than promoting diversity on the reef, and it may well be that human activities have contributed to this. Some crown-of-thorns outbreaks in the Pacific seem to be related to periods of heavy rainfall, during which more nutrient run-off finds its way into coastal waters, leading, in turn, to an increase in the phytoplankton, upon which starfish larvae feed. Run-off now occurs more often as a result of land clearance, intensive agriculture and the destruction of rainforests and mangroves, which could account for recent outbreaks on some reefs, although it obviously does not explain outbreaks on reefs remote from land or around coral atolls.

Alternatively, outbreaks may be caused by over-fishing and collection of the fish and molluscs that normally eat the crown-of-thorns and keep its numbers in check. The giant triton is a spectacular snail up to fifty centimetres long that occasionally feeds on the starfish and it has been heavily collected for the ornamental shell trade, leading some people to suggest that its increasing rarity is leading to crown-of-thorns outbreaks, but there is as yet no conclusive evidence for this. Perhaps more likely is the overfishing of predators such as triggerfish and pufferfish, which are taken for both food and the marine curio trade, and the hump-headed (or Napoleon) wrasse, which has been a popular quarry with spear fishermen in the past, and is taken in large quantities by commercial fishermen on the Great Barrier Reef. A great deal more research is needed to make definite links between overfishing of certain species of fish and crown-of-thorns outbreaks, but research being carried out in the Red Sea and the eastern Pacific is beginning to point in this direction.

When reefs have been damaged by crown-of-thorns starfish, they rapidly lose their appeal for tourists. Many of the reefs affected (for example in Australia and the Maldives) are used extensively by divers and snorkellers, and as a result considerable effort has gone into finding ways of controlling outbreaks. Labour-intensive though it is, there have even been projects that involved injecting the offending starfish with a variety of poisons, such as formaldehyde, copper sulphate and sodium hypochlorite. Although this method is effective, it is too expensive and time-consuming to be widely used. The most cost-effective method known at present is to enlist the help of amateur divers and remove the starfish by hand. In the Maldives, several diving resorts are running this kind of programme: divers are given a crab hook and protective gloves with which to prise the starfish off the reef; the starfish are then left to dry out on the beach. During 1990 in one

Crown-of-thorns starfish (Acanthaster planci) – several are shown opposite on a reef in Australia – can cause vast damage when they occur in large numbers. Above: a crown-of-thorns starfish feeding on coral, leaving behind a denuded white skeleton. Right: the giant triton, seen here attacking a starfish, has been collected in large numbers for the shell trade; it has been suggested that this may have contributed to crown-of-thorns 'plagues' but it now seems more likely that overfishing of fish predators has had a more important effect.

resort alone, Nakatchafushi, 18,700 starfish were removed. But poisoning or removal by hand are likely to remain temporary and highly localised measures, tending to be used only in popular tourist areas and providing cosmetic, short-term solutions, which prevent further reef damage only until the next outbreak.

## Other Reef Predators

The crown-of-thorns starfish is not the only creature to attack coral. Other starfish, sea urchins, some molluscs, fish, hermit crabs and worms all feed on coral but not usually on such a large scale. Outbreaks of coral-eating gastropods *Drupella* have occasionally caused localised damage on reefs, for example, in the Caribbean and in Japan and Micronesia in the early 1980s. The encrusting sponge *Terpios* has killed corals and sedentary animals on some reefs; at one site in Guam it spread along a kilometre of reef and prevented coral re-growing for about thirteen years. *Terpios* has also occurred on reefs in American Samoa, Belau and the northern Marianas in the past although it has not caused any problems recently in these places. In the Maldives, some northern reefs have been affected by the spread of the sea anemone *Rhodactis*, which prevents corals settling and coral colonies expanding.

Under normal conditions these creatures have a positive impact on the reef, providing the minor disturbances which contribute to reef diversity, keeping seaweed at bay, ensuring space for coral growth, and forming sand and sediments by eroding dead coral skeletons, mollusc shells and calcareous algae. But if populations of bioeroders, herbivores or predators change dramatically this can cause serious damage and slow down recovery from other disturbances suffered by reefs. The recovery of some of the reefs damaged by the 1982/83 El Niño was delayed by the grazing of pufferfish: once highly selective in what they ate, the pufferfish have adapted to feed on a wide variety of other corals and are removing small coral colonies before they have a chance to become established. In Jamaica, recovery of reefs after Hurricane Allen was slowed down by coral-eating snails, worms and sea urchins. Even herbivorous damselfish can have an impact as they often remove small coral colonies that start to grow in the 'algal gardens' within their territories (although certain coral species seem to be allowed to remain).

The number of sea urchins that a healthy coral reef can sustain seems to be particularly finely balanced. In the 1970s and early 1980s, the abundance of the fierce-looking spiny black *Diadema* urchins began to increase significantly in the Caribbean. Densities of up to eighty urchins per square metre were found. With such enormous numbers of urchins multiplying on the reef, it looked as if they would do more than just keep the reefs clear of seaweed, and that the corals themselves might be eroded. At these densities, sea urchins are capable of lowering the reef surface by six millimetres a year. But before any lasting damage was done, a mass die-off swept through the urchin populations, eliminating some and reducing others to less than a tenth of their former numbers. The order in which populations were affected around the Caribbean was found to correlate closely with the currents and water circulation patterns,

*Pufferfish like this* Arothron nigropunctatus *are among the few predators on sea urchins and are thought to play an important part in controlling their numbers. Over-fishing of pufferfish may be an explanation for some of the urchin population outbreaks.*

*Opposite: black band disease – the black line marks the forward edge of the disease, leaving behind it whitened dead coral.*

Diadema *sea urchins have caused colossal damage on some reefs where their numbers have suddenly increased.*

which led to the conclusion that the plague was caused by a water-borne disease. On some reefs, the urchins died out completely, and by 1985 their disappearance was reflected in the growth of abundant seaweed on the reefs. This in turn led to a decline in some areas of certain coral species, coralline algae, and sponges, which were unable to compete with the seaweed. Even today, urchin populations in the Caribbean have not fully recovered and there have been recent reports of further die-offs, although not on the scale of the earlier one.

Meanwhile, on reefs elsewhere in the world, some populations of urchin are on the increase and causing damage. Urchin-induced erosion has been reported in Mauritius, Kenya and the Red Sea and in the eastern Pacific, where outbreaks seem to have been triggered by the reef damage caused by El Niño (which resulted in increased seaweed growth on the dead and bleached corals that provided a major food source for the urchins). In the Galapagos, sea-urchin grazing has been so severe, with such a quantity of coral removed in the process, that coral growth has stopped altogether in some areas. Elsewhere, for example in the Red Sea and Kenya, urchin outbreaks may well have been sparked off by overfishing of triggerfish and pufferfish which are predators of urchins.

## Coral Diseases

On the reefs of the Florida Keys, vast areas of elkhorn coral have been wiped out by disease. In 1981, delicate cyclindrical branches of elkhorn covered extensive areas of reef and made up ninety-six per cent of reef cover in places. By 1986, this had been reduced to three per cent of the reef cover, leaving mainly dead coral which was rapidly overgrown by seaweed.

Two main coral diseases are known. They are both widespread in the Caribbean and more recently have also been reported in the Red Sea. Black Band Disease is caused by a bacterium which produces a black mat of fine filaments where it attacks the coral. Found mainly in massive brain corals and gorgonians, it appears to kill the coral tissue with poison, and seems

to be more frequent on reefs under stress from other impacts, such as bleaching. White Band Disease occurs mainly in branching coral; it kills and bleaches the tissue in parts of the colony, leaving behind a white skeleton. Its cause is unknown, although bacteria have been found in diseased colonies.

Other disease-like conditions, possibly also caused by stress, have been reported in the Caribbean and Hawaii. Corals have been seen with cancerous growths (called neoplasms) in which the skeleton develops an unusual structure and forms lumps or tumours. Very little is yet known about these problems, except that some corals seem to be resistant to disease, for reasons which currently remain obscure. If diseases are indeed triggered by stress, they could well become more common. The interconnectedness of the oceans means that disease can spread widely through populations of marine animals, as demonstrated by the rapid demise of sea urchins in the Caribbean. The very mechanisms that allow corals to colonise the oceans may also carry the seeds of their destruction.

In Florida a few attempts have been made to control the spread of White Band and Black Band disease. One technique is to use an aspirator to suck the diseased tissue off the coral, which is then

disposed of on land. Another is to coat the infected area with moulding clay or cement. Both techniques are expensive and time-consuming and are unlikely to be feasible for treating large areas of diseased reef.

## Upsetting the Balance

Natural disturbances such as hurricanes and predators are part of the normal life cycle of the reef, but the combination of human and natural stresses can be devastating. The ability of reefs to recover from natural disturbances is easily upset by the addition of human impacts. Reefs may well be able to survive single, isolated catastrophes such as hurricanes, and continuous low-level pressures such as urchin grazing. They have a considerable capacity for regeneration, provided that stresses and disturbances do not persist for long periods or, crucially, that several stresses do not operate at once.

The difference between just one disturbance and several can be seen in comparing the platform reefs around two very similar coral cays, Heron Island and Green Island, on the Great Barrier Reef. Reefs around Heron Island are still in good condition although the island has

been a tourist resort for nearly forty years. In contrast, reefs around Green Island, which has also been used by tourists for many decades, have never fully recovered from outbreaks of crown-of-thorns starfish in the 1960s and 1980s. The various disturbances caused by tourism seem to have been enough to prevent recovery from the starfish attacks. The proximity of Green Island to the coast may also have made the reefs more vulnerable to nutrient run-off from the sugar plantations and intensive agriculture on the Queensland mainland, compared to the more remote reefs around Heron Island.

## Ciguatera

Ciguatera is the commonest type of fish-poisoning in the tropics and is much feared by coastal people and sailors. Known since at least the sixteenth century, it is especially prevalent in the Caribbean and the Pacific. Some believe that ciguatera outbreaks are increasing and that this is almost certainly a signal that the health of coral reefs is under assault. Ciguatera is caused by poisons (or a poison) produced by tiny plants or dinoflagellates (most commonly *Gambierdiscus toxicus*), that live on seaweeds on the reef. 400 species of fish are known to feed on the seaweed and from them the poisons are passed up

the food chain through the carnivores and animals that eat decaying plant and animal remains. It is most prevalent in carnivores, many of which are the most popular food fish with humans, although it can also be carried by herbivorous fish. Common 'ciguatoxic' fish are groupers, mullet, parrotfish, triggerfish, surgeonfish, wrasse, emperorfish, barracuda, snappers, jacks and trevallies – all widely eaten by humans. In the Caribbean, various shallow-water fish including such popular commercial species as snapper and yellowfin grouper are notorious for carrying the poison and are often not sold because of the risk.

Ciguatera is virtually undetectable by taste or smell and can have seriously debilitating consequences on humans. The results of poisoning are extremely unpleasant. Symptoms begin about six to twelve hours after eating the fish, with diarrhoea, stomach cramps and nausea, normally followed by neurological disturbances including dizziness, tingling or numbness in the mouth, hands and feet, and extremities, headaches, skin rash, muscle weakness, itching, sweating and general pain. Severe cases can lead to shock, paralysis, and in rare cases even death. Recovery normally occurs naturally but takes anything from two days to a week in mild cases to several weeks for

more severe attacks. Furthermore, people appear to become 'sensitised' to the toxin, so that subsequent attacks are worse than the first. Symptoms are, however, extremely variable and seem to be related to the type of fish eaten, suggesting that in fact several poisons are involved. About two out of every thousand people in the Pacific are known to be affected each year but many cases are not reported and incidences may be ten times as high. In the Caribbean, reported incidences have been as high as 4.2 cases per thousand as in the US Virgin Islands in the early 1980s.

No antidote to the poison is available, though extensive research to find one is underway. The drug mannitol can alleviate some of the symptoms, but in some coastal communities there are traditional remedies which are held to be effective – pharmacological scientists in Australia and New Caledonia are looking at these for possible sources of cures. The breakdown of traditional lifestyles in many tropical island countries, and the growing dependence of local people on fish bought in town markets rather than caught by themselves has meant that local knowledge of how to avoid ciguatera is being lost. This ranged from not fishing on known affected reefs and avoiding fish species that are likely to be toxic, to practical actions such as feeding a sample to the household cat first and watching the result! When a ciguatera outbreak happens, it can have a number of far-reaching, indirect effects. Fear of the poison and the need to avoid fish after an outbreak has led to increased dependency on imported food, which has an obvious impact on the local economy, and it can be a major obstacle to the development of fisheries. Even the tourist industry can be affected.

In recent years, outbreaks of ciguatera seem to have been increasing in some areas. This could be put down to better reporting of the problem, as more people are attending clinics for help, but a worrying correlation has been noticed by scientists studying the disease. Many of the severe outbreaks coincide with some major form of disturbance on the reef. Ciguatera does not inevitably follow all stresses on reefs, but outbreaks have been correlated with hurricanes, storms, freshwater run-off, wrecks, dumping, blasting and construction.

Evidence for a link between reef damage and ciguatera was first noticed on the atoll of Hao in French Polynesia. Between 1966 and 1968 an outbreak affected some 280 of the 650 inhabitants shortly after large-scale construction had taken place to build a staging base for nuclear testing on the atolls of Moruroa and Fangataufa. An army camp was built for 2,000 soldiers, with a large airfield and a 3,500-metre runway which had required the dredging of large amounts of coral. Outbreaks also occurred in the 1960s and 1970s following similar construction work in the Gambier Islands, again in French Polynesia. (It is after these islands that the dinoflagellates involved in ciguatera are named.) Between 1968 and 1987, 3,000 cases of fish-poisoning occurred on Mangareva, the largest of

these islands, and coincided with the construction of military facilities.

Reef disturbances often result in increased seaweed growth, and this provides even more habitat for the dinoflagellates that produce the poison. Why ciguatera outbreaks accompany some disturbances and not others is not at all clear. In the Pacific, many of the major outbreaks have been associated with intense military activity, and the reasons for this remain obscure. Certainly military projects seem to have provoked the largest outbreaks of poisoning, and this could be linked to the fact that the construction activities involved are on a larger scale than most others in the area. It may simply reflect the fact that where the military has been present, both the impact on the reef and the health of the local human population are

well documented – teams of scientists have worked in both the US and French territories in the Pacific; it is quite possible that correlations between outbreaks and reef damage exist elsewhere but have simply never been recorded.

Another query hangs over the question of whether radioactivity may play a role in ciguatera outbreaks in French Polynesia, which have frequently appeared to be linked with both the building of military bases and the development of the nuclear-testing programme. Ships contaminated during atmospheric tests at Moruroa were often washed down afterwards in the lagoon at Mangareva, and all manner of waste materials were dumped here without being checked for radioactivity. In the Marshall Islands, where there are at least three cases of ciguatera poisoning per thousand people each year, outbreaks have appeared to be linked with both military activities and nuclear testing on Kwajalein, Bikini and Enewetak atolls.

The view of some local people and environmentalists in the Pacific, however, is that ciguatera represents a largely hidden human tragedy that is directly related to military activity. Wherever it occurs, it seems, at the very least, to indicate that something is wrong with the reef, and the evidence suggests that in many cases this may have a human origin.

# CHAPTER FOUR

# DEVELOPMENT & POLLUTION
## Halting the Destruction

In the 1860s, the biologist Sir Alfred Russell Wallace visited Ambon Bay on the island of Ambon (then known as Amboyna) in Eastern Indonesia and was overwhelmed with the rich diversity of the shallow reefs he saw there. 'The clearness of the water afforded me one of the most astonishing and beautiful sights that I have ever beheld', he wrote. 'The bottom was absolutely hidden by a continuous series of corals, sponges, actiniae, and other marine productions, of magnificent dimensions, varied forms and brilliant colours . . . In and out of them moved numbers of blue and red and yellow fishes, spotted and banded and striped in the most striking manner . . . It was a sight to gaze at for hours, and no description can do justice to its surpassing beauty and interest. For once, the reality exceeded the most glowing accounts I had read of the wonders of a coral sea . . . there is perhaps no spot in the world richer in marine productions, coral shells and fishes than the harbour of Amboyna.' As far as the modern reader can tell, Wallace was describing a reef in well-nigh pristine condition.

Just over a century later, marine biologists studying the Ambon Bay reefs discovered that although some of them on the outside of the bay were still in good condition, elsewhere large areas of coral had been blasted away or smothered by silt and rubbish washed off the now well-populated coastline. In 1984, an expedition of Dutch and Indonesian reef scientists visited the same area and found only fifteen coral species in the whole bay, compared to seventy or more on other reefs they had looked at on nearby islands.

Ambon Bay is typical of numerous tropical locations where reefs are now being destroyed or threatened. People have always been drawn to coastlines, as coastal plains provide fertile agricultural land, and the shallow waters above the continental shelf offer abundant fisheries. As maritime trade developed, ports were built, and towns and cities were often sited on river deltas to ensure good communications with inland areas upstream.

These patterns of settlement posed few problems in pre-industrial times, but a combination of modern industrial development and fast-growing populations is now putting enormous pressures on coastal ecosystems. The world's current

*Opposite: a jetty and boat channel built over and through reefs in Tarawa, one of the many atolls that make up Kiribati in the Pacific Ocean. Even small coastal constructions in remote areas can have a local impact on reef health.*

*The reefs of Indonesia, lying in the region of highest reef diversity, amazed early naturalists such as Wallace with their exotic and colourful inhabitants like this fish, a particularly striking species of scorpionfish (Dendrochirus biocellatus).*

All centres of population and industry nowadays, even agricultural land, produce a range of waste products and effluents. In coastal areas, these are habitually discharged into the sea and in many cases the impact on tropical coastlines is still largely unknown. Studies that have so far been carried out have often produced conflicting results, which can make it difficult to use the data to convince people that potentially harmful practices should be changed. The seriousness of the effect of a pollution incident depends on many variables such as weather and not just on, say, the size of a toxic discharge. For example, in open water and on well-flushed coastlines, pollutants are dispersed far more easily than in enclosed bays and lagoons. A further complication is that it is often difficult to separate the effects of different pollutants, of which sewage is a case in point: both the nutrients in sewage and the chemicals used to treat it can damage corals.

A single brief pollution incident can cause short-term, localised damage (and often much media attention) but the affected reef may recover surprisingly rapidly. When a Greek freighter ran aground on a reef in the north-west Hawaiian Islands in the early 1980s, 2,200 tons of powdered kaolin clay were jettisoned overboard in order to refloat the ship. Huge plumes of suspended clay streamed from the site and caused widespread public alarm. Two weeks later, the area of reef in the immediate vicinity of the damage, up to a radius of fifty metres, was indeed found to have been badly damaged, but beyond that there was no sign of the silt, which had been thoroughly dispersed by ocean currents. On the other hand, steady, chronic pollution, such as repeated minor oil leakages from a refinery, can cause enormous damage, even if the quantity of pollutant entering the sea at any one time is generally low.

In spite of the fact that the depredations of many pollutants are difficult to measure exactly and that it can even be hard to identify their precise origin, it is well known that many substances used in a range of industrial, domestic and agricultural contexts are harmful to human health and cause damage to other natural

population is estimated at 5.3 billion, of whom 3 billion live in coastal areas. By the year 2050, the number of those living near coastlines is expected to be approaching 7.2 billion, and the greatest increases in population are likely to take place in the poorer developing countries in the tropics.

Coral reefs and other habitats associated with them, such as mangroves and seagrass beds, are therefore increasingly coming under severe stress. Many have been destroyed outright through coastal development – where ports, airports, tourist resorts and urban and industrial complexes are built quite literally on the reef itself or on areas of land reclaimed from shallow water, which can include mangrove swamps or seagrass beds. More insidious damage is caused less directly. A major hazard for reefs is pollution: sediments and toxic chemicals wash on to them as side-effects of a wide range of human activities. And there are also less well understood forms of environmental stress. When channels are dredged and jetties built out over the reef, for example, it is not unusual for the

natural pattern of water circulation to be changed. This is likely to alter the distribution of oxygen and food to the reef inhabitants as well as having an effect on the transport of the larvae of various reef species to or from the reefs. Other reef animals may become starved of important nutrients, which are no longer swept into the water around them, and recolonisation by new animals may be hindered.

It has been estimated that about forty per cent of marine pollution derives from the land, and a huge proportion of this – around ninety per cent – tends to collect in shallow coastal waters, rather than being swept into the deep ocean where it might do less damage. This means that, like other shallow water habitats, reefs are extremely vulnerable to the threat of pollution. Fringing and patch reefs and any reefs close to the shore are most at risk, especially those around high volcanic islands and indeed anywhere with steeply sloping coastlines. Even reefs some distance from land may be at risk from land-originated pollution – if it is easily transported in sea water.

the corals, as oxygen and vital nutrients are prevented from reaching the polyps. Equally importantly, silty waters prevent sunlight reaching the zooxanthellae in the polyps, which means that photosynthesis is impeded and coral growth is slowed down. Sediment lying on the hard surfaces of the reef prevents young corals from settling there and forming new colonies, as well as blocking up the crevices and depressions in the coral rock that would normally be used as sheltering places by fish and other creatures.

Star coral (*Montastrea cavernosa*) is one of the most resistant to silt, but the majority of corals will eventually be damaged or killed if silt levels remain high over a protracted period. Some, like the beautiful elkhorn coral (*Acropora palmata*) are extremely sensitive and die off very quickly in silty environments.

Most of the heavy sediment that settles on reefs comes from the land. The heavy rain that periodically falls in the tropics ensures that any soil not stabilised by a covering of vegetation is only too vulnerable to erosion. The causes of erosion, which include mining, construction sites and development projects of all kinds, are numerous. It is now common, for example, to build roads close to the coastlines of islands, allowing motorised transport to reach communities that had previously depended on boats for trade and communication. In the initial stages of development, roads tend to be unpaved (because of the high cost of hard surfacing) and constructed of sand and crushed coral. A certain amount of damage happens during construction, but this is not the end of the problem. With

habitats. It is critically important that steps are taken to choose alternative methods of development or to find non-toxic equivalents of harmful substances so that potentially damaging activities can be avoided.

## Silting up the Reefs

Corals have to be able to tolerate some degree of silt, as they are naturally subject to sediments stirred up from the seabed by currents and waves and, during storms, to a certain amount of soil run-off from the land. Normally the coral colonies are soon washed clean by tides and currents, a process sometimes helped by the corals themselves through movements of the polyps and tentacles and through the production of mucus by the polyps which

traps particles of sediment. Some, such as *Goniopora* and *Euphyllia*, which are among the few corals still surviving in Ambon Bay, seem to be particularly silt-tolerant and can be found in very muddy environments. Quite how they survive is still not clear; in some cases it may be because they have large polyps that are especially good at removing silt. Some corals have been known to produce particularly large quantities of mucus at times of stress to prtect themselves. However, this is an energy-intensive activity, and so it is not necessarily beneficial for corals to be forced to react in this way.

Most corals, however, are very sensitive to high or increased levels of silt, rapidly becoming damaged or even dying. Large amounts of sediment effectively smother

*Above: although some reefs can survive a certain level of sedimentation, most, like this one in Belau, will rapidly deteriorate. The silty surface that develops in situations like this prevents coral larvae from settling and so impedes the development of new colonies.*

*Opposite, top: the beautiful elkhorn coral* (Acropora palmata), *flourishing here on a Caribbean reef crest, succumbs extremely fast in silty conditions.*

*Two types of coral that are particularly resistant to silt –* Goniopora (left) *and* Euphyllia (right).

the first rainstorm, the unstable surface will begin to be washed away and the sediment will start to land on the reef below.

In Guam, the building of just one road on the south coast of the island resulted in the death in some localities of up to ninety-five per cent of the corals. In northern Queensland, Australia, a road was built along the coastal edge of the Daintree rainforest in the early 1980s, on a steep slope that drops directly onto the reef. Although the corals here appear to be highly tolerant to silt, the increased rates of soil run-off may be pushing them near the limit of survival and even a small increase in soil run-off could have fatal consequences. Where roads must be built, opting for a stable surface would vastly decrease the amount of silt created by them.

The destruction of rainforests has shown us how easily the thin, fragile layer of topsoil on which they grow can be lost, and if reefs are anywhere near the run-off from them, the effect can be disastrous. Where forests and other vegetation are cleared, it is essential that steps are taken to avoid erosion.

Often the sources of sediment that ends up on a reef can be relatively far inland; much of the soil washed off the land flows first into streams and rivers before it is carried into the sea. The practice of slash-and-burn, poor farming methods, intensive agriculture and the raising of plantation crops can all have devastating effects in terms of soil erosion. In Kenya, land clearance and deforestation in upland areas have led to a huge loss of topsoil into the Sabaki and Tana Rivers, which disgorge up to 8.4 million tonnes of silt a year into the sea. Reefs to the north of Malindi, as well as many in the Malindi-Watamu Marine Park, are now very badly affected. The water here is sometimes so thick with silt and visibility so poor that even fish cannot be seen.

Similar activities are thought to have caused the sediment damage found on over half the reefs in Thailand and to explain the fact that in some coastal areas near forests around Puerto Rico, reefs close to shore have high levels of silt and little coral; those furthest away from shore (eighty metres or so) have strikingly less silt and more coral. Large areas of coral

*This coastal road was carved through the Daintree rainforest, in Queensland, Australia – a prime example of a badly planned road posing a serious threat to the coral reefs nearby. The road was never finished so that when it rains, soil washes off it down the steep slopes to the fringing reef below.*

on reefs on both the Caribbean and the Pacific coasts of Costa Rica, for example, have been killed by silt resulting from forest destruction. On the Pacific coast, the Esquinas River drains into the Golfo Dulce which once had healthy reefs. Forest cover in the drainage basin is now down to ten per cent of the area that was forested in the 1940s. The trees have been replaced

by banana plantations, and reefs in the vicinity of the estuary are now largely dead. The only remaining live reefs in the Golfo Dulce are along the coast drained by the Rincon river, whose watershed still comprises pristine rainforest.

Much of the soil run-off that happens during logging operations is due not so much to tree-felling as to the construction

*Mud from eroded land upstream being washed into the sea at Airai, Babeldaob Island, Belau – an increasingly common sight all over the world. There is already major concern about the impact of erosion on the land; its effect on marine life is less often appreciated, but outflows of silt like this in the tropics can easily damage vulnerable coastal habitats such as reefs.*

of the dirt roads, camps and other infrastructure that support the enterprise, especially where the activity takes place on steep slopes. This is just what happened in Bacuit Bay on Palawan Island in the Philippines. Surrounded by steeply forested slopes, this beautiful bay is dotted with massive limestone islands, whose pinnacles rise vertically out of the crystal blue water to heights of 500 metres or more. Below water, the rocky cliffs of these islands provide a firm base for flourishing coral reefs, which support a wealth of food fish that are harvested by the small local community; they have also become a prime dive site. Logging began in this previously untouched location in 1985. A large area of forest was cleared some three kilometres inland for the logging camp, and a network of dirt access tracks was built through the forest. On the coast, soil was bulldozed down the steep hillside into the sea to build a large earthen pier where heavy machinery and logs could be loaded on and off. Within a year, siltation on the reefs in Bacuit Bay had increased by as much as 200 times the normal rate, and some of the reefs were already dead.

On small islands, where flat land is at a premium, airports are often built on reef flats or shallow reefs. Even if the whole reef is not destroyed in the course of being levelled, silt from the site often kills corals on adjacent reefs. The airport that is planned for Hong Kong and that proposed for the island of Ishigaki in southern Japan could have major impacts on nearby reefs.

Military bases have frequently been built on remote atoll islands, and the construction, dredging and dumping associated with this often causes heavy sedimentation on the surrounding reefs. In the Pacific, reefs were damaged during the construction of US bases on Johnston Atoll (see box), Palmyra, Wake and Midway atolls, and in the Indian Ocean, the British and US bases on Diego Garcia, the southernmost atoll in the Chagos Archipelago, may have affected adjacent reefs.

Mangroves naturally trap some soil runoff from the land, thereby protecting reefs behind them, but all too often they are removed or filled in as a prelude to development, so the problem of sedimentation is exacerbated.

*Greenpeace's flagship, the Rainbow Warrior, sailing to Johnston Atoll in June 1990 to protest at the activities of the US army chemical weapons incineration facility there.*

Johnston Atoll, an unincorporated territory of the United States, lies 1,300 kilometres south-west of Hawaii in the Pacific Ocean. In 1926, part of the Atoll, now called the Johnston Atoll Wildlife Refuge, was declared a nature reserve 'for the protection of native birds'. Eight years later the military began to use the island. Since then, what was a relatively small area of land has grown dramatically through land reclamation so that it is now ten times its original size and comprises two artificial islands. The construction activities associated with this, involving large-scale dredging of the lagoon, have been responsible for the devastation (through sedimentation) of vast areas of reef. An estimated 28 million square metres of reef and lagoon have been seriously affected, and a further four million may have been totally destroyed.

The military facility played a central role in the US nuclear testing programme (1946-63), and in 1972 large quantities of a chemical defoliant, Agent Orange, were brought from Vietnam to Johnston Atoll for disposal. A number of contamination incidents involving both plutonium and dioxin have been reported over the years, though little is known about the extent of contamination, and more incidents may have occurred.

At present the Atoll is being used to test a prototype incinerator which will burn the 400,000 chemical weapons currently stored on it, including 100,000 US chemical weapons withdrawn by NATO from West Germany in 1990. Since 1983, Greenpeace and most of the Pacific Island Nations have expressed strong objections to the presence of the incinerator. The concern is that toxic residues from the incinerator may pollute the sea and accumulate in marine organisms, ultimately affecting the health and viability of the entire food web. Thermal discharges – a by-product of the process – may raise the sea temperature above a level that corals can cope with, and there is the ever-present risk of a major accident that could lead to extreme pollution of the environment. In 1986 Johnston Atoll Wildlife Refuge earned the doubtful honour of being declared by the US Fish and Wildlife Service one of the ten sites in the US and affiliated areas most in need of a clean-up.

In response to pressure from Greenpeace and peoples in the Pacific, the US government has given some assurances that once the current stockpile has been disposed of, no additional chemical weapons will be brought to Johnston Atoll, and the incinerator will be dismantled. But the fear is that this expensive facility will continue to be a dumping ground for hazardous wastes. Greenpeace is committed to observing and recording the impact on corals and other marine life of incinerator operations and to demanding that detailed monitoring of the marine environment be carried out on a regular basis around the Atoll.

## Healthy Land – Healthy Reefs

On many Pacific islands, the link between activities in the inland forests and the health of coastal waters has long been understood. In some cases, the land has traditionally been divided among clans and tribal groups in wedges, so that a community has control over at least part of the catchment area that drains to the coastal area where it has fishing rights. In others, inland communities are held accountable to people living on the coast for any damage caused by poor land use. One coastal community in Marovo Lagoon in the Solomon Islands, for example, is threatening to take action against a group of inland ('bush') people who have considered selling their traditional forest rights to a foreign logging company. The coastal people allow the inland people to fish on their reefs, in exchange for the inland people taking care of the forest in such a way that the reefs and lagoons do not suffer. The inland people stand to lose their fishing rights if they pursue the economic incentives offered by loggers and give up their forest.

Stopping the run-off of soil, fertilisers, pesticides, herbicides and other agricultural pollutants from land is a major task and involves a wide range of people and organisations that may have little to do with the shore and the reefs. Ultimately, it requires a move away from intensive farming practices and deforestation to more sustainable forms of agriculture and forestry, and education of those involved about the links between their activities and the health of the reefs.

Preventing siltation from deforestation means protecting forests on steep slopes and implementing sustainable forest management. One strategy is to opt for uses of forests that do not involve cutting down trees, and instead harvesting rattan or plants of medicinal value, for example. Where timber has to be extracted, this is best done through small-scale, community-based operations which have minimal impact on the forest as a whole, reduce erosion rates and have the important advantage of benefiting local people directly,

unlike the huge commercial projects which are almost always controlled by outsiders.

A return to traditional methods of 'agro-forestry' on some of the Pacific Islands might help to reduce soil run-off: crops are grown between and beneath timber species to maintain ground cover. There is also a whole range of erosion control measures that should be observed in all watersheds, such as contour planting of woody species to stabilise soils in agricultural areas, and prohibiting the removal of natural forest and vegetation along the banks of streams and rivers. The ecological importance of forests near coral reefs must be recognised and taken into account in management plans.

Small-scale farmers can be supported in using methods that involve minimal tillage of the soil, such as planting seeds in holes rather than broadcasting them on tilled, bare soil. Where agriculture is already intensive, careful dialogue is necessary between the farmers and those managing the reefs. A start has been made in Queensland in Australia, where the Great Barrier Reef Marine Park Authority is discussing with sugar farmers methods to decrease the amount of fertiliser that leaches out into the sea from the acres of cane sugar fields along the mainland coast.

## Dredging

Reefs can also suffer if the sediments that normally lie on the sea floor are disturbed too much. This can happen during dredging for ports and harbours, or mining for coral and coral rock. Dredging usually takes place in the course of clearing channels for shipping, and in the shaping of marinas and ports. It is also used as a method of obtaining sand and coral rock for building roads, runways and other coastal infrastructure. When dredging happens, huge clouds of silt can form, which are then swept along the coast in currents, sometimes causing damage miles away from the dredging and construction sites. When a deep-water port was dredged at Phuket in Thailand in 1987, sediment killed over a third of the corals on the nearby reefs within a single year. In this case, the impact was relatively brief and the reefs recovered a year or so after completion of the port. Undoubtedly this had a lot to do with the fact that the reef flats were dominated by massive corals (*Porites*), which are among the most resistant of corals: even if only a small amount of live tissue is left, new polyps grow back quite rapidly over damaged areas. Had the corals been more fragile, damage could have been longer-lasting, possibly even permanent.

There are measures which can be taken on site to lessen the amount of silt that escapes onto surrounding reefs when dredging and construction activities are in progress – silt screens can be erected and suction pumps used. While these can never be completely effective, they do afford a certain protection, though only if properly installed and operated; this means that the people using them must be properly trained. Where possible, marinas and other harbours should be excavated in the dry, from the landward side, so that the sea is allowed to enter only when the works are almost finished.

Channels are often dredged through reefs to allow boats to reach shore or to anchor in the sheltered waters of a lagoon. Quite apart from the siltation that may be caused during construction, artificially created channels can radically alter water circulation, tidal flow and even water level, causing changes to the environment that corals may not be able to withstand. When a boat channel was blasted through a reef at Nanumea on Tuvalu in the Pacific

in the 1940s, for example, the subsequent drop in sea level at low tide in the lagoon of the atoll resulted in the death of many corals, and the reef had still not recovered over forty years later.

Where channels must be dredged, they should preferably be built where the reef is already damaged. In no circumstances should they be built between the sea and a lagoon in which the water at low tide is above sea level, as this will drain the lagoon. Boat channels through the reef and even harbours can be constructed with deliberately uneven sides and bottoms to encourage reef animals and plants to settle.

If engineering and construction activities must take place on the coast, it is essential that a full and careful assessment of all the natural habitats that would be affected is made, so that sites that are particularly rich or diverse, or have important ecological roles – as spawning grounds, for example – can be avoided. Wherever possible, areas that have already suffered damage should be chosen, in order to spare healthier reefs.

## Coral Mining

In atoll nations, where the country consists of a large area of water dotted with tiny islands, the available land is far too precious to be mined for building material. Even where terrestrial sources can be used, reefs may still provide the cheapest building materials. On Chuuk (Truk), in the Federated States of Micronesia in the Pacific, crushed rock taken from inland quarries for road construction and surfacing costs about thirty-three US dollars per cubic metre, whereas coral and dead coral rock mined by dredging cost only half that much.

Historically the use of coral as a construction material probably had relatively

*Opposite: devastation caused by logging in a forest in Milne Bay Province, Papua New Guinea. Tracks and camps built by logging companies are a major source of silt and erosion. Left: a silt screen in position to contain sediments produced during dredging in Bonaire, the Netherlands Antilles. Dredging can result in nearby reefs being inundated with sediment, so using silt screens is an important method of damage limitation. Above: coral miners doing their job under water in the Maldives – the one in the foreground is in the process of moving a big coral colony.*

little impact because population densities were low and building was on a fairly small scale, but in recent years, coral mining has increased dramatically as a direct result of the rapid growth of tourism and the building of resorts.

In the Maldives, coral is traditionally mined by villagers from the island of Maamigili in Alifu Atoll who travel around the atolls to supply other islands in need of construction material. Once they have selected a suitable reef, corals are dislodged from the reef, broken into manageable sizes using iron bars, and taken ashore by boat. The massive species such as *Porites* and the more sturdy branching corals such as *Acropora humilis* are most commonly used.

It is usually very straightforward to extract coral boulders from nearshore reefs. On many islands, local people may justify removing coral on the grounds that it will eventually regrow; what they often do not realise is that current extraction rates are so high that the reefs cannot keep pace with demand, given how slowly they regenerate. In addition to this, their fisheries may be affected as major dismantling of reefs may remove the crevices and overhangs in which reef creatures can shelter, so affecting their abundance. In the Maldives, for instance, reefs that have been mined for coral have fewer fish than unmined reefs, particularly of the small species that shelter among shallow water corals, many of which are valuable as bait in the commercial tuna fishery or in the aquarium fish trade.

Coral is much used in the construction of roads and office blocks in the Maldivian capital, Male, and for ports, harbours and jetties on several islands. Over 93,000 cubic metres (over 3.2 million cubic feet) of coral rock have been extracted from the Maldivian reefs in the last twenty years, most of it from around North and South Male atolls where there is rapid tourist and industrial development.

Many reefs which have been mined show only minimal signs of recovery even after ten years and may take more than fifty years to regenerate, always assuming that there is a minimum of disturbance during that period. Some may never recover. It has been estimated that if coral mining continues at the

present rate, North Male Atoll could be barren of all shallow reefs by the year 2014.

Elsewhere, huge quantities of coral are being removed for similar purposes: in Mauritius, Sri Lanka, the Comores, India, Malaysia, Indonesia, the Philippines and many of the Pacific Islands, major damage is being caused by mining.

Preventing coral and sand mining is difficult in countries where there are few alternative sources of building materials. In the Maldives, there is a plan to mine an entire 'sacrificial' reef. A reef has been selected that is not used for fishing or tourism and will be excavated down to the fossil coral, perhaps fifty metres below sea level. It has been estimated that this could provide sufficient building material for North Male atoll for at least a century. This will be a costly solution in terms of equipment and technology and will inevitably depend on overseas aid.

In many countries, schemes such as this are not feasible and so it is important that other alternatives are sought. A return to more traditional forms of construction may be a solution in some areas, using fast-growing indigenous trees and plants such as coconut palm fronds – which have long provided relatively sound housing in tropical countries. Buildings may not last as long, but at least they have the advantage of being easily renewable.

Coral was traditionally mined in Sri Lanka from fossil deposits found inland, but during the 1970s and 1980s these supplies were largely depleted by a boom in the construction industry as a result of a

massive World Bank-supported housing programme for local people and the development of tourism along the south west coast. By the mid-1980s, over 2,000 tonnes of live coral were being removed each year from the reefs and 7,000 tonnes of coral rubble were being taken from beaches, to complement the 10,000 tonnes a year still available from the fossil deposits. In addition, over 34,000 cubic metres of sand were being removed annually from beaches and inshore areas.

Mining of live coral from the reef and the removal of coral rubble were made illegal in Sri Lanka in 1983, but these practices still continue (despite the existence of alternative sources of building material inland) and have proved extremely difficult to prevent. In the 1980s over a thousand people depended for their living on coral mining and the lack of suitable alternative employment has made enforcement of the law practically impossible. Attempts have been made to stop coral mining by penalising collectors and confiscating corals but these have invariably failed against a background of a continuing market for the material and the lack of alternative work. Some coral collectors have been offered jobs elsewhere, but since these have been mainly agricultural, based inland and away from their homes, the acceptance rate has been low. Any attempt to discontinue coral mining will need to involve the miners and their families directly in finding or setting up acceptable alternative employment in the same area.

Two of the thousands of creatures that lose the essential protection of overhangs, caves and cracks in the reef, when coral is mined: above, a leaf scorpion fish (Taenianotus triancanthus), which can sometimes be seen rocking from side to side in the swell, bearing an uncanny resemblance to algae waving in the currents; right, a box fish (Ostracion tuberculatus) – its characteristic shape is formed by protective bony plates making it almost completely rigid; only its mouth and side fins can move. Boxfish can exude a toxic mucus from their skin, making them immune from attack by all but the larger predators on the reef.

Opposite: massive corals mined from reefs in the Maldives and piled up on the shore to dry in the sun before being broken into smaller pieces and used for building walls and houses.

## Reefs as Natural Barriers

Reefs act as natural breakwaters between the ocean and the land, affording much-needed protection, both to the natural habitats behind them and to the people living in such areas.

Mining coral removes the basic framework of the reef and so destroys, or at the very least weakens, the natural breakwater that protects the shore from the erosive power of waves. The removal of coral also means the removal of the material that would eventually have broken down to form the sand for beaches, which themselves also play a part in protecting the coast. Removing coral rubble and sand from beaches and dredging sand from lagoons and seagrass beds reduces protection from waves and storms still further and increases the rate of erosion.

The south-west coast of Sri Lanka is swept by the winds and rains of the annual monsoon from May to October. In the last two decades, erosion has affected around seventy-five per cent of the beaches along the 350-kilometre stretch of coast between Colombo and Hambantota. There has been extensive flooding which has killed villagers and left thousands homeless. Much of this is due to poorly planned coastal development, badly sited jetties and the like, but coral and sand mining have been major contributing factors.

Growing fears about rising sea levels and more frequent storms resulting from global warming have made erosion a major issue especially in low-lying countries such as the Maldives, but also in coastal areas close to sea level in general. Many of these nations are comparatively poor and any artificial barrier to the sea

*Left: this aerial picture of waves breaking on the weather side of One Tree Reef on the Great Barrier Reef in Australia clearly shows their function as breakwaters, leaving the tranquil waters of the lagoon beyond undisturbed by the ocean breakers. Opposite: barrel sponges; sponges obtain most of their food by filtering minute particles out of the water and are not dependent on clear water. They stand a better chance than corals of surviving in water polluted by nutrients and may even initially benefit.*

to replace damaged reefs would be prohibitively expensive to put into position, even if it could be made to work.

In some circumstances coral-mining can actually benefit marine life if carried out with sufficient care and on a small scale. In the Pacific, atolls such as those in the Marshall Islands are often surrounded by a broad reef flat from which dead coral and coralline algae are mined. With a reef of this nature, if suitable sites are chosen and the coral 'rock' is quarried to leave holes between two to four metres deep, these will attract reef animals seeking shelter and over a period of twenty years or so thriving reef communities will develop inside them.

## Sewage and Fertilisers – Pollution from Nutrients

The tropical waters where reefs flourish are normally low in nutrients such as nitrates and phosphates. The fertilisers and sewage which are dumped in the oceans, however, contain very high levels of these compounds, causing a condition known as eutrophication, which means that the water is enriched with mineral and organic nutrients. Many of these nutrients are essential to the maintenance of life, but in excessive amounts, they result in reef creatures being starved of oxygen. Seaweeds benefit from high nutrient levels and can tolerate low oxygen levels, but corals have difficulty surviving in such conditions. Nitrates in large quantities are toxic to corals, and phosphates inhibit skeletal growth. So in waters that have become nutrient-rich, seaweeds may soon come to dominate a reef, further hastening the demise of corals as they shade out the sunlight. The tiny plants (phytoplankton) that float in the upper layers of the sea also benefit from nutrients and increase under these conditions, reducing the amount of light reaching the corals still more. Plant-eating fish and sea urchins may keep the seaweed in check for a while, but in heavily fished areas, or where sea urchin populations have declined, the reefs may rapidly take on the appearance of seaweed beds.

For coral reefs, eutrophication is now a global problem, and much of it is due to sewage pollution. Billions of litres of sewage are pumped into the sea daily worldwide, much of it barely treated, or containing toxic chemicals from treatment processes. Often advocated is tertiary level treatment, which cleans the water most thoroughly (though it may still leave some contaminants), but this is so expensive that it is only rarely used, even in the industrialised world. Many treatment plants discharge only partially treated sewage, septic tank systems often develop faults allowing sewage to leak into the groundwater, and even simple village privies can overflow in heavy rains. Sewage pollution constitutes a major health hazard for people swimming in the sea where the outfall ends up, causing outbreaks of viral hepatitis, cholera and typhoid (notoriously picked up from filter feeders like mussels and oysters that take up sewage), but is also a major cause of reef damage.

On open coastlines washed by strong currents, the impact of a sewage outfall on corals may be minimal if the effluent drifts rapidly away from the reefs. It can even be beneficial for certain species of fish which will congregate at such spots to feed on the organic matter. But sewage can have a disastrous impact in enclosed bays or in calm, shallow waters like lagoons where it remains in contact with the reef over long periods.

A well-documented example of this kind of damage was at Kaneohe Bay on the island of Oahu in Hawaii, which has been heavily developed in the last few decades. The rich volcanic soils of the lower mountain slopes are intensively farmed, there is a large military base on the shore, and new roads have been built to allow residents to commute daily to Honolulu. By 1970 the number of people living around the bay had risen to 100,000.

The bay also happens to be the location for the marine laboratory of the University of Hawaii, so the changes that have taken place on the reefs have been extensively studied. In the early 1970s it became apparent that seaweed was taking over the reefs, and that there was less and less living coral. The water of the bay grew increasingly murky, with large amounts of floating organic matter. By 1977, the water was so dirty that even the seaweed was dying off, through lack of sunlight. There was still plenty of life on the sea bottom, but by now it consisted of large populations of sponges, barnacles and other animals that feed by filtering particles of organic matter out of the water. All the organisms that depended for their survival on light had vanished. The source of the problem was the main sewage outfall for the human residents of the area, which was discharging into the southern end of the bay.

Following protests from the public, the outlet was diverted in 1978 so that the effluent flowed out into the open ocean, well outside the bay and down current from the reefs – a common method of limiting sewage pollution. An extraordinary reversal then took place as the water became clearer and the level of nutrients in the bay dropped. First the sponges disappeared as there was no longer any floating food for them, and by 1982 the seaweed had returned. By 1985, the waters of the bay were approaching their former purity, corals had reappeared and the reefs began once more to flourish. Soon tourists began to visit in large numbers again.

But the story is not yet over and the happy ending not secure because in 1990, for no apparent reason, the seaweeds started to increase again. It is possible that the causes could be increased nutrient run-off from the land provoked by further coastal development and the construction of golf courses, which are heavily treated with chemical fertilisers, but so far it has proved difficult to determine the reason.

Little is known about the impact of the extension to the outfall pipe on the ocean outside Kaneohe Bay, and while it is clearly no longer affecting the reefs in the bay, the fact that relocating the pipe was seen as an acceptable solution to the problem of sewage pollution reveals an attitude that many environmentalists regard as fundamentally flawed. Using fresh water in large quantities to flush away human excrement and urine is quite a recent practice that was developed in rich western societies to cope with the problems of poor hygiene and sanitation in the urban environments of the nineteenth century. Until then, throughout human history, human waste had mainly been returned to the soil, where sunlight, soil bacteria and high or low temperatures killed off any disease-causing bacteria or viruses, and the remaining matter acted as a valuable fertiliser.

The costs of waterborne disposal systems make them highly unsuitable for small islands surrounded by coral reefs. They are expensive to build and operate, and they use huge quantities of fresh water (it has been estimated that on average it takes 140 litres of water per person per day to carry sewage to a treatment plant), which is often a precious commodity, especially in heavily populated areas. Even where they are working well they usually do not make the sewage entirely harmless to animal and plant life, and the more sophisticated the treatment, the more expensive and energy-consuming the equipment and process is likely to be. Equipment problems are of particular concern in remote island settings where parts and expertise are not typically at hand.

Agricultural fertilisers are probably as serious a pollutant as sewage, but their effect is much more difficult to measure. Unlike the contents of outfall pipes, they

do not enter the sea at particular points in quantities that can be measured, but leach through the soil and run off the land when it rains or are carried out via streams and rivers along wide areas of coast. Identifying fertiliser pollution is made even harder by the fact that coastal areas where there is heavy use of fertilisers often have relatively dense populations and so produce quantities of sewage. A variety

## Biological Toilets

For most people in the developed world, having access to a flush toilet is one of the fundamentals of modern living. The fact that marine pollution is largely invisible to most people means that the huge pollution problems that result from this way of dealing with sewage are rarely confronted. Many poorer countries aspiring to the lifestyles of the developed world or hoping to attract people from these countries as tourists, consider sewage treatment plants as a prerequisite of their own development. But somehow a way must be found to transform the perception of human waste as just that, something to be disposed of, into the idea that it is material with a valuable use that need not pollute the environment.

Composting or 'biological toilets', which are safe and odourless, make use of a controlled biological process to kill pathogens and to transform human excrement into an inoffensive and harmless residual that can be used as a high-quality soil fertiliser. Some dry treatment systems are based on the process of composting (mixing the waste with earth so that bacteria and fungi break it down to

form humus), others involve the burning or drying of the waste. There are also water-based systems that use very small quantities of water which can then be recycled. Since a supply of water is not needed to operate the system, clean water sources can be used primarily for drinking and cooking. Biological toilets do require some maintenance to ensure that they work properly, but are relatively simple, unlike large, centralised water treatment plants, which use highly complex technology that is inevitably subject to costly breakdown and failure. They could be a significant bonus on islands or atolls where soil fertility is poor. The sewage could be treated either at the municipal level, or perhaps more simply on a household-by-household basis, using dry toilets made of locally available materials. Tourist operators or hoteliers could take the lead in the introduction of these systems by installing dry toilets in resorts so that residents and visitors alike could appreciate their value and acceptability; it would also obviously help to cut down on potential sewage pollution on the local reefs.

## Chemicals, Metals and Other Industrial Pollutants

Tests relating to some of the chemicals and metals that occur in the effluents from industry and mining have been carried out on corals and other reef animals, both in the laboratory and on actual reefs, but very little is known about long-term impacts. In any case, evaluating the effects of potentially dangerous substances is a gargantuan task: there are now about 60,000 synthetic chemicals in use across the world, and another 1,000 are added each year. Even in countries with relatively little industry, businesses involved in boat-building, printing, photography or clothing manufacture, for example, all release effluents, often containing toxic compounds. The solvents used in degreasers, paints and stains and for dry cleaning, for example, all evaporate during use to become air pollutants and eventually find their way to the water. Left-over paints, oils and cleaners, when thrown away at the dump, seep into the water table or are flushed directly into coastal waters.

Heavy metals and certain minerals, frequently found in mining wastes and industrial effluents that are discharged into the oceans, are known to damage sensitive habitats such as coral reefs, but there is much variation. In Thailand, iron has been found in bands within skeletons of corals on a reef flat. The bands correlate with periods of heavy discharge from a tin-smelting operation. The impact of this on the health of the coral is still not known but it could well be deleterious.

of industrial processes, including even small-scale island industries like fish, fruit and coconut processing, also produce effluents that cause nutrient enrichment.

The high nutrient levels in water surrounding the Great Barrier Reef are being put down to a combination of sewage effluents and agricultural run-off. The increase in phosphates over the last 172 years can be seen in changes in banding patterns in coral skeletons which correlate remarkably closely with the steady increase in coastal populations (in particular, the growth of tourist resorts along the coast around Cairns and Townsville and on offshore islands), the intensification of agriculture and the development of the sugar cane industry over the same period. The steady deterioration of the Florida reefs over the last fifteen years is almost certainly partly due to similar factors, although separating these from the more direct impacts of tourism and overfishing is difficult.

Algal blooms or red tides often appear where nutrients build up from sewage or agricultural run-off. These are large slicks of tiny plants such as dinoflagellates and diatoms, which make up much of the phytoplankton and flourish in nutrient-rich waters. Where there are large build-ups, other marine life may suffer: the algae found in the blooms are often toxic and the mucus that tends to accompany them

has a smothering effect. There are few reported cases of damage to reefs, but in 1985, a severe dinoflagellate bloom in the eastern Pacific, off the coasts of Panama and Costa Rica, caused widespread coral mortality.

*Opposite: sign put up by a hotel on a Pacific island that has become the victim of its own sewage.*

*Above: a chain diatom (*Chaeroceros sp.*) with long spines, an organism that is part of the phytoplankton and does well in nutrient-rich waters; ultimately, diatoms can form huge slicks that adversely affect other life on the reefs.*

*Right: a section of* Porites lutea *coral collected in an area within 50 metres of a tin smelter at Ko Phuket in Thailand. The thick brown layer around the upper edge shows the depth of skeleton that was occupied by the coral animal. The thin orange band is iron, deposited at a time when the coral was subjected to particularly high levels of iron in the washings of tin ore, which are discharged from the smelter directly onto the reef flat, forming pools there when the discharge happens at low tide.*

Some persistent chemicals, which are resistant to natural degradation and so gradually build up in the environment, such as PCBs, DDT and chlorine-based compounds, are an obvious cause for concern. Chlorine-based substances are known to be poisonous to many reef animals, especially to planktonic larvae. Many herbicides and pesticides are toxic and make the impact of agricultural run-off even worse: not just silt, but toxic silt is produced.

## Thermal Pollution

Warm water discharged from power plants may heat water to temperatures above the limit that corals can survive and cause bleaching. In Guam, discharge at a temperature of about 34°C from a power plant built in 1971 caused damage to some 20,000 square metres of coral and killed 10,000 square metres; clear evidence of this is still visible over twenty years later.

In Taiwan, a power plant built in 1987 caused bleaching on reefs to five metres depth in the area of discharge of the coolant water. In both cases, action has been taken to halt the damage and there has been some coral recovery. In general, though, the danger of corals being exposed to excessive temperatures as a result of thermal pollution is now considerably less than the threat of the same conditions being created by global warming.

## The Microlayer

One aspect of marine pollution that has only recently begun to be investigated is the impact it has on the sea's surface, in particular the microlayer, which is the topmost layer of what is sometimes referred to as the water column (the various levels in the sea from surface to seabed). This extremely thin layer of water, only about a tenth of a millimetre deep, has enormous importance in marine ecology: nutrients and minerals are brought to it from deeper water by bubbles of air and stimulate the growth of plankton. The eggs of many marine species also float to the surface and congregate there. These sources of food in turn attract an immense variety of larvae of fish, crustaceans and other invertebrates which gather in the upper few inches of the ocean. Exactly which reef species live in these upper layers during their larval stages, and are dependent on the microlayer, is not known but certainly lobster larvae and the larvae of some reef fish such as blue tang are found there and possibly coral larvae.

Many pollutants tend to concentrate in the microlayer, after either floating through the water or being deposited from the atmosphere, in particular, hydrocarbons. Most research into pollution of the microlayer has taken place in northern temperate waters, where it has been found that larvae from a polluted surface are often deformed or develop slowly and that eggs may fail to hatch. There is every reason to believe that similar disturbances will arise or are already happening in tropical waters, and there is a great need for research into the impact of sea surface pollution on coral reef ecology.

*Blue tang (Acanthurus coeruleus), whose larvae live in the microlayer, are at present common throughout the Caribbean, and can be seen foraging for food in large numbers over the reef, but populations could be threatened if pollution in the area continues to escalate.*

## Curbing Industrial Pollution

As far as toxic chemicals are concerned, a useful rule of thumb is to assume that any toxic chemical brought to a small island will end up as a pollutant in the marine environment during either its use or its disposal. Adequate assessments of the impact of individual chemicals on human health alone are possible for fewer than one per cent of the substances because of

*Spraying pesticides in Florida Keys.*

lack of toxicological data, and even less is known about the effects of mixtures of chemical pollutants. Some idea of the impossibility of obtaining comprehensive and conclusive scientific data in this field can be gained from a recent estimation in the United States that a minimal study of the effects of a mixture of twenty-five chemicals would require more than thirty-three million experiments which would cost more than three trillion US dollars. Arguably, the only way to prevent toxic chemicals from becoming pollutants is not to produce or use them.

The key to preventing pollution from toxic chemicals is to identify the activities that make use of them and to try to find alternative ways of achieving the same ends using non-toxic materials. Safe substitutes exist for many toxic chemicals. In many industries, waste pollution can be dramatically reduced and even eliminated by cleaning up production methods. Even if the impact of many industrial effluents and other wastes on reefs is still poorly understood, this approach should be used to avoid potential problems. Public pressure, political will and even financial incentives are required to force or persuade polluting industries to implement the necessary changes. Where clean production methods cannot be introduced immediately, temporary improvements can be made by siting outfalls away from reefs and giving

thorough treatment of wastes to render them as harmless as possible, but these are strictly damage-limitation exercises and should not be relied upon as permanent solutions.

## Oil Pollution

Despite the popular image of the Caribbean as a tropical paradise of idyllic beaches and clear blue seas, it is also a region of significant oil pollution. Oil production is concentrated in the Gulf of Mexico (mostly off the coast of Louisiana and in Mexico's Gulf of Campeche) but dispersal of oil by currents and the high volume of tanker traffic in the region spread the damage over a wide-ranging area. Large quantities of tar float in the major current systems, and surface waters have very high levels of dissolved hydrocarbons. Exposed beaches and coastlines on the windward side of the islands are particularly vulnerable to oil being washed ashore. A similar situation exists in the Red Sea and the Arabian (Persian) Gulf which are subject to repeated oil pollution from the vast amount of tanker traffic in the region and the expanding infrastructure of coastal refineries and off-shore oil rigs. Many other areas of the tropics are now being explored for oil and, as in the Caribbean and Middle East, the target areas often coincide with vulnerable coastal habitats such as coral reefs.

Although dramatic oil spills arising from tanker accidents grab the headlines,

there has so far (perhaps miraculously) been no serious damage to coral reefs from incidents of this kind. Tanker accidents account for about twelve per cent of the oil entering the sea each year. They have tended to cause acute but often temporary and localised pollution. This is not to say, of course, that the risk of damage from a tanker spilling its often colossal load is insignificant. But low-level, chronic oil pollution, caused by regular leakages from tanks or pipelines on land or in the sea or by deliberate spillage is currently a far greater problem. About forty-five per cent of marine oil pollution is from the routine flushing of tanks and bilges of ships at sea. Half of the floating tar found in the Gulf of Mexico comes from tanker ballast washings, and an analysis of beach tar in Jamaica found that most of it is from similar sources, despite regulations that make such discharges illegal. Just under a third of marine oil pollution stems from day-to-day leakages at land-based operations such as outfalls and refineries, which pose a particular threat to fringing reefs.

As an oil spill spreads, the lighter components in it evaporate. Light, refined oil such as petrol and diesel may evaporate almost entirely; crude and heavy lubricating oil may lose half its volume over a period of days, leaving behind tar; other forms of oil may scarcely evaporate at all. The lighter oils, although they evaporate more easily, tend to contain more toxic substances and these often dissolve in the water where they may affect marine life and pose a threat, in particular to the microlayer. Most damage occurs if oil comes into direct contact with plants and animals, either by being washed ashore or by coating the sea bed at low tide. Some animals are affected more than others: seabirds are particularly vulnerable, because once their feathers

*Above left: hawksbill turtle* (Eretmochelys imbricata) *on a tar-covered shore, where it may well have come to lay its eggs, in the Arabian Gulf, June 1991. Above right: the wreck of an Iraqi mine layer at Umm Al Maradem, Kuwait, photographed in 1991 against a soot-laden sky. Below: a bridled tern* (Sterna anaethetus) *on the coral island of Kubbar, off the coast of Kuwait in the Arabian Gulf, which remarkably escaped the worst effects of the oil spill during the Gulf War. This and three other tern species breed here in their thousands at the beginning of the summer. Seabirds are among the first to suffer from oil pollution; if they do not perish from being covered in oil, they often fail to survive cleaning and de-oiling processes. Opposite: brittle star on soft coral in the Gulf of Aqaba, the Red Sea – an area at daily risk of oil pollution.*

are coated with oil they can neither fly nor float, and if they ingest it while trying to clean themselves they are often poisoned.

The response of corals to pollution is very variable and depends on a whole range of factors such as the type of oil, the depth of the water over the reef, and the kind of cleaning-up operation undertaken. Under some conditions, oil spills have had remarkably little short-term impact on reefs. In the 1991 Gulf War, millions of gallons of oil were •intentionally discharged from tankers and storage tanks on the Kuwaiti coast by the Iraqi military. A huge slick moved south along the coast of Saudi Arabia, coating the intertidal mud flats and beaches and causing immense damage to invertebrates and shorebirds. The reefs in the area lie mainly around the offshore islands of Kuwait and Saudi Arabia, and for some weeks after the war it was assumed that these would be devastated. The reefs around the Saudi islands have yet to be fully surveyed (as this book goes to press), but Greenpeace has received reports that oil reached some of these and that there has been some damage. On the northern Kuwaiti islands, oil coated some beaches, but, extraordinarily luckily, had bypassed most of the reefs. In some cases, oil floated past reefs, which were sufficiently deep to avoid contamination even at low tides. In the long term, however, damage could still appear if oil and toxins leach out from sediments in shallower waters. Levels of hydrocarbons and other toxins were already high in Gulf waters before the war as a result of chronic oil pollution; the enormous volumes of smoke which billowed out before the wells were eventually capped contained similar substances, some of which undoubtedly entered the sea and could put further stress on the coral reefs in the area.

Reefs are most affected if the oil settles out on the corals or leaks out onto the reef over time. Reefs adjacent to and downstream from a large refinery on Aruba in the Netherlands Antilles have noticeably less living coral than those further away or upstream from the refinery. This was the case on the east coast of Panama where a storage tank at the Texaco refinery at Bahia Cativa ruptured in 1986,

dumping an estimated 50,000 barrels (eight million litres) of crude oil into a huge region of coral reefs, mangroves and seagrasses to the east of the Panama Canal. Mangroves, seagrasses, seaweeds and many marine invertebrates were soon smothered and died. Up to ninety-six per cent of corals on the most heavily polluted shallow reefs died, and even at depths of twelve metres, forty-five per cent of the corals died. Many of those that survived have suffered toxic effects and have been left with bleached and diseased patches. What had happened was that sediments around the mangroves that backed the reefs had soaked up the oil, and several years after the spill, it was still leaking out on to the reef, particularly after heavy rain and high tides, and so impeding recovery.

In off-shore oil exploration, a mixture of fine mud and chemicals ('drilling mud')

is pumped into bore holes to act as a lubricant. This is then flushed into the sea, where it may kill corals nearby. At one exploratory site in the Philippines, drilling mud killed ninety per cent of corals within a radius of 100 metres from the wellhead. Chemical dispersants used to clean up oil spills can cause even more damage than the oil itself, as many of them are toxic to corals. Some effort can be made to clean up rocky shores or sandy beaches by mechanical means but this is of course impossible with fragile coral reefs.

## Combatting Oil Pollution

There are a number of international and regional agreements and treaties covering pollution and contamination from ships, particularly oil pollution. The most important is the International Convention

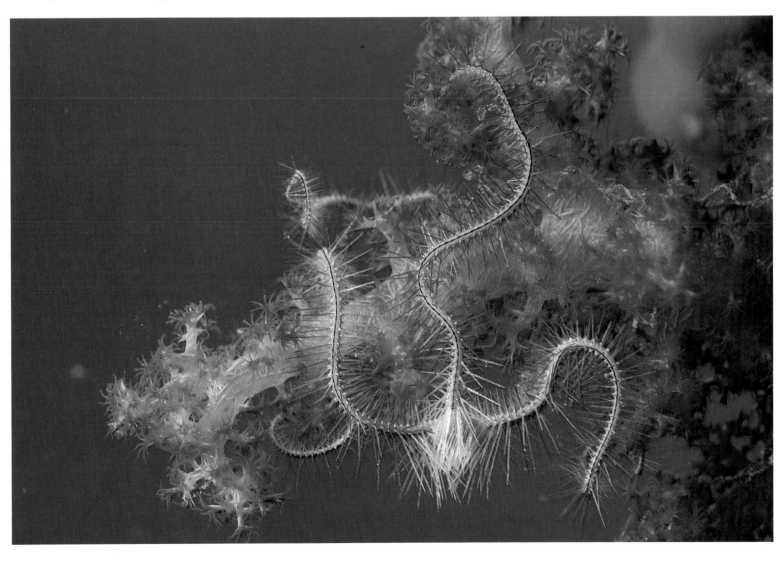

for the Prevention of Pollution from Ships, known as MARPOL and drawn up in the 1970s, of which many countries are signatories. It requires that they introduce national legislation to limit pollution from ships within their waters and from vessels registered by them. Areas that are particularly at risk from pollution have been identified, and within these waters it is illegal for ships to discharge oil. Ports must also provide facilities for dealing with oily wastes, so that ships are not forced to discharge them at sea. The Red Sea, The Arabian (Persian) Gulf, the Gulfs of Aden and Oman and the Great Barrier Reef have all been designated protected areas in this respect and the Gulf of Mexico and the Caribbean may shortly join the list.

As well as introducing preventative measures, oil-spill contingency plans must be drawn up to deal with accidents, should they occur. These need to specify the types of cleaning method that are appropriate according to the vulnerability of the habitats, and which areas should be tackled first, as well as providing information as to the directions in which the oil is likely to spread according to prevailing currents and winds. Finding out quickly which type of oil has been spilt is very important: in some cases it may be best to take no action, but to allow the natural breakdown of the oil by bacteria, although this can take a very long time. In other cases, it

will be necessary to act immediately: for example, by encircling the spill with booms and then pumping it away before it comes into contact with vulnerable habitats such as reefs.

In Australia a national plan to combat oil spills was drawn up following the grounding of the tanker Oceanic Grandeur in the Torres Strait on the Great Barrier Reef in 1970. Equipment such as booms, chemical dispersants and absorbent granules was provided for use in an emergency. In

1987, an oil-spill contingency plan called Reefplan was implemented specifically to protect the Barrier Reef which includes a computer model that can predict where an oil slick might travel on the basis of information about tides, winds and the type and volume of oil. But these precautions are designed to be effective only for spills of up to 2,000 tonnes, and many of the ships travelling through the reef contain cargoes of some 10,000 tonnes of oil. If a

*Top left: crude oil washing on to Galeta Reef on the Caribbean coast of Panama in January 1989 following the oil spill from the refinery at Bahia Cativa. Left: an oil-soaked beach in Saba Marine Park, Netherlands Antilles, after a spill from a tanker, the Vista Belle, in March 1991.*

*Some of the remarkable reef life in the Caribbean: an area with a high level of oil production and transport. Top right: squirrelfish (Holocentrus rufus), and opposite, a trumpetfish (Aulostomus maculatus) mimicking a branch of gorgonian while it hangs in wait for the smaller fish on which it preys to pass.*

spill occurred on offshore reefs, which can be as much as 200 kilometres from land, it would be almost impossible to take effective action. Legislation has been introduced requiring compulsory pilotage for larger vessels but conservationists have called for a total ban on tanker traffic within the Great Barrier Reef as the only effective way to prevent further spills and avoid the risk of a major catastrophe. Unfortunately, in developing countries with few resources, adequate contingency plans are rarely set up and regulations seldom enforced, although great efforts are now being made to rectify this.

Oil pollution from shipping is actually declining as a result of treaties such as MARPOL. But oil pollution from land-based sources is increasing and the piecemeal action being taken by the oil-production companies is insufficient to cope with this.

It is essential that oil companies take measures to clean up all the processes involved in oil extraction. Exploratory drilling for oil was prohibited in the Great Barrier Reef Marine Park when it was established in 1975 and was recently banned on all reefs in Florida as part of the establishment in 1991 of the Florida National Marine Sanctuary. Elsewhere, controls on drilling are inadequate. If drilling occurs, all steps should be taken to reduce leaks and discharges at each stage of the production process. There is, for example, a water-based lubricant now available for use in drilling muds, and techniques have been developed to recycle the mud more often. All industrial waste, of which drilling muds are one example, should be brought ashore for treatment and disposal and never discharged at sea, and atmospheric pollution associated with offshore drilling must not be ignored.

Regardless of what protection is in place, coral reefs will continue to be damaged by oil for as long as it remains a primary source of energy. Fortunately practical steps can be taken to improve the situation. Efficiency techniques can dramatically reduce energy consumption, and renewable energy technologies already exist that can provide the power we still need. The problem is one not of technology, but of political will.

## Litter and Rubbish

The same currents that carry the larvae of marine creatures across the oceans now carry another, less desirable burden – the refuse of twentieth-century civilisation. Much of it is plastic and virtually indestructible. During their annual clean-up of beaches in the United States in 1990, members of the Center for Marine Conservation collected over four million items of garbage, of which over sixty-four per cent was plastics. This washes around the sea for years and fouls even the most remote beaches and atolls. On Ducie Atoll in the Pitcairn group of islands (which lie in the middle of the Pacific ocean nearly 300 miles from the nearest inhabited island and 3,000 miles from the nearest continent) a visiting expedition in 1991 collected 953 items of litter including 100 buoys, 250 bottles and several hundred plastic items on just one-and-a-half kilometres of beach.

Litter can kill wildlife. Fish, birds and turtles die after becoming entangled in nylon fishing lines, nets and plastic 'six-pack' rings. Seabirds and turtles suffocate and die after feeding on plastic bags, balloons and other items which resemble jellyfish, one of their normal food sources.

Reefs inevitably attract flotsam and rubbish, being close to the surface, and those popular with tourists are rarely visited without some piece of detritus being left behind. Divers and snorkellers are well aware of how extremely unattractive rubbish on the reef can look, but in small amounts it probably has little impact on corals and reef life. But where it is persistent or occurs in large quantities, it can break and damage coral colonies, At Daymaniyat, in Oman, over half of some coral patches have been destroyed by lost and abandoned monofilament fishing nets that have become entangled around the corals. At Musandam, close by, one third of the reefs that were surveyed in 1990 were affected by rubbish abandoned by fishermen and small boat traders: sheets of lino, plastic, fishing gear, paint-cans and even at one site about 120 pairs of trousers, a consignment from an Iranian trading boat that had presumably been lost overboard!

## Radioactive pollution

The Pacific, ironically, was named 'El Pacifico' or 'The Peaceful Ocean' some four-and-a-half centuries ago by the Portugese explorer Ferdinand Magellan, but in this century it has become the focus of intense military activity including missile testing, bombing practice and the construction of bases; nuclear testing has been concentrated on the atolls of Bikini, Enewetak, Johnston, Kiritimati (Christmas), Moruroa and Fangataufa.

This has had long-term consequences both for the local people and the reefs and islands in the American, British and French territories where these activities have been concentrated, far away from western populations. The cynical assumption was that the lives of island peoples in the region were unimportant and that they had limited political power to oppose these activities. Much of the damage has been the result of the construction of military bases, airfields and ports but nuclear testing has been a particularly insidious threat.

Reefs have suffered from all three types of nuclear testing: atmospheric, underwater and underground. Not surprisingly, underwater explosions have had the greatest impact on reefs, blasting craters in which all life is destroyed and throwing up a 'soup' of sand and corals that suffocates adjacent corals and other filter feeders. Even when the blast is in deep water far below the level at which corals grow, the resulting shock waves can topple huge blocks and send them hurtling down the sides of the reef.

In atmospheric testing, the explosions or 'air bursts' scorch polyps, fuse coral skeletons into lime, burn fish in shallow lagoons and send shock waves through the

*Nuclear bombs inevitably kill a wide range of reef life. Bony fish, like this school of fusiliers (Caesio sp.), die as the pressure from the shock waves ruptures their airbladders. Corals and gorgonians are shattered and ripped from the reef.*

*Dumping rubbish in or near the sea is a worldwide dirty habit. Even the most remote coral island may be adorned with plastic bottles, old tyres and other detritus of modern civilisation, carried in on the tides. Opposite, top: children on Mejato in the Marshall Islands play with parts of old motor vehicles – unwanted scrap that is notoriously badly dealt with on islands without appropriate recycling facilities.*

*Opposite, bottom: mushroom cloud from the eleven megaton nuclear test code-named Romeo at Bikini Atoll in March 1954.*

water, fracturing and toppling fragile corals. Fish are killed in all types of explosions by shock waves bursting their air bladders, livers and kidneys, or causing haemorrhaging, and they may be crushed inside collapsing caves or by falling blocks of coral.

Atmospheric testing was ended by the US and Britain in 1963 (in the wake of the Partial Test Ban Treaty) and by France in 1974. Underwater testing has also now ceased but underground tests have continued in French Polynesia, where on the atolls of Moruroa and Fangataufa, there have been 196 nuclear blasts to date. Since 1972, Greenpeace, together with the peoples of the Pacific, has been involved in trying to bring an end to French nuclear testing in the area. In April 1992, shortly after Greenpeace's ninth protest voyage to Moruroa, the French government announced the suspension of

its thirty-two year programme of nuclear weapons testing in the South Pacific until the end of the year, indicating that an extension of the moratorium to 1993 could be considered if other nuclear powers (notably the US and China) were to follow suit.

On Moruroa, there is known to be major structural damage. In 1979, an explosion dislocated about one million cubic metres of coral and rock from the side of the atoll, causing underwater avalanches and tidal waves. The atoll is now said to be as riddled with holes as a Swiss cheese: cracks have started to appear in the surface, and radioactivity may be leaking into the surrounding environment. Jacques Cousteau surveyed the Moruroa lagoon in 1987 and discovered high levels of radioactivity, the only feasible source of which could have been the underground explosions. In October 1990, Greenpeace found high levels of this same artifical radioactivity (Caesium-134, which has a half-life of two years) in plankton in water outside the twelve-mile exclusion zone round the atoll; the location and type suggested that it had been flushed out of the lagoon on tidal currents and had probably originated from the underground caverns where explosions have taken place.

Radioactivity from test explosions initially contaminates phytoplankton and seaweeds, and is then passed up through the food web at increasing strengths to invertebrates, fish and eventually humans. Humans exposed to radiation suffer a wide variety of ill effects, as discovered following the bombing of Hiroshima in World War II, the atomic testing on Bikini and Enewetak in the 1940s and 1950s when many Marshall Islanders were subjected to fall-out, testing in French Polynesia, although the latter has been poorly documented, and most recently after nuclear power station accidents and leakages such as the one at Chernobyl. The immediate effects include nausea, vomiting and bleeding. Those who survive these may later suffer cancer, miscarriages, cataracts, sterility, leukemia, and the birth of handicapped children. Radioactive contamination of reef species used for food may well contribute to many of these sicknesses, but this has been little studied. Efforts to stop people eating such food have often been ineffective if suitable alternatives have not been provided or if there are strong cultural reasons for eating them.

The impact of radioactivity on the reef and its inhabitants is much less well documented, but it seems that even corals could be directly affected. On Enewetak, highly radioactive, long-lived isotopes were found to have accumulated and become concentrated in inorganic materials on the reef, and some long-lived corals can no longer reproduce. It was perhaps some doom-laden clairvoyance that led the early Polynesians to give Moruroa its name, which means 'Place of the Great Secret'.

## Damage from shipping

Reefs have always been a major navigational hazard for shipping but until recently the focus of concern has naturally enough been the threat to human life, rather than damage to the marine environment. Although damage is normally restricted to one locality when a ship grounds on a reef, the destruction at the point of impact may be total and extremely long-lasting. A Japanese fishing boat went aground off Yap in 1990 and directly destroyed 3,000 square metres of reef, damaging a further 500 square metres with coral rubble.

The Straits of Tiran in the Red Sea are notorious for shipwrecks because reefs are scattered right across the major shipping route linking the Gulf of Aqaba with the body of the Red Sea. In 1989, the freighter Safir went aground here, damaging about 500 square metres of reef; two years later, another freighter, the Mayflower, went aground in the same area and damaged a further 320 square metres. And in late 1991, another ship, the Lastovo, grounded, destroying another 270 square metres. Despite the fact that a relatively small area was affected, the reef may well take twenty years to recover.

The reefs of the Florida Keys are highly vulnerable because of the crowded traffic in adjacent shipping lanes. In 1984, the freighter MV Wellwood hit Molasses Reef in Key Largo National Marine Sanctuary. This small reef area was one of the most popular dive and snorkel sites. Nearly 1,500 square metres of reef were destroyed

and a further 850 square metres damaged; some of the underlying reef framework was even fractured by the weight of the ship. At first the ship attracted large numbers of fish, much as an artificial reef would, but once the wreck had been removed, the damaged area quickly became covered with seaweed. Five years after the grounding, although the number of coral colonies was approaching three-quarters of the original number, coral cover overall was still under a quarter of what it had been before the accident.

## Coastal Development

Development that takes place along coastlines, whether for tourism, industry, transport needs, agriculture or the local community's housing needs, must obviously be controlled if some of the problems that have already been outlined are not to have damaging, even catastrophic, results for the reef. An integrated approach that takes account of all the human activities that are likely to have an impact on the health of coral reefs and the sea around them, as well as the needs of the people living close by, is essential. Development will inevitably need to happen. What is important is that the ways in which it is pursued should be chosen with proper regard to their implications in the sea as well as on land, and that local people should be able to take the initiative in regulating it to minimise any harmful impact on their lives or on their environment.

## Preventing Reef Destruction

'Prevention rather than cure' is widely recognised as a sound approach to human health, and the same dictum applies to natural ecosystems and the health of the planet. Retrospective action to repair damage is in many cases impossible and, where it can be done, usually prohibitively expensive. Out of this approach has come the idea of the precautionary principle, which, broadly speaking, means preventing pollution at source by cleaning up production methods and calling a halt to other sources of degradation, even in the absence of conclusive scientific evidence that such activities are harmful to the environment. At present, legislation in most countries is based on the opposite premise, that an activity must be conclusively proven to be harmful before any control is initiated. The precautionary approach shifts the burden of proof on to whoever is proposing an activity which might cause potential damage – a developer for example – thus giving the environment the benefit of the doubt. There is now considerable pressure on governments and regulatory bodies concerned with the environment to adopt a precautionary approach when assessing development plans.

An important aspect of this approach is the careful analysis of the implications for the natural environment that any development activity might have before permission is given for it to start. If it appears that there might be some damage, permission

should be refused unless the developers can produce an alternative plan that does not cause harm. The process of such surveys and analysis is often called environmental impact assessment (EIA) and in many countries it is now mandatory before any development or change of use of an area takes place. Unfortunately, all too often the principles are abused, in developed and developing countries alike, with EIAs being carried out that do not reveal the full consequences of a project or that are not appropriately acted upon. Sometimes, the supposed EIA is carried out by a consultant who is actually hired by the developer, and in these cases the report is unlikely to be fully objective. In many tropical countries an additional problem is that the sheer number of development projects underway and the lack of qualified people available to carry out EIAs make the process far from effective.

Many forms of development have a range of far-reaching impacts, and studies need to take account of all of these. Few people realise, for example, that there is naturally a certain amount of movement in a coastline. All coasts are subject to a natural drift of sediments, with waves and currents moving them from one area to another. On an undisturbed coastline not suffering from human activities, this dynamic process means that at any one

time a variety of habitats is likely to be found there as, for example, one part of the coast is eroded and another has sand deposited on it. On a developed coastline, with piers, harbours, hotels and other structures built directly on the shore and with artificial channels in shallow waters, these natural processes are disrupted. Leaving aside the catastrophic effects this can have in terms of the ecosystems that are disturbed, if the dynamic nature of the coast is not considered at the planning stages of a construction project, there can be serious economic consequences: harbours may silt up and the foundations of hotels and buildings on the shore may be eroded.

Following up environmental assessments with appropriate action is crucially important if development is to proceed in an environmentally sound manner. Techniques for prevention at source of many forms of pollution and habitat destruction are now available or being developed and must be promoted. Education and training in correct EIA techniques is being made a high priority in many countries, so that local people are equipped to assess proposals for themselves. In the Pacific, for example, training courses on EIA are being run for islanders and guidelines are being published, often with particular emphasis on coral reefs, which are one of the most vulnerable habitats. Equally, developers,

*Above: beach erosion at a holiday village in Jamaica which was clearly unforeseen by the owners or developers.*

*Opposite: the freighter MV Wellwood aground on Molasses Reef in the Key Largo National Marine Sanctuary, Florida, in 1984.*

*Development of coastlines and islands is inevitable if the local people are to improve the quality of their lives. On many small islands, as on Ebeye (below) in the Marshall Islands, land reclamation is often chosen as the solution to overcrowding. Careful planning and a full understanding of the impact of such activities on the land, the sea and the lives of the people themselves, can, however, go a long way to minimising the damage to ecosystems like reefs.*

engineers and industrialists need a better understanding of the links between their activities on the shore and the health of the reef, and must appreciate that short-term economic gain is generally counter-productive to long-term sustainable development, and in a few countries, notably Australia, guidelines and codes of practice are beginning to be published.

## Repairing the Damage – the Last Resort

The highest priority in reef management is to remove or at least minimise human causes of reef destruction, and to improve conditions so that natural regeneration of the reefs takes place as quickly as possible. However, where damage has already occurred, active efforts to help reefs recover may be of value. It is most unlikely that a reef could be restored to its original state in anything other than a timescale of decades, but it may be possible for it to be helped towards a stage where normal processes can start to function.

Large-scale replanting of corals has proved difficult to carry out successfully, largely because of the amount of diving labour required. When a reef is damaged by a hurricane much of the regrowth takes place by regeneration of the broken coral fragments but large numbers also die. Similarly, when a reef is being replanted manually, numerous fragments of coral have to be planted if a significant number are to survive. With manual replanting, the coral fragments are carefully attached to a hard surface (quick-setting glue is sometimes used for this purpose) or wired to metal stakes. If the fragments are left so that they are able to move or roll around, the polyps are quickly killed.

Because of the scale of the damage caused by hurricanes, manual restoration is rarely a feasible option under these circumstances, although voluntary replanting of coral fragments by divers may help. On Cozumel, an island eight miles off the Yucatan Peninsula in Mexico, one dive operator in particular, German Mendez, has been painstakingly trying to reverse some of the effects of Hurricane Gilbert, which in 1988 ravaged the reefs on the south-west coast of the island. With the help of his colleagues, he has removed sand and debris swept on to the reefs from the shore and, by a system of trial, error and educated guesswork has replanted some of the pieces of coral that had been broken off the reef.

Active reef restoration is perhaps most useful and cost-effective where there is a need to increase populations of very rare coral species, or to repair reefs in marine parks or in locations where a great deal of money is earned from tourism. A reef in front of a large hotel in Moorea (French Polynesia) for example, was badly damaged when a boat channel was dredged through it, and corals are being replanted there.

Restoration of this kind may also help after ship groundings, where damage is restricted to a small area. Large corals that have been fractured or dislodged can be cemented back together. A quick-setting cement has been used in Florida at the site of the Wellwood grounding to reattach dislodged corals and repair large broken colonies. This also helps to prevent further damage to the reef from the movement of loose boulders and rubble.

## The Polluter Pays

One principle increasingly being recognised in the battle to protect the world's natural resources is that whoever is engaged in activities that could harm the environment pays, both to install the equipment or technology to prevent pollution and other degradation, and to repair any damage that is caused. In several countries, this principle of mitigation is now enshrined in law, and anyone who damages an area of natural habitat is obliged to restore, improve or protect an equivalent area. Shipowners are now often liable for cleaning up oil spills and paying compensation for any damage caused.

Calculating the monetary value of damage to reefs is a complicated business but is now increasingly being undertaken, notably in the case of ship groundings, in order to obtain compensation from the company involved which can help towards restoring the reef. There is no standard system of valuing coral reefs; each case has to be assessed according to its characteristics and its potential as well as current uses.

Reefs used for tourism are most obviously of high economic value. Molasses Reef in Florida, on which the MV Wellwood grounded, was valued at US $2,000 per square metre, a notably high value because of its importance as the most popular dive site in the Key Largo National Marine Sanctuary. The Cypriot company that owned the ship reached an out-of-court settlement with the US Federal Government of over US$6 million for the 1500 square metres damaged, US$3 million of which was allocated for reef restoration. Taken over the whole region, Florida reefs have been calculated to have a value of US$15.75 per square metre of live coral based on direct income from diving, snorkelling and boating or US$85.00 if the revenue from travel and accommodation costs for reef users is taken into account. If fishing, other activities, and the vital role of protecting the shore are also included, the value would be even higher. In 1990, a dredging company paid US$1 million compensation to the local authorities in Florida for scraping coral off one hectare of reef whilst pumping sand to replenish beaches, a settlement that is also being used for reef conservation.

It may be more difficult to calculate values of reefs used primarily for fishing (particularly subsistence fishing), unless detailed catch statistics are available, which they are often not. A damaged reef in Yap in the Pacific was valued at $20 per square metre, the same as for agricultural land which was considered equivalent in food value. In the Red Sea, following an oil spill from a tanker that affected about 50 kilometres of the Saudi Arabian coastline in 1989, the reef was valued at only US$0.10 per square metre on the basis of its potential fishery yield. It is perhaps even harder to put prices on scientific or aesthetic value – some remote and pristine reefs might be considered especially valuable now for their rarity value.

Clearly the process of valuation is complex and the results at present are variable and highly dependent on the site in question and the amount of information available. But it can provide an indicator of the conservation value of the reef and underlines the importance of preventing damaging activities.

# CHAPTER FIVE

# HARVESTING THE REEFS

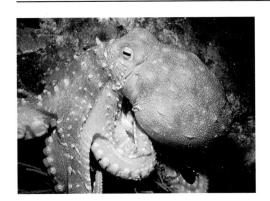

*Octopus is hunted for food around the world; this one was photographed in the Turks and Caicos Islands in the Caribbean.*

*A typical south-east Asian fishing village (in Palawan, the Philippines), whose inhabitants depend on the reefs for much of their food and income.*

The octopus is an elusive creature, full of tricks to outsmart predators. It possesses a high degree of control over the tiny sacs of pigment beneath its skin which allows it to change colour and blend in with whatever bit of reef it finds itself in. Humans, though, have made it their business to learn about the creature's habits, because the octopus is a valuable food source as well as making good bait.

In the Pacific, fishermen hunting octopus scan the seabed for upturned pebbles with pink coralline algae growing on them; these particular algae normally grow only on the underneath of pebbles, so for the fisherman this is a sure sign that the octopus has passed by, turning the pebbles over with its suckers. The search is then on for fragments of clam or crab shell nearby, which the octopus sometimes leaves outside its burrow. Once the burrow is located, the octopus is either speared, helpless inside its burrow, or, if it has gone too far inside, a natural toxin, prepared from the skin of another reef creature, the sea cucumber (*Holothuria atra*), may be used to force the octopus out into the open where it can be caught.

## Traditional fisheries

Coral reefs provide the fish, crustaceans and molluscs on which coastal peoples in many countries depend for food or to make a living. Over the centuries, fishermen have acquired extensive knowledge and skills which enable them to exploit reefs to best advantage. In some cases – as on Pacific atolls which would be uninhabitable were it not for the harvest from the reefs – the local people possess a rich storehouse of detailed information and fishing lore which far exceeds scientific knowledge of many of the species involved.

Although off-shore species such as tuna are taken in some traditional fisheries, many coastal and island people depend on the hundreds of edible species that live around shallow, near-shore reefs and lagoons, and it is largely here that the fishermen's expertise comes into its own. On Pacific atolls, fish generally make up at least twenty to thirty per cent of the diet, and, if other reef species like molluscs and crustaceans are taken into account, the reefs may easily provide over half the daily protein eaten by local people. In

*Bamboo rafts at Bolinao in the Philippines – one of the simplest ways of fishing over shallow reef flats and seagrass beds. Fine nets are used for fish, and molluscs and sea urchins are collected by hand. The catch is piled up on the raft and paddled or towed on foot back to shore.*
*Below: spiny lobsters are one of the most prized food species on reefs, relished by local people and visitors alike; recently their value has soared, so the bulk of the catch in most countries supplies restaurants or the export market.*

south-east Asia, fish provide up to a quarter of the total protein consumed, and the proportion is probably considerably greater for people living on the coast.

The variety of species eaten reflects the extraordinary richness and diversity of reef life. At Bolinao in the Philippines, over 150 different species are taken in one local fishery, and in the Tigak Islands in Papua New Guinea an astonishing 250 reef species are fished. Unlike fisheries in temperate and open-ocean waters, like those for tuna or cod, it is rare in a reef fishery for one or even a few species to dominate the catch. Fish are the most important food, but numerous other species are harvested, including marine turtles, octopus, bivalves, gastropods, shrimps, spiny lobsters, sea urchins, sea cucumbers, seaweeds and jellyfish. In American Samoa, a study of eleven villages found that

clams, octopus, gastropods and other invertebrates comprised over a third of their reef catch.

Understanding reef life is vital for traditional fishermen. They rely heavily on their knowledge of the behaviour and life cycles of their prey: where exactly the animals go to feed, breed and spawn, for example. They also have to understand the intricacies of local tides and currents, and how these affect the feeding and migration of reef creatures.

Many reef fish spawn according to the phases of the moon. During spawning they not only congregate in large numbers – sometimes in their tens of thousands – but also become sluggish and easier to catch. Marine biologists 'discovered' this phenomenon only comparatively recently, but fishermen have been aware of it for centuries. When Bob Johannes set out to

record the knowledge of Micronesian fishermen in the 1970s for his book, *Words of the Lagoon*, he learned that his chief informant, Ngiraklang, knew of many more lunar spawning cycles of fish than marine biologists were aware of throughout the world.

In traditional fishing communities, the more adventurous fishing activities, involving prestige animals such as shark and dugong, as well as most of the fishing done from boats, have mainly been carried out by the men. But the women also play a part in harvesting the reef. Often accompanied by their children, they go out on to the reef flats and shore at low tide to glean or gather a wide variety of invertebrates, seaweeds and small fish. In Western Samoa, for example, they collect sea urchins and numerous molluscs including octopus, as well as jellyfish, seaweeds, crustaceans and sea cucumbers (only half of the sea cucmber is twisted off, so that the other part can be left on the reef to regenerate). These activities provide a surprisingly large, and most importantly very steady, contribution to the community's food supply, and in the case of species like *Trochus*, it may even produce some cash income. The women also tend to process the catch – cleaning, gutting and preparing the animals for cooking or for market, an occupation which has given many of them a very precise knowledge of the

creatures they handle, not least of their reproductive cycles.

A wide range of different fishing methods have traditionally been used according to the shape, size, habits and preferred foods and habitat of the species sought. Line-fishing is common, using a variety of hooks, lures and different types of bait according to the prey. Nets are deployed just off the reef or in channels and lagoons, either from boats or by 'seining': surrounding fish in the shallows just off the beach. Lobsters and smaller fish are caught using circular throw nets. Hand spears (as opposed to spear guns) are rarely used now, but when they are, the spears are thrown from boats on shallow reef flats or while standing in shallow water to catch surface-swimming fish, or swimming underwater to catch larger fish like groupers. Before goggles were invented

*Sharks are fished by traditional fishermen, sport fishermen and also in commercial fisheries, and in many places populations are declining; but whether reef species, like this white-tip reef shark (Triaenodon obesus), in hot pursuit of a soldierfish (Myripristis sp.) on a reef in the Seychelles, are also decreasing in numbers is not known for certain.*

*Below left: reef gleaning is usually carried out by women and children, as here at Kilifi in Kenya. At low tide, reef flats can provide rich pickings in the form of a wide variety of invertebrates and small fish.*

*Below right: local people in Oro Bay, Northern Province, Papua New Guinea, fishing in the shallows with seine nets; although women rarely go out fishing in boats, they take part in many other aspects of subsistence and artisanal reef fisheries.*

fifty to sixty years ago, spearing was a highly skilled activity; sometimes fishermen chewed on coconut flesh and spat the oil onto the surface of the water to create a lens through which they could see the fish better.

Fish corrals or weirs – structures built across reef flats or tidal channels to catch fish as they followed the receding tide – have now mainly disappeared. Built from stone or wood, these used to be common in the Pacific, but required considerable maintenance and have now been mainly superseded by nets. Portable traps, that can be moved around the reef, are particularly common in the Caribbean, the basic design essentially unchanged since it was introduced by slaves from Africa. There are many local variations in shape and size: Z-traps are used in Jamaica, S-traps in Cuba and arrowhead traps in much of the eastern Caribbean. Smaller fish tend to enter the trap first, seeking cover, in turn attracting bigger, more valuable species such as grouper or snapper.

Sometimes natural poisons derived from plants or other marine creatures, such as the sea-cucumber toxins mentioned earlier, are used to catch particular species. The sea cucumber can also simply be cut up and placed in shallow pools on the reef flat so that it exudes poison into the water: as the intoxicated fish float to the surface, they can easily be collected. The root of the derris plant (*Derris elliptica*) is used in a similar way, without apparently causing any harm to people who eat the fish.

*Aborigines in Australia, where their people have made use of the reefs for thousands of years, returning from fishing with traditional hand spears.*

*On many atolls, fish traps like this one at Tarawa, Kiribati, in the South Pacific, are built on the reef flat using coral boulders; the fish enter at high tide and are caught and collected as the tide recedes.*

## Modern fisheries

The introduction of cash economies and growth in human populations mean that relatively few coastal people these days practise purely subsistence fishing, unless they live in extremely remote places. More often, those fishing on a small scale will fish partly for subsistence, but will also sell any surplus catch to other members of the community or tourist restaurants. Compared to the capital-intensive, export-oriented fisheries for species such as tuna and prawns, though, few reef fisheries are commercialised on a large scale, and in many areas such as remote Pacific atolls, catches still rarely reach the cash market. The fact that coastal peoples are often among the poorest has ensured that subsistence fishing is still extremely important. In the Caribbean, for example, where tourism and industry provide the primary sources of income, there are still about 60,000 small-scale fishermen who operate, often on a part-time basis, to provide extra food for their families or to earn a bit of extra cash. Nevertheless, the form and scale of reef fisheries worldwide have changed dramatically this century. The availability of imported and canned food has decreased the immediate dependence of coastal people on their adjacent reefs, and the development of export markets for reef species like grouper and spiny lobster and the tourist industry – both accelerated by the growth in air travel – has provided strong incentives for intensive fishing.

In many places, modern technology has radically altered fishing patterns. New methods have been introduced to increase catch rates and, in attempts to improve yields and generate income, government fisheries departments provide loans and subsidies to upgrade fishing gear, motorise boats and train fishermen. Unfortunately, these moves often have negative effects in the long term. In many mainly subsistence cultures, people fish on a part-time basis, as and when they need to; tending their gardens, pursuing social activities and harvesting other resources are often equally important. This makes it very hard to introduce the steady flow of produce that an export market normally demands, and in any case the remoteness of many of the communities puts them beyond the reach of frequent visits from cargo boats and regular supplies of ice. Of most concern, though, is that new technology often stimulates over-fishing.

Traditional fishing methods generally had relatively little impact on the reef habitat, but many of the more modern techniques accelerate over-fishing and damage to the reef itself. Modern fishing methods often require little knowledge of reef life, and so many traditional skills have been lost, along with the deep understanding of the reef that is so valuable to conservation programmes. Nylon nets have taken the place of nets woven from vegetable fibre or plaited coconut fronds, and if lost or discarded pose a real threat to corals, easily becoming entangled round them. In Oman, the introduction of synthetic fibre gill nets has caused an immense amount of littering on the reefs; local dive clubs removed about two to three kilometres of nets in a single weekend cleaning-up operation. Nets with much finer mesh are being used, so many more immature fish are taken in each catch. The fine 'karu-kod' nets used in the Philippines take very small juveniles of a wide variety of fish which are used to make fish paste. Fishermen in Madagascar are increasingly using modern beach seine nets with small mesh sizes on the extensive reefs near Tulear in the south-west, catching ever smaller fish, with the overall result that since the 1970s catches have fallen and the variety of species taken has declined. Most fishermen avoid trawling near reefs for fear of damaging their nets and gear on coral, but with large commercial fishing fleets, this may not be a prime concern. Although some fishermen still use sailing boats or dugout canoes, these are rapidly being replaced by boats with outboard motors which extend the range further afield.

Goggles and spearguns (and often the Hawaiian sling, where the spear is powered by a rubber thong) have replaced throwing spears, and underwater flashlights (for night-time spearfishing) have further expanded the potential for catching food. The use of scuba gear has dramatically increased the amount of fish taken by spear-fishing or collecting by hand and has also enabled local divers to go deeper in search of their prey. Spearfishing is highly selective on large fish such as groupers; when sport fishing with spear guns was banned at Looe Key National Marine Sanctuary in Florida, snappers doubled in number and grunts quadrupled.

Most countries have made spearfishing with scuba illegal, but the regulation is difficult to enforce. The Maldives has banned the import of spear guns, which is perhaps the best way to stop overseas visitors using this method. In Hawaii, spearfishing is still permitted on many reefs; where it is banned, however, as in the Hanauma Bay Marine Life Conservation District, reef fish are significantly larger and more abundant. Collecting with scuba should also be banned for all sedentary (and therefore vulnerable) reef animals like sea cucumbers and queen conch, even if this means bringing conch fishing to a halt in some areas.

Portable traps are now made with wooden or metal frames covered in wire mesh instead of from woven cane, and motorised boats are capable of handling twice as many traps as canoes. Traditional fish traps decay quite rapidly if lost on a reef, but the modern wire versions do not break down, continuing pointlessly to catch fish and often moving around as ghost traps and damaging corals, especially in rough weather.

*Trawlers, like this Taiwanese vessel, generally avoid reefs because of the risk of damage to fishing gear. If they do fish near corals and reef communities, they can cause immense damage to the habitat, as illlustrated by this huge incidental catch of sponges which will simply be discarded.*

*This rock cod (*Epinephelus merra*), photographed in Mozambique, is, like other groupers, one of the easiest targets for spear fishermen because of its habit of lying virtually motionless, ready to ambush the small fish on which it feeds.*

Natural poisons have been used for fishing in the Pacific for centuries without causing any apparent harm to the reefs, but the more powerful commercial poisons now being used, usually sodium cyanide and chlorine-based products such as bleach, kill corals and other invertebrates and fish, and lead to subsequent overgrowth of the dead corals by seaweed. Poisons are used mainly to collect aquarium fish, but in some places, such as the Philippines, sodium cyanide is used for food fish with as yet undocumented health effects on the consumers, and in the Caribbean and Hawaii bleach has often been used to catch lobsters.

Regulations are now being imposed in the Caribbean to prevent damage from fish traps. Traps are being introduced with 'biodegradable windows', often made of plant fibres that break down rapidly in the water, so that if they are lost on a reef any fish that is subsequently caught can escape. Nets and traps in the Caribbean must now have certain mesh sizes to prevent large numbers of juveniles being caught. In Discovery Bay in Jamaica, enforcement of this regulation is being helped through a project in which fishermen can exchange one of their small mesh traps for enough large mesh to make two new ones. This helps to offset costs for the fishermen, and, by enabling them to make two traps in exchange for one, it ensures that catches do not drop too dramatically even though small fish can no longer be taken and, of course, protects fish populations by cutting the number of juveniles caught.

## Dynamite Fishing and 'Muro-Ami'

Two very destructive methods used for food fish are dynamite and 'muro-ami' fishing. Both have developed as part of the vicious cycle of declining yields leading to ever more intensive fishing methods; dynamite and muro-ami are used on some of the most heavily exploited reefs in the world where the temptation to increase low yields can prove irresistible. Highly wasteful practices of this kind, that both devastate the reef and kill large numbers of unwanted reef creatures, make the reef

even less likely to regain its former level of abundance, whether the original cause of the low yields was over-fishing or destruction of the reef habitats.

Blasting reefs with dynamite or other explosives to stun the fish is probably the most damaging method of fishing commonly employed today. The reason it is so widely used is that it allows fishermen to scoop up large quantities of fish in one go, particularly on reefs where fish abundance is so low that methods like the hook and line are no longer practical for making a living. Bombs consist of small charges of explosive powder in bottles, or dynamite ignited with fuses. Dynamite fishing using abandoned ammunition became common after World War II particularly in the Pacific and south-east Asia. Villagers in the Padaido Islands in Irian Jaya, eastern Indonesia, have made a profitable industry out of the thousands of live bombs dumped in the lagoon by the Americans at the end of the war. Hundreds of fish bombs can be made out of a single large bomb, and these are sold to traders who distribute them throughout the Indonesian islands. Elsewhere, dynamite is now often obtained from construction sites. In the Philippines, nitrogen-based fertilisers or powdered urea foam used in boat-building, mixed with small amounts of gasoline and gunpowder, are commonly used.

*Dynamite fishing is bad for reefs and also highly dangerous. Many Philippine fishermen have lost their arms through this practice.*

*Opposite: fusiliers (Caesio sp.) feed on plankton in large schools just off the edge of the reef during the day. This makes them particularly vulnerable to methods like muro-ami, which scoop up huge numbers of shoaling fish at a time.*

Most common food fish have air bladders which give them buoyancy. A bomb thrown into the water and exploding in a school of fish will cause immense damage by rupturing air bladders, as well as breaking bones. After the explosion, the fish are gathered up with nets or by hand, but usually far more are killed than are collected.

Dynamiting also has a high human cost, as home-made bombs often go off prematurely in mid-air, killing or maiming fishermen. In some parts of the Philippines, one out of every five or six dynamiters has lost one or both arms in this way, and a significant number have been killed. Making fish bombs is therefore a skilled business: the mixture must burn at a high enough temperature to go off underwater, but not so fast that it explodes in mid-air.

A bomb the size of a beer bottle can destroy corals over an area three metres in diameter; one of the larger, five-litre

bombs that are commonly used can destroy an area ten metres in diameter, which may take decades to recover. During the peak fishing months in the Philippines, an average six blasts an hour can be heard on reefs in the Bolinao area; over half the coral on the reef slope here has been damaged and total damage is probably even greater if the impact of cyanide poisoning is included. In Tanzania, damage caused by dynamiting on the fringing reef of a small, sandy island was so severe that the island itself eventually disappeared: once it no longer had a reef to protect it, the waves simply washed it away. A number of Tanzanian fishermen have now moved north and are dynamiting the Kenyan reefs. A dynamited reef at Mwamba Midjira, near Kenya's southern border, was found to have only about a twentieth as much living coral as normal healthy Kenyan reefs, and only a tenth as many fish.

Despite the fact that dynamite fishing is banned almost worldwide, it is still practised widely because of poor enforcement and lack of awareness of the effects of the damage. Efforts are being made in the Philippines through education programmes and the retraining of fishermen to use more environmentally sound methods. Greenpeace, in association with the Melanesian Environment Foundation, is sponsoring a literacy and awareness project that will teach coastal communities in Papua New Guinea about the dangers and problems of dynamite fishing and the alternatives to it. In Indonesia, posters indicating the ecological, economic and social impacts of dynamiting have been produced for distribution in Irian Jaya, with funding from the Worldwide Fund for Nature (WWF). The local government has called for a stop to the bombing, and local rural development agencies have been asked

whether they would distribute free hooks and lines to ensure that alternative equipment is available. In St Lucia in the Caribbean, dynamiting has been successfully stopped at least around the Maria Islands Reserve, by enforcing the penalty of prison for offenders. In this area there is an energetically run programme to involve fishermen in management issues, and peer pressure plays an important role in discouraging damaging methods.

Muro-ami is commonly used only in the Philippines but has exceptional capacity for robbing the reef of life. Brought to the Philippines before World War II by the Japanese as a method to increase yield without using trawls (that snag on reefs), the method employs hundreds of boys and young men to swim over the reef, pounding the coral with lumps of coral or rock tied on the end of 'scarelines' flagged with white plastic streamers. The combination of noise and the advancing wall of streamers drives the fish into a semi-circular net or 'muro-ami'. On the already impoverished reefs of the Philippines, this method results in the removal of practically all the larger reef species such as surgeonfish and parrot-fish, though an even greater negative effect is the damage done to the reef habitat. Another method, 'kayakas', uses bamboo poles instead of scarelines and lumps of rock.

Although outlawed since 1986, at least thirty muro-ami boats or 'masterships' still operate in the Philippines. The boys, who may be as young as ten years old, are expected to work for ten months at a stretch, on the basis of a paltry advance of between 200 and 600 pesos (US$9 and $26) given to their families which will be deducted from their subsequent earnings, and represents a tiny share in the profits of the catch. An estimated 15,000 people are dependent on muro-ami for their livelihood. The boats are now moving further and further out into the South China Sea both to escape the law and to find new reefs.

An alternative to muro-ami called 'pa-aling' has recently been devised, which works on the same principle, but uses compressed air bubbles to scare the fish rather than weights on scarelines. Unfortunately, while it may cut down on damage to the reef itself, if it is effective (which is as yet un-proven) it will still result in huge quantities of fish being taken unselectively, so only accelerating the problem of over-fishing.

## Commercial Fisheries

Commercial fisheries now compete with local fisheries in many areas, due to their greater efficiency, often encroaching on fishing grounds that have traditionally supported only local people, and hastening over-fishing, which can ultimately encourage the use of destructive fishing techniques. Outboard motors can bring remote fishing grounds within easy reach of individual fishermen, but they require a large capital outlay and can be expensive to maintain. Subsistence fishermen may have to work for other people if they cannot afford the equipment required; in Haiti, for example, boats are often owned by middlemen, who exploit the fishermen and pocket most of

the profit. In the Lingayen Gulf in the Phil-ippines, about 14,000 people fish the reefs, generating over US$2 million annually from the catch of fish, invertebrates and sea-weed. But although this works out at about $170 per fisherman per month, each family earns only about US$20, and most of the profits go to the middlemen who control the distribution and marketing of the catch.

When people fished just to feed their families or to supply local markets, reefs

could provide a continuous supply of food. But the combination of the introduction of modern technology, the creation of export markets, demands from the tourist industry, growing local populations and worsening poverty have vastly increased the pressures on reef resources. Out of about a hundred countries with reefs, over-fishing has been reported from eighty of them. Growing coastal human populations and a huge worldwide demand for fish and other marine products means that exploitation is now at an all-time high, and populations of some reef species are now being re-duced to dangerously low levels.

The most valuable reef fish are groupers, snappers and emperors, which, as good food fish, are heavily in demand for local consumption, the tourist industry and ex-port markets. The shallow-water species (such as the red hind, Nassau grouper and yellowtail snapper in the Caribbean and the coral trout on the Great Barrier Reef) are usually found at depths of fifty metres or less; the deep-water species (such as red snappers in the Caribbean) live on the outer reef slopes at depths of up to about 300 metres. These food fish are vul-nerable for several reasons. They are large (often reaching a metre in length), long-lived and slow-growing, which means that once populations are reduced they take a

long time to build up again. Some species congregate to spawn in vast numbers, often in their thousands, and fishing on these sites during the spawning period can decimate populations. The two spawning aggregations of the Nassau grouper in the US Virgin Islands, for example, have all but disappeared over the last two decades.

Snappers and groupers are becoming much rarer on reefs across the world. The Nassau grouper is now rarely seen in Puerto Rico, where catches of all groupers have been declining for a decade, and fishing now concentrates on less desirable species such as parrotfish, squirrelfish and triggerfish; in Papua New Guinea, low-value rabbitfish are now more abundant in catches than groupers or snappers. In Haiti, traps that once caught groupers now mainly yield parrotfish, butterflyfish and damselfish, and on heavily-fished reefs in Guam, large snappers have declined,

*In some countries, fishing communities are among the poorest groups of society; people living in the fishing villages around Santiago Island at the mouth of the Lingayen Gulf in the Philippines lead a hand-to-mouth existence. Bamboo rafts and simple sailing boats are used each day to gather what can be found from the reefs and seagrass beds. Any excess left over after feeding the family is sold to middlemen in the local town of Bolinao. Even small children, like this little girl sorting the sea urchin catch, are involved.*

*Opposite, top: Nassau grouper (*Epinephelus striatus*) congregate in vast numbers to spawn and at this time are particularly easy prey for fishermen; bottom: another valuable food fish, the red-throated emperor.*

*Coral cod* (Cephalopolis miniatus) – *one of around 400 species of grouper, many of which are food fish. Like a number of other reef fish, groupers spend their first years as females, and then become males. It is possible that taking too many younger fish may have a detrimental effect on the balance of the sexes, and thus on populations.*

*Opposite, top: an increasingly rare sight – a reasonable-sized giant clam* (Tridacna *sp.), on a reef in Belau, Micronesia. Most of the large species of giant clam have been overfished throughout much of their range, and even small ones are now in demand for their meat.*

along with parrotfish and surgeonfish. Over-fishing is now spreading to the smaller, less valuable species, and catches are continuing to decrease despite the same or even greater effort being spent on fishing.

As yields of shallow-water groupers and snappers have grown smaller, so fishermen have started to go after the deep-water species. Fisheries departments have invested heavily in gearing up and encouraging fishermen to exploit these new fishing grounds often with the encouragement of multi and bi-lateral aid and foreign investment. In the Pacific some thirty deep-water species are now taken on the outer reef slopes and seamounts in Hawaii, French Polynesia, Vanuatu and other countries, and large numbers are also being fished in the Caribbean. But the deep-water species appear to be just as susceptible to over-exploitation as their shallow-water counterparts: catches of red snapper in US waters, for instance, fell by over half during the 1980s.

Many countries, particularly in the Caribbean, now have to import fish to supply growing tourist markets. Tourism has stimulated demand for high-value species such as snapper, grouper and spiny lobster (in the mid-1980s, visitors to tourist hotels in Haiti were responsible for consuming 135 to 180 kilos of fish, 115 to 160 kilos of lobster and 90 to 125 kilos of conch per week). Of the reef invertebrates, spiny lobsters and conch are now the most valuable commercial species in the Caribbean. Spiny lobster in Belize, for example, made up two-thirds of the value of the 1989 total fishery catch, worth nearly US$18 million. Despite the fact that elsewhere in the Caribbean, particularly around some of the small islands, lobster stocks have already been wiped out, and many islands that once exported them, now import them, intensive fishing of these species continues unabated where catches can still be made.

The queen conch (*Strombus gigas*), which lives in seagrass beds adjacent to reefs, was once an important part of the subsistence diet in the Caribbean. It used to occur in huge populations on the shallow banks around the Bahamas, Florida (where the Keys became known as the 'Conch Republic') and the Turks and Caicos. Traditionally, people fished for conch either by wading out into the shallows and collecting them by hand or, during this century, by taking a boat out, looking through a glass-bottomed bucket held over the side, and hooking up the conchs with a long pole. Over the century, exploitation has been so great that most of the big populations have now disappeared. The introduction of snorkelling equipment and outboards made conch fishing much more efficient, and the invention of scuba gear dealt the final blow as it brought deep-water populations within range. In many areas scuba gear is now essential, so deep are the remaining populations. Conch is now generally considered a luxury food, commanding high prices on the export market and in tourist restaurants. As a result, despite widespread declining populations, about ten to fifteen million conch are still being harvested each year.

The seven species of giant clam, whose meat is highly nutritious, have long been an important food source in the Pacific, as is evident from the vast quantities of their shells excavated from middens (prehistoric rubbish dumps). Smaller ones have generally been used for day-to-day consumption; the larger specimens have traditionally been collected from the reef and placed in groups or 'clam gardens' in shallow lagoons and reserved for eating at special ceremonies or when the weather was too bad for fishing on the outer reef. In many areas, the maintenance of clam gardens has ceased, partly because clams have become so rare and partly because islanders now have numerous other sources of food in the form of packaged goods, but in some areas such as Fiji, clam gardens may still be set up if big council meetings and feasts are planned.

The greatest demand for giant clams now comes from restaurants in Asia, which use 500 tonnes of clam meat a year. The adductor muscle, fetching well over US$100 a kilo, is highly prized, and is often served as sushi (it is also considered an aphrodisiac in some places); the remaining meat is used in salads and soups. Being slow-growing, sedentary and highly visible on reefs, giant clams are extremely vulnerable to over-harvesting. As populations along the Pacific coasts of the Asian countries have disappeared, fishing vessels – predominantly run by the Taiwanese, who dominate the giant clam market – have raided the reefs throughout the Pacific, often taking clams illegally from fishing grounds in remote areas where fishing communities lack the resources to police their reefs.

The two largest species, *Tridacna gigas* and *Tridacna derasa*, have now virtually disappeared from much of Indonesia, the Philippines, Belau, the Federated States of Micronesia and Japan. Populations in most other Pacific countries have dwindled, and *Tridacna gigas* recently became extinct in Fiji. The status of the other five species of clam is less well known, but they too have been overexploited in many localities.

Many more reef species, often less obvious sources of food, are now being intensively exploited. Reef sharks in the Pacific have traditionally been fished for their meat and skin, but were not widely considered subsistence food. A village chief might request shark meat for a special occasion, and in some communities shark fishermen gained prestige from hunting them, but at this level, their exploitation had little impact on populations. There is currently a lack of information on the impact of modern commercial shark fishing on reef sharks, but it is known that many species of shark are now intensively fished, and

*Two stages in the making of* bêche-de-mer *or trepang: diving for sea cucumbers at Ashmore Reef, N.W. Australia (an area to which Indonesian fishermen have come for this purpose since the 17th century), and drying the gutted animals in the sun to preserve them.*

many thousands are killed for their fins (which can fetch up to US\$170 per shark). There are many reports of reef sharks dwindling; in the Florida Keys, for example, there now seem to be fewer lemon sharks, which are used as bait for crab-fishing. What is certain is that sharks are highly susceptible to over-exploitation because they do not have planktonic larvae, produce only small numbers of young, and are slow-growing.

When gutted, dried and smoked, sea cucumbers are known as trepang or *bêche-de-mer* and are considered a great delicacy by Chinese communities. They are now exported in huge numbers from reef lagoons in the Philippines, Indonesia, and Malaysia to restaurants throughout Asia. To cope with growing demand, small fisheries are being started up in many Pacific countries, even though local people rarely eat sea cucumber themselves. In New Caledonia, sea cucumbers are collected at low tide from the reef flat; until recently, the harvest was mainly made up of the sandfish *(Holothuria scabra)*, said to make the best-quality *bêche-de-mer* and fetching about US\$30 a kilogramme, but recently catches have consisted largely of the 'blackfish' *(Actinopyga miliaris)*, for which collectors can get only US\$10 a kilo, which may be an early sign of overcollection of the more valuable species.

The best baitfish for commercial tuna fisheries are anchovy, which are found in estuaries and muddy coastal areas, but where these are not available, sprats and sardines, together with a variety of other small reef fish, are taken from lagoons. Fisheries for these exist in the Solomon Islands, New Caledonia, around the Maldives and in Sri Lanka, and at present they do not seem to be suffering any decline, but there is concern that juvenile fish of a range of other food species may also be being taken, which could affect other aspects of the reef fishery.

Over recent years, there has been a huge growth in sport fishing, a popular activity among local residents and tourists alike, particularly in Australia, Hawaii and the Caribbean. Although the big oceanic game fish such as marlin are the most sought-after catches, many reef fish are also taken. Recreational fishing on the

Great Barrier Reef in the 1980s took three times as much fish as the commercial boats, and in one part of the reef alone the catch amounted to 2,000 tonnes in a single year. Between the 1960s and the 1980s, the average weight of coral trout on the Barrier Reef declined by a kilogram, and in some areas these popular fish have almost disappeared. In locations such as Florida and Hawaii amateur fishermen flock to the reefs in their thousands at the weekend and in holiday periods, adding substantially to other pressures on fish stocks. Lobsters are also a prime target for amateurs and are so simple to catch that their numbers are easily decimated. An experiment in Florida showed that it took two years after the closure of a lobster fishery for stocks to recover to even seventy per cent of their previous level.

Although many reef fishermen are well aware that fish stocks are declining, marine biologists have found it difficult to quantify this. Reef fish produce large numbers of young, but only a few reach maturity because of the high rate of predation, so at any one time there may be only a few individuals of a particular species on a

reef, or even none at all. Local populations may even become temporarily 'extinct'. Fluctuations of this kind are a natural part of the ecology of the reef, but if any one reef species reaches an especially low abundance, it becomes extremely vulnerable to exploitation. Fortunately, very few reef species are likely to become biologically extinct from over-fishing, although numbers may drop below the level at which they can be fished. As the planktonic larvae of reef animals are carried long distances on ocean currents, populations on unfished reefs can potentially replenish over-fished reefs.

Even so, over-fishing has several serious consequences, both for the reef and for the people who depend on it. If catches are so high that fish and invertebrate populations cannot replace themselves naturally (which is already happening in many areas), and the ecological balance is upset, future generations of fishermen will find that they catch less and less despite ever greater effort. The first sign that fishing has passed a sustainable level is a decrease in the size of fish caught – small individuals and small species begin to predominate. As fishing intensifies, an increasing number of juveniles will be taken, so that more and more fish are taken before they have been able to breed. In some cases, the decline may be dramatic and the fishery may 'crash', which effectively means that the particular species has become commercially extinct. The question of what is a sustainable harvest is difficult to ascertain, but fishery scientists think that, on average, reefs can sustainably yield about fifteen tonnes per square kilometre a year. This would mean that theoretically reefs worldwide, if managed sustainably, could yield about nine million tonnes of fish, crustaceans and molluscs per annum, or just over a tenth of the current world total fishery catch.

Few records have so far been kept of the amount of fish taken from reefs, but from the little information available, it has been estimated that yields are immensely variable. On some reefs in the Philippines, for example, thirty to forty tonnes per square kilometre a year are taken. In other places, such as some Pacific

Coral trout (Plectropomus leopardus), *like this one at Heron Island, are enormously popular with recreational fishermen on the Great Barrier Reef and populations have declined markedly since the 1960s.*

*When a fishery crashes, it means that the normal food fish have for all practical fishing purposes disappeared. Then the catches will consist only of less well-favoured and particularly of very small fish like this butterflyfish* (Chaetodon melannotus), *at Batangas in the Philippines. While decorative, they are not sustaining as nourishment for humans.*

islands, catches may be only two to four tonnes per square kilometre a year. Unfortunately, these figures reveal little about the health of the reef unless other information accompanies them. A high yield may equally reflect a reef with abundant fish that is being lightly harvested or one with small populations that are being very intensively fished. And a reef with a low yield might be one with few fish (some over-fished reefs in the Philippines now yield only about five tonnes per square kilometre a year, despite the large numbers of fishermen using them), or a reef where little fishing takes place.

An additional complication is that intensive fishing can have complex repercussions that ripple through the intricate web of reef life and alter the entire ecosystem. Over-fishing of any one species can cause a dramatic population decline or explosion in another, often causing a domino effect as each species in turn is affected. For instance, removing herbivorous fish such as parrotfish or surgeonfish can cause an increase in seaweed growing on the reef; the seaweed then outcompetes the corals, since there is no natural check on its growth. Similarly, in the Caribbean, the queen triggerfish (*Balistes vetula*), which is a key predator on sea urchins, now accounts for some ten to twelve per cent of reef catches, allowing urchin populations to increase, and ultimately accelerating reef erosion through the feeding habits of urchins. In many parts of the world, including the Caribbean, the Red Sea and Kenya, over-fished reefs are frequently

characterised by excessively large populations of sea urchins. Over-fishing could even be a contributory factor to the outbreaks of the crown-of-thorns starfish. Although it was initially thought that over-collection of the giant triton, a mollusc popular in the ornamental shell trade and one of the few known predators of the starfish, might have been responsible, more recent work is suggesting that over-fishing of commercial food fish such as emperors and triggerfish, that feed on juvenile crown-of-thorns starfish, may be more significant.

## Mariculture

A number of techniques have traditionally been employed for increasing yields of certain species. Giant clam gardens involve giant clams being collected from reefs and then placed in shallow lagoons near villages to grow to maturity before being harvested, and this could be considered an early form of farming. For many centuries, people trapped young fish and crustaceans by blocking off mangrove swamps and estuaries to create temporary ponds in which their catch could be kept until large enough to be eaten. Eventually, more permanent ponds were built to act as larders stocked with fish or crustaceans collected in the wild.

Mariculture, the farming of marine plants and animals, has become increasingly important in the tropics with demand for fish and marine foods, both for burgeoning populations and forever-expanding export markets, continuing to grow while natural

stocks decline. Mariculture of reef species is attracting more and more interest: it can be a source of employment, reduce pressure on overexploited stocks, provide a reliable source of protein and be used to restock depleted reefs. Today the range of species farmed is considerable, with production increasing annually as mariculture expands in tropical developing countries. In south-east Asia, milkfish *(Chanos chanos)*, and giant tiger prawns *(Penaeus monodon)* are cultivated extensively, though, unfortunately, with major environmental consequences, as these brackish water species are often raised in ponds created by cutting down mangroves. In addition to this, the shrimp farms often use large quantities of fresh water which sometimes limits supplies to local people. In the Philippines, at least 156,000 hectares of mangroves have been uprooted to make way for milkfish farms. Once the mangroves have gone, wild populations of some reef species decline because their nursery habitat has vanished, there are fewer young fish and crustaceans available for collection to stock the mariculture ponds, and subsistence fishing declines.

Modern commercial mariculture uses intensive production techniques which can be extremely damaging, as has been well documented in the salmon fish farms in the northern hemisphere. Animals and plants are kept at much higher densities than in the wild, and fertilisers and fishmeal are often applied to boost their growth or that of species on which they feed. This, combined with the high levels of waste matter that are generated, creates pollution in neighbouring habitats. Chemicals and antibiotics are often used to control the diseases that arise in crowded conditions, which may subsequently constitute a health hazard to humans as well as affecting the surrounding environment. Diseases may spread to populations outside the farm, and there is a considerable danger of farmed animals escaping and becoming established in the wild outside their natural range where they may outcompete indigenous species or weaken genetic strains.

Nevertheless, there is potential for carefully managed mariculture of some reef species, particularly if it is carried out at low intensity, and preferably at a scale compatible with management by local communities. A comparison can be drawn with farming on land, where small-scale traditional methods generally have low-level impacts on the environment, whereas large-scale monocultures can have widespread and long-term consequences. Hatcheries in Belau, the Federated States of Micronesia, the Solomon Islands, the Philippines and Turks and Caicos, among others, are experimenting with several kinds of food farming of giant clams, conch, seaweed and fish.

In some parts of the Caribbean, harvesting seaweed from the wild has already led to declining supplies and rising prices, so it is fortunate that seaweed is one of the easiest tropical marine organisms to farm: cuttings or small pieces are attached to nylon lines suspended in grids (normally called rafts) over reefs and lagoons and left to grow. The red seaweed *Euchema* is grown extensively in south-east Asia, Japan and the Pacific, either in large commercial farms or on a smaller scale (as in Kiribati in the Western Pacific where there are around 500 small-scale seaweed farms) and processed commercially to make alginates and agars; these are then used as thickeners in a huge range of products from ice cream to shoe polish and as a medium for the culture of microbes in hospitals and laboratories. In the Caribbean, several species of *Gracilaria*, known locally as seamoss, have traditionally been blended with milk and spices to make a drink or pudding. Seamoss farming started in St Lucia in 1981, and there are now 300 rafts in operation on small-scale farms. Even seaweed though, can cause problems in the ecological balance. In Hawaii, for example, after *Euchema* had been farmed for some years, there were escapes into the wild that developed into heavy infestations, leading to a reduction in fish and invertebrate populations.

The development of queen conch farming in the Caribbean was a direct response to the loss of wild stocks. In the Turks and Caicos Islands, a captive population of 200 male and 200 female conch are kept together in an underwater 'pasture'. In this sheltered habitat, where they are protected from predators and the males and females are able to find each other easily,

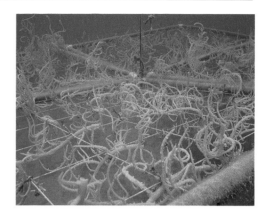

female conch produce between six and eight egg masses every year, each containing up to half a million eggs. Once the eggs have been collected, they are hatched out at the conch farm and the baby conch reared until they can be transferred to shallow tanks. Here they are fed on algae until they are about five to seven months old when they are released into another larger underwater pasture to grow to maturity, and finally harvested when they are three to four years old.

Hatchery-reared juvenile conch have been exported from the Turks and Caicos Islands to re-seed reefs elsewhere in the Caribbean. A simple, low-cost method of increasing conch populations would be to create egg farms upstream from potential habitats for adult conch. Male and female conchs could be penned together, as they

are in the Turks and Caicos, but instead of the eggs being collected they could be left to re-populate adjacent areas naturally. The advantage of this system would be that greater reproductive rates are achieved by keeping numerous males and females in a semi-enclosed habitat than in stock farming conditions.

Giant clam farming in the Pacific may prove to be the key to the future survival of these reef creatures, producing them both as food for local people and export, and as stock with which over-fished reefs can be replenished. The yield can be substantial, with production rates of as much as sixty tonnes of clam meat per hectare per year. All seven species are being cultured, but best results have been obtained with *Tridacna derasa,* one of the largest species. Adult 'brood' clams are kept in tanks where they spawn; the juveniles are then reared in tanks and raceways (tanks with running water) for six months to a year until they are about five millimetres long, when they are transferred to cages or 'nurseries' floating in the reef lagoon. At this age, they grow quite rapidly, about 4 to 10 cm a year, and once they have reached about 20 cm or more they can be placed directly out onto shallow reefs, in areas often referred to as clam gardens (after the traditional giant clam gardens maintained by Pacific islanders).

*Large adult giant clams being placed in a floating tank to spawn at a hatchery on Mili Atoll, Marshall Islnds.*

*Opposite, top: seaweed farming project in the lagoon at Majuro in the Marshall Islands.*

*Below: culturing microalgae inside a geodesic dome to feed larval queen conch at the Caicos Conch Farm, Providenciales, Turks & Caicos Islands. Opposite, left: recently released hatchery-reared queen conch in a pasture fenced off from the open sea at the conch farm.*

The main hatcheries producing juvenile clams are in Belau and the Solomon Islands, with some smaller operations in countries such as the Philippines. Thousands of juveniles are now being distributed from the hatcheries to numerous countries in south-east Asia and throughout the Pacific; in most cases, they are being sent to villages and communities which have expressed interest in clam farming. Local people are shown how to keep the young clams in quarantine for a month, in tanks away from the natural reef, to ensure that they are free from disease and other problems. The clams are then planted out at a selected spot, and the community ensures that they are protected until they have grown to a suitable size for harvesting. To help introduce these ideas, Greenpeace has joined forces with ICLARM (the International Centre for Living Aquatic Resources Management) to produce a handbook on giant clam conservation and management for villagers. This will give detailed instructions on rearing clams through to harvestable size and explain how successful clam production requires pristine waters and an undamaged reef environment.

In the Philippines, the first hatchery-reared giant clams were planted out on a reef in the community-run marine reserve on San Salvador Island in 1990, and clams are now being introduced to a number of other community-managed reserves. In

the Pacific, communities have been particularly enthusiastic about clam farming, and the traditional system of rights and ownership of reefs helps to ensure that the clam gardens are protected. In Yap, more than forty villages have established clam gardens, and numerous others have been set up in the Solomon Islands. The clams provide a welcome source of cash to communities previously largely dependent on subsistence fishing, and give a powerful incentive for careful management of the coast and marine environment, so that unsound development (in the form of agriculture, industry, road-building and so on) is avoided.

Farming reef fish has proved to be rather more difficult, largely because very few will spawn in captivity and so little is known about their life cycles. Floating net cages are used to raise the grouper *Epinephelus tauvina* in Thailand and Malaysia, and aquarium fish enthusiasts are contributing to efforts to rear other species. Fish that lay their eggs on the substrate rather than spawn, such as damselfish, are easier to breed. Leaving aside the practical problems, any project involving breeding fish in captivity needs to be properly assessed so as to discover likely economic and social consequences as well as ecological implications, and effective monitoring schemes need to be in place before farming starts, so that it is properly regulated.

## Artificial Reefs

Another method used to boost the harvest of a variety of reef species is artificial reefs. Probably the first – if unintentional – artificial reefs were shipwrecks. Any sunken ship in the right location will quickly become a magnet for life and will be rapidly colonised by numerous plants and animals. In tropical waters, shipwrecks can rapidly acquire the appearance of a reef: the metal provides a smooth, hard surface for coral larvae to settle on, and parts of the structure offer shelter and breeding sites for fish and invertebrates. Other species will eventually arrive in search of food and the shipwreck soon becomes a thriving artificial reef.

Purpose-built artificial reefs are now fairly frequently placed either on damaged reefs (where they may aid recovery) or on the sea bed near reefs. By creating additional habitats, they allow a greater number of larvae to settle, seek shelter and survive predation. In the Philippines and in Thailand, artificial reefs are being installed on

*It is difficult to breed reef fish in captivity but species like these damselfish that lay their eggs on a hard surface are easier; many of the main food species, however, spawn in mid-water.*

many damaged reefs where fishing yields have declined, and are being managed by local fishing villages. No artificial reef, though, can compete with a natural coral reef for productivity, and the prime objective must be to prevent damage to these in the first place.

Artificial reefs can be made from a variety of readily available, low-tech materials. Bamboo structures are popular and cheap in countries where there is abundant bamboo, as in south-east Asia, and provide a good habitat for fish, although corals do not settle on them.

There is however, a great temptation to use waste materials when building artificial reefs; this can clearly be counterproductive if it causes pollution. Bundles of old tyres have been widely used because they are so easily available and have proved very effective: coral larvae readily settle on them. But the risk is that as the tyres gradually break down, they will release toxic substances, becoming a hazard to the very creatures and plants they were supposed to attract, though no research has yet

Although not in the tropics, Greenpeace's first Rainbow Warrior is now an artificial reef, having attracted large numbers of sub-tropical plants and animals, though not, of course, reef-building corals. Destroyed in 1985 in Auckland harbour by bombs placed by French secret service agents, while in the course of a mission to the Pacific to protest against French nuclear testing, in 1987 it was cleaned of all oil and pollutants and towed to Matauri Bay off the coast of northern New Zealand, where it was sunk.

*The wreck of the old Rainbow Warrior (which was sunk in its final resting place in 1987), already colonised by jewel anemones.*

been carried out into this. In Florida, several proposals have been put forward to use municipal solid waste ash from incinerators to build reefs. This is highly risky because of the impact that toxic residues in the waste could have. In 1987, one company initiated an 'experiment', to see how waste could be used in this way. Bricks made of ash from an oil-fired power plant, solidified in concrete, were dumped in the sea off Vero Beach in Florida. Oil ash is rich in the toxic heavy metal vanadium as well as a variety of other hazardous substances and, despite the company's claims that these would have no ill effects, there is clearly a potential risk. In 1991, Greenpeace used the MV Moby Dick to dismantle part of the reef and retrieve some of the bricks and put pressure on the company to remove the rest. As a result the 'experiment' was abandoned, but no action has been taken to remove the remaining bricks.

A range of sophisticated, specially-designed artificial reef structures are now available which seem to be highly efficient, although they are expensive. Pre-cast

concrete structures have been used to attract groupers in Salt River Canyon in the US Virgin Islands, and in the Maldives an artificial reef has been made from square concrete blocks, concrete 'mattresses' and chain-link fencing held in place by paving slabs – within a few months of its installation it had been colonised by seaweeds, fish and invertebrates including some corals that had settled. It is hoped that in a low-lying country like the Maldives, artificial reefs of this kind will have the added benefit of protecting the shore from more damage and flooding.

A form of artificial reef has traditionally been used to increase lobster harvests in Cuba: mangrove boughs are interwoven and stacked together to form lobster shelters, which last about a year once underwater. Some 200,000 of these in the Gulf of Batabano produce an annual harvest of 14,000 tons of lobster. In Belize, Cuba, the Bahamas and Mexico, similar lobster shelters, known as *casitas*, are built from concrete and plastic tubing.

One of the drawbacks of artificial reefs is

the possibility that they may attract species from adjacent areas where they could have been fished under natural conditions with less expense and effort. But ideally, artificial reefs can provide additional habitats in which marine life can reproduce and flourish.

Another way of increasing fish yields is by installing Fish Aggregration Devices, or FADs. These are objects of various shapes which float on or below the surface in the open sea and provide a visual reference point around which fish can congregate. Although principally used in deeper water for pelagic species, they can also be positioned above or near reefs. The FAD may be a simple bunch of palm fronds tied together, a complex, purpose-built raft, or a durable plastic cone. In Barbados, bundles of sugar cane are tied beneath fishing boats to attract schools of flying fish, and in Jamaica standard fish traps are suspended in the water to catch rainbow runner, barracuda and jacks. By concentrating the fish, FADs save time and effort for fishermen, as well as increasing the catch.

*Ships and anchors can cause great damage when they first hit a reef, but, given sufficient time, their hard surfaces can form the basis for a new 'artificial' reef. This anchor (left) will eventually disappear from view as the corals and other reef animals growing on it proliferate.*

*Above: schools of barracuda are often seen near reefs, where they may find a ready meal of fish. They can also provide tasty food for humans, and are one of the species that can be attracted to Fish Aggregating Devices.*

# Traditional Fisheries Management

In the past, traditional fishing generally exploited reefs at a level that allowed each species easily to replace itself, and this is still the case in remote areas, especially where fishing is mainly for subsistence. Even if local over-exploitation occurred – and this may have happened in some places, with particular species like, say, giant clams, and when certain techniques were used – people would have been able to move on to other areas and allow the depleted reefs to recover. A wide variety of species was taken from the reef which helped to maintain the ecological balance.

In many parts of the world, reef fisheries have traditionally been managed on a communal basis. In the Pacific, fishing rights applied to numerous species, including fish, giant clams and other invertebrates, and were handed down through the generations within family or kinship groups. Regulations included measures such as live storage in ponds, the freeing of surplus fish caught in spawning migrations, closed seasons during periods of spawning, 'taboos' or prohibitions on fishing in certain areas, and the setting aside of stretches of sea near particular sections of coast for fishing in bad weather only. Fishing rights were usually overseen by village leaders, religious leaders or in some cases by special fishery 'experts'; in some societies, the king or chief had ultimate control. Punishments for infractions included ostracism by the community, the invoking of supernatural curses, fines or confiscation of the catch, and even corporal punishment or death.

Such traditional management practices appear to be less common outside the Pacific, although more informal communal arrangements do exist elsewhere. In the Caribbean, fishing is an individual pursuit and by law anyone can fish anywhere. But in some places, as in Jamaica, fishermen can lay claim to certain areas for reef fishing, based around their local community and 'fishing beach' or landing site. Fishing communities of this kind are close-knit, helping each other out and lending a hand with the building of one another's boats. If a stranger's trap is found within an area habitually fished by one of these communities, it is likely to be removed or damaged. This system may, at least in part, account for the unexpectedly high yields of reef fish that have been caught here over a long period. In the Indian Ocean, on the south-east coast of Oman, the reefs of Barr al Hikman still have large populations of fish species that have been fished out elsewhere in the country, largely, it appears, because the local people prohibit commercial fishing on the reefs, and allow fishing for domestic use only in times of hardship.

Fishermen in such societies generally have a good understanding of management principles. Many of the old fishing methods and ways of husbanding the reef are now disappearing, or – in some places – have vanished altogether; in Barr al Hikman, for example, traditions are just beginning to break down, as a result of fishermen (with no knowledge of or respect for local customs) coming in from outside to use the reefs. Where well-tried practices do still exist, they can provide a sound basis for modern reef fishery management. Fishermen on the atoll of Woleai in the Federated States of Micronesia regularly ban certain fishing methods on reefs that show signs of being over-fished. As in other parts of the Pacific, there is a long tradition of group fishing here, whereby forty men at a time join together to fish large quantities, generally before a celebratory feast held on the occasion of a wedding, funeral, high-school graduation (and even when girls start to menstruate). Large numbers of fish are gathered, either by the men forming a circle and forcing the fish into the centre where they are killed by spearing, or by the use of a seine net with scarelines of coconut fibres to enclose the fish (a precursor of the modern muro-ami method). Inevitably, as with modern intensive methods, the reef is rapidly depleted by this kind of mass fishing, but traditionally these reefs would have been left 'fallow' to recover over several months or more. Nowadays, though, growing populations mean that feasts occur more often, and the fishermen are now having to work out more long-term management strategies, based on traditional regulations, such as prohibiting spearfishing in certain areas.

In areas like the Caribbean and much of south-east Asia, where there is open access to fisheries, efforts are now underway to introduce communal management. In some countries, fisheries for spiny lobsters and other reef products are run on a cooperative basis, a system chosen to ensure equitability, improve efficiency in processing and marketing, and distribute

profits evenly. It also provides a framework for community involvement in the management of the reef fishery. In Japan, for example, there are some 4,000 co-operatives based around communities that traditionally have rights to fish in certain areas, and in southern Japan, on certain reefs. These fishing grounds cannot be sold, although the government has on occasion given the community cooperatives large sums of money in exchange for their rights, when it has wanted to use the area for landfill or some other development initiative.

Under Mexican law, lobster, conch and shrimp may only be fished by cooperatives in allotted areas. At Sian Ka'an, on the Yucatan coast, each fisherman in the two cooperatives there is responsible for protecting his own territory where he sets up his lobster traps or *casitas*. Territories can be bought and sold among cooperative members, though they are usually passed down through families. The cooperative sets certain rules relating, for example, to closed seasons and the type of equipment that can be used, and it can expel members or confiscate their gear for poaching in other members' territories. Joint manage-

ment of this kind provides clear incentives for improving fishing methods. Lobster *casitas* in Sian Ka'an are traditionally made out of *chit* palm, a local tree that is now badly over-exploited; alternative materials, such as cement and steel, are now being investigated.

Where coastal peoples have no traditions of community management, considerable work may be needed to improve awareness and understanding of its aims and benefits and to break down the natural distrust and rivalry between poor fishermen. Several cooperatives have failed because they were set up too rapidly for local people to appreciate or understand the benefits they could bring. Local management is soundest in terms of sustainable use of the reef if there is no pressure vastly to increase yields. When there are development projects (often sponsored by aid agencies or foreign companies) aimed at maximising output potential (so as to gain foreign currency), the fishery is likely to become a victim of its own success, and risks concentration of ownership of equipment and boats, negation of conservation measures and reduced reliance on local food.

*Approaching storm clouds as a small fishing boat heads for home in Butaritari Lagoon, Kiribati, South Pacific; traditional boats like this are increasingly being replaced by modern motorboats.*

*Opposite, left: fishermen at Hikkaduwa, on the west coast of Sri Lanka, using a traditional method of fishing with hook and line.*

*Below: communal activity in Kiribati in the Pacific, as fish are caught with a seine net in the shallows.*

## Fishing Reserves

One of the most frequently used methods in traditional management of reef fish or other resources of the reef used to be the establishment of 'taboo' or no-go areas. Fishing would be prohibited either on a permanent basis, or just at certain times of year, providing safe havens for breeding populations of fish and invertebrates or spawning aggregations and helping to ensure that adjacent exploited reefs have been replenished.

The concept of closed fishing areas has been lost among many western fishing communities, and both commercial and recreational fishermen often take great exception to being told where they can and cannot fish. But if the entire community understands that the closure is to their long-term advantage, the idea may be readily accepted again. Modern fishing reserves are being set up in many parts of the world under a variety of names: reserves, parks, management areas or sanctuaries. Recommendations have even gone forward to make a fifth of the reefs in Florida and the Gulf of Mexico into fishing reserves.

In the Philippines, community-managed marine parks, where local fishermen have decided to allow only non-damaging methods, also contain small sanctuary areas where all fishing is banned (to protect breeding stocks), an initiative that has led to noticeably better catches. At Pamilacan on the island of Bohol, where a marine park, managed by local people and including a sanctuary was set up in 1985, the density and abundance of fish is now several times higher than on adjacent unprotected reefs. At Sumilon Island, off Cebu, fish catches on the reefs that remained open to fishermen increased noticeably after the reefs on the other side of the island were closed to fishing completely in 1974.

Community management of these small reef areas based, in the Philippines, on villages, is an essential component of their success, often leading, ultimately, to a more community-based attitude towards the care of natural resources. The reserves that have worked best are those where the local people, especially those who fish, are closely involved with managing the reefs, so that they benefit directly from enhanced yields; often the most effective way of enabling them to do this is, initially, by the provision of education and support. The reserve at Sumilon failed in 1984, when it was invaded by about 100 fishermen, led by their newly elected mayor, using dynamite and muro-ami in addition to less damaging methods. Within two years they had reduced fish populations by nearly one half, and even butterflyfish (which had not been specifically targeted), had declined because large areas of coral, their food, had been killed. This happened partly because the island has only a very small resident population. The fishermen who use the reefs come from Cebu, three kilometres away, and when decisions about the reserve were made by biologists at Silliman University, who set up the project, the fishermen were not consulted about management or enforcement of new regulations. By contrast, fishermen who live on the island of Apo (also off Cebu) took the initiative in organising a reserve here and, as at Pamilacan, control management of the reefs around the island; in 1988, for example, they requested that scuba divers should be banned from the sanctuary area because they had been unable to stop Japanese tourists taking spearguns there.

Closed areas can be established on a seasonal basis. A variation on this method involves rotating closed seasons on different reefs, effectively creating temporary fishing sanctuaries to protect breeding populations and to allow stocks to recover after short but intense fishing seasons. Under the new coastal zone management plan currently being prepared for the Belize Barrier Reef, spawning sites for the Nassau grouper (*Epinephelus striatus*) will be closed to all fishing during the spawning periods. Belize fishermen are well aware of the significance of such areas, where anywhere between 30,000 and 100,000 grouper may gather just after full moon in December or January each year. Until recently, these spawning aggregations were regularly decimated by fishermen, many of whom came from Honduras and fished illegally on the Belize fishing grounds. The closure of the area during the spawning season will ultimately benefit all fishermen through increased populations on a year-round basis, and will ensure that Belize fishermen can be more certain of the future of their own stocks.

Fishing reserves, whether community-managed or overseen by a government authority such as the Great Barrier Reef Marine Park, can be combined with tourism, as marine parks, making them more cost-effective: the presence of visitors and park wardens deters illegal fishing and makes enforcement easier. Fishermen and their families can also benefit from the additional income they can earn by providing a range of services from boat trips to accommodation for tourists.

## Healthy reefs – healthy fisheries

Unfortunately experience has now shown that the success of fishing reserves and closed areas can be severely compromised if the reefs within them are being damaged by other factors. In Kenya, for example, fish populations on reefs within the marine parks are no higher than on those outside, probably because the reefs along much of the coast have been damaged by pollution, siltation and heavy tourist use, regardless of whether they are protected within a park. If mangroves and seagrass beds, adjacent to reefs are removed or filled in, the loss of these habitats which act as nurseries for so many juvenile fish can reduce fish yields as much as over-exploitation.

A dead coral reef may initially shelter a healthy fish population, particularly if there is a heavy growth of seaweed, but fish rapidly move away as the coral skeletons break down. Broken coral provides less shelter for fish and invertebrates, and

heavy silt blocks up the cracks and holes in which they hide. In the Maldives, fish populations are much lower on reefs that have been mined for corals than on unmined reefs. One theoretical calculation suggests that if the Philippine reefs were not so badly damaged they could potentially provide over 150,000 more tonnes of fish a year, and a further 125,000 fishing jobs.

Since fishermen themselves are also a major cause of reef damage, encouraging them to use non-damaging methods should be a big priority in fisheries management. This requires education programmes to help fishermen understand the damage they can (sometimes unwittingly) cause, and to provide them with alternative non-damaging methods – sometimes fishermen know they are acting destructively but know no other way of achieving a reasonable catch. Any regulations in place, such as bans on dynamite fishing, must be properly enforced, so that those who keep to them are not penalised while offenders are rewarded with higher short-term yields.

*Healthy reefs are vital for the maintenance of good reef fisheries; damaged reefs provide less food and shelter for both food fish and the many other species that make up the reef, such as this cardinal fish (top) and (above) the hawkfish* (Paracirrhites forsteri), *which moves from perch to perch on corals where it waits for the fish on which it preys to pass.*

*Opposite: a white margate* (Haemulon album) *over a seagrass bed at Hol Chan Marine Reserve, Ambergris Caye, Belize. Protection from fishing in the reserve allows this species to thrive there.*

## Controlling the Harvest

Management of reef fisheries is a much more complex challenge than temperate water or open ocean fisheries management because of the huge number of fish and invertebrate species caught. The problems of managing the world's major commercial fisheries, such as herring in the North Sea and tuna in the Pacific and Indian Oceans, stem mainly from the competitive nature of the industry and the huge economic incentives for some of the large companies involved. Even so, because only one or two species are involved it is comparatively easy to obtain the information about their biology and populations that is needed in order to set quotas, restrict

numbers of fishing boats through licences and introduce other measures to limit the amount of fish that is taken.

In many countries, fishermen may only operate with a licence, and it is then open to government to limit the size of the fishery by restricting the number of licences issued. But this is of little use in countries where there is a high proportion of subsistence fishermen who have to continue fishing, licensed or not.

For most reef species, information about populations and biology is still too sparse to be used to set suitable size limits or catch quotas. Even if this were possible, enforcement of such regulations over a wide range of species would be impractical. In the case of a small number of reef

animals, though, especially those taken commercially or for export in what are essentially single species fisheries rather than as a basic food, size limits and quotas could be a useful adjunct to the management approaches mentioned earlier, though they will never constitute an exclusive solution and enforcement remains a problem.

Size limits are most useful for animals such as molluscs and crustaceans that can be put back into the water still alive and uninjured if they are below the legal size limit. Most Caribbean countries have a minimum size limit of 1.5 cm carapace length for spiny lobsters, as well as a ban on the taking of egg-bearing females. Unfortunately, under-size individuals are frequently taken; for example, in Belize, they are sold directly to tourist restaurants, thus by-passing local markets and harbours where fishery officers may be checking catches. For conch, the recommended size limit is 18 cm in length or a minimum meat weight of 225 gm if landed without a shell, although in many countries, conch fishing has been banned entirely. Recreational conch fishing is still fairly widespread and is often regulated through quotas. Quotas have been used to try to limit the take of molluscs such as conch, both for the commercial market and for private consumption. For example, in Saba in the Netherlands Antilles, each licensed recreational collector can take a maximum of 20 a year and in the US Virgin Islands, sport fishermen can take two lobster and two conch a day.

Sustainable management of reef fisheries in most countries will probably be successfully achieved only if a carefully chosen combination of methods is adopted. Most importantly of all, fishing communities which depend on the fisheries must be involved in setting up management programmes, so that their day-to-day concerns are addressed along with the long-term aim of sustainable development. If local people have a vested interest in the stewardship of marine resources, and are aware of the benefits of improved habitats and fish stocks, responsible fisheries management is far more likely to be successful than if it is imposed by outsiders, however well-meaning.

## Marine curios

The shells of reef molluscs have been used since prehistoric times for a wide variety of purposes, including jewellery, decoration, tools and even currency. People have always been fascinated by the many forms and shapes that shells take, sometimes even endowing them with magical and religious attributes: the egg cowry (*Ovula ovum*), for example, is considered a symbol of fertility in parts of the Pacific. On Yap, cones and cowries were used as scrapers, augers and mitre shells as adzes, the giant triton (*Charonia tritonis*) as a trumpet, and pearl oysters, the egg cowry and many other species for beads and jewellery. The money cowry (*Cypraea moneta*) served

*Opposite: grunts, shown here with some spectacular tube sponges, are a good food fish. Conserving stocks of fish of this kind is an essential component of fisheries management plans. Their name derives from the curious grunting sound (amplified by the air bladder) that they make when they grind their teeth.*

*Above: yellow sea fan (or gorgonian) on Peleliu Wall, Belau, in the Pacific. Sea fans are widely collected and sold as ornaments.*

until recently as currency in many countries; in Papua New Guinea, the pearl oyster was once used as currency and its name, 'kina', still survives as a high-value denomination in present-day currency. Traditional trading rings, through which coastal people in Papua New Guinea obtained products from other islands or the mainland, involved a variety of reef molluscs: the 'Kula Ring' in the Milne Bay area, for example, used armlets of a cone shell (*Conus leopardus*) and necklaces of money cowries and other shells.

In the Caribbean, the shell of the queen conch (*Strombus gigas*) was used as a tool and, like the giant triton in the Indian and Pacific Oceans, as a trumpet. Giant clam shells have served as bowls and basins for all kinds of purposes: the Torres Straits islanders used them to catch rainwater under pandanus trees.

Europeans have long been fascinated by such treasures from tropical seas. Giant clam shells can be found in churches all over the world as fonts and holy water basins – one of the largest pairs, weighing a total of 250 kilos, is in the church of St Sulpice in Paris. Pearls, shells and other curiosities were brought back by sailors in the early days of exploration and trade from what were then considered far-off lands. By the end of the last century, shell-collecting was a well-established hobby, and

*Above: porcupine fish (*Diodron hystrix*) for sale to tourists, Veracruz, Gulf of Mexico. Opposite: cowries are among the most popular shells in the curio trade, but few people realise that the living animal expands the soft part of its body, called the mantle, out and around its shell completely covering its surface. The black spotted cowrie (*Calpurnus verrucosus*) is not a true cowrie, but is in the closely related family of egg or false cowries; its shell is pure white, the black spots are on the mantle. Below: hermit crab (*Dardanus sp.*), making rather better use of this gastropod shell than would be made of it on a mantelpiece.*

the Victorians enthusiastically sought and displayed their collections of the remains of strange animals from foreign seas.

The fascination with corals and shells has, if anything, grown, and the ease with which the marine curio trade can now be conducted together with the growth of the tourist industry have made it into a multi-million dollar international business. Walk into almost any resort hotel in the tropics and you will find a souvenir shop stocked with marine curios from reefs: exotic shells, dried pufferfish and seahorses, starfish, mother-of-pearl, black coral jewellery and entire pieces of coral are among the many items on sale. Reef curios are also often sold by beach vendors, or from market stalls or specialised shops, many of the latter catering to short-term visitors such as cruise-ship passengers. But this trade is not just restricted to tropical holiday resorts. In the USA, huge emporia with hundreds of square metres of floor space are devoted to little else but the sale of marine curios. In coastal towns around Britain, marine curio shops are part of a seaside holiday, though much of their stock comes from thousands of miles away.

Numerous reef species, including shells, pearls and aquarium fish are valued specifically for their aesthetic appeal which has led to high prices being paid for them, and with this has come increasing collecting pressure, just as growing demand for food from the reef has caused intensification of fisheries.

## Ornamental shells

Ornamental shells are as popular now as they have ever been, with around 5,000 species, most of them reef molluscs, traded all over the world. Many are sought avidly by shell collectors for their rarity value, whilst others are turned into jewellery, craftwork and trinkets – often a sad mockery of their former beauty. For many years, the Philippines has dominated the shell trade, but other suppliers include Indonesia, India, Mexico, Haiti and Kenya. Peak exports from the Philippines averaged 3,000 to 4,000 tonnes a year in the early 1980s, but exports declined to 1,500 tonnes in 1986, over ninety per cent of which went to the USA. In Florida alone, there are thousands of retail outlets for shells, most of which come from the Philippines. Although most shells are exported to the USA, Japan and Europe, large quantities also go to other developing countries for sale to tourists. Often countries that prohibit removal of shells from their own reefs import shells from elsewhere: it is ironic that reefs in the Philippines, already over-stressed, are carrying the burden of supplying shells to Florida, where there is a ban on collection.

Many reef molluscs are exploited for shellcraft (including inlay work), for which the shells are worked or carved to make a variety of items like buttons, jewellery and decorative boxes. Most shellcraft comes from the Philippines, which, during the mid 1980s, was exporting 4500 tonnes (excluding mother-of-pearl) each year.

Mother-of-pearl is the 'nacre' or thick iridescent layers found inside the shells of several mollusc species, and has been sought after for decorative purposes in many countries for centuries. The thickest and most durable mother-of-pearl – and therefore the best – comes from *Trochus niloticus,* pearl oysters (*Pinctada maxima* and *Pinctada margaritifera*) and green snail (*Turbo marmoratus),* all of which are found on reefs in the Indian and Pacific Oceans. The main suppliers are Indonesia, Australia, the Solomon Islands, New Caledonia, the Philippines and Papua New Guinea; other countries in the South Pacific supply smaller amounts. Most mother-of-pearl is exported to Japan and Korea for processing, although the Solomon Islands and Vanuatu have factories for making rough-cut buttons. Shells are cut into various shapes, and the dull outer layers removed by cutting and grinding. Although the mother-of-pearl market declined earlier this century with the development of plastics, it is once again much in demand, even for buttons, as it appears to withstand detergents and frequent washing better than plastic.

Like fishermen, shell collectors often damage the habitat of the animals they are seeking, trampling across reef flats, overturning coral heads and leaving the undersides exposed to the sun, and breaking corals either accidentally or intentionally in search of shells. How far the impact of intensive harvesting of molluscs affects the balance of reef life is not yet fully understood, but as with food fisheries, it may well have repercussions for the reef ecosystem. It has been speculated, but not proved, for instance, that heavy fishing of the giant triton on the Great Barrier Reef may be responsible for outbreaks of the crown-of-thorns starfish, as the giant triton is one of its few natural predators. But it is difficult to tie down fluctuations in mollusc populations to the attentions of shell collectors because many of the creatures involved are preyed upon by other reef animals. In Kenya, for example, there are fewer commercially valuable shells in marine parks where collecting is prohibited than on unprotected reefs where collecting still takes place. This may be because there are more fish that feed on molluscs in the marine parks, where fishing is banned, than on unprotected reefs where it is intense.

There have been many (largely anecdotal) reports of over-collection in particular locations. Among molluscs that are most at risk from over-exploitation are those that live exposed on reef flats and so are easy to collect, such as spider shells (*Lambis* spp.) and egg cowries, and species such as the giant triton, which are naturally rare to begin with. Molluscs that do not produce planktonic larvae have quite restricted distributions, so they can be vulnerable to over-collection. Volutes in the family Volutidae, for example, lay eggs from which tiny snails hatch directly; Australia has about 140 endemic species of volute, all of which could be threatened if intensively collected. Some molluscs have declined in numbers for reasons other than shell collection, but if their populations have already been hit, the shell trade can have an extremely serious impact. Giant clam populations have been decimated in most countries, mainly for their meat; in the Philippines they are still taken in large numbers for their shells – single giant clam shells are worth at least US$100 each.

All commercial mother-of-pearl shells have been widely over-exploited. *Trochus* has declined in Belau, Yap, the Cook Islands, New Caledonia and Australia, and

*Florida's conchs are protected from collection, as this sign near the reefs warns. But this does nothing to inhibit a vast trade in shells in Florida Keys based on foreign imports principally from the over-exploited reefs of the Philippines.*

*Trochus are traditionally collected by hand by divers, who often have an amazing ability to hold their breath under water. But as the animal becomes rarer, the temptation to use scuba gear becomes stronger, which could eventually lead to its disappearance in some localities.*

is particularly vulnerable because of the ease with which it can be collected and because it is slow to recover from over-harvesting. *Trochus* may only move a distance of about 100 metres throughout their entire lifetime and so the chances of them repopulating over-collected reefs are low. Green snails, which have been seriously over-exploited in Japan by scuba divers, also have poor recolonisation capabilities because the planktonic stage is brief and they settle quickly on the reef without travelling far. Scientists think that their current rarity throughout much of the Pacific is due to widespread over-exploitation in the past. Wild stocks of pearl oysters have also plummeted in many areas, especially in the Cook Islands and French Polynesia.

## Ornamental corals

The delicate and attractive shapes of coral colonies have made them a prime target for collecting for sale to tourists or for export. The Philippines has been the main exporter of ornamental corals since the 1950s, and concern over the impact of coral collection on its reefs led to a ban on collection and export in 1977; despite immense efforts to enforce it, though, coral is still being smuggled out at an alarming rate. In 1988, the USA imported a record 1,456 tonnes of ornamental corals, compared with annual imports of about 200 tonnes in the 1960s, most of it from the Philippines.

Other important suppliers include several south-east Asian countries (notably Indonesia) and some Pacific nations, such as New Caledonia and Fiji, which are now stepping up exports. As with shells, many countries with reefs import corals rather than exploit their own: large quantities of Caribbean and Indo-Pacific corals are sold in the Florida Keys and Hawaii where collection of corals is banned under state law. Considerable amounts of coral are also imported by European countries and Japan.

Much of the ornamental coral trade focuses on abundant and widespread species of coral, so the main problem posed by collection is that removal of large quantities can damage the structure of a reef and cause loss of habitat for other reef

animals. In New Caledonia, where the slow-growing brain corals are most in demand, harvesting is at a level ten times greater than what might be considered a 'sustainable' rate, in terms of the reef regenerating itself. A few of the coral species taken have very restricted distributions. The harvest from the Pacific coast of Costa Rica includes some species with narrow ranges, and, in cases like this, the ornamental coral trade could potentially cause extinction, particularly if the reefs are also under pressure from habitat destruction. Recent work has shown that many coral species occur in much smaller (though often very scattered and widespread) populations than previously believed; where studies have been made in Indonesia and Japan, about one third of the corals are found only rarely on reefs, even though they occur in several locations.

Coral is also used extensively in jewellery, but this is mostly black coral rather than reef-building coral. The Philippines exports large quantities to Taiwan for processing; nearly half a million pieces of black coral jewellery are exported each year from Taiwan to the USA, the main consumer. Other countries make jewellery on a smaller scale for sale locally as souvenirs or for limited export.

*Above: corals destined for the curio trade being collected and drying in heaps in the Philippines. Below: conch shells, sea fans, a dried pufferfish and a small shark for sale in the Cayman Islands. The impact of the marine curio trade on populations of reef creatures is still poorly understood. With more information, it may be possible to develop ways of managing their exploitation in a more sustainable way, but at present it may be better to discourage such a wanton use of reef life.*

There have been many anecdotal reports of over-collection of black coral, particularly in the Caribbean, and there is concern about over-exploitation in the Philippines. Like stony corals, black corals have a slow growth rate and may take many years to reach their full size. Unfortunately, only the thicker branches and the main stems produce enough material for turning into jewellery, so the wastage rate is high, with many of the more delicate branches being discarded.

## The Aquarium Trade

Keeping fish in an aquarium tank is one of the world's most popular hobbies. In the UK alone there are around five million home aquaria. Although freshwater fish are still more popular (they are cheaper and easier to keep), several hundred marine species are collected, and most of these originate from reefs. The most popular are butterflyfish, angelfish, surgeonfish, wrasse, moorish idols, basslets, squirrelfish, damselfish and triggerfish. The USA is the largest importer of tropical fish in the world and obtains about eighty per cent of its supplies from the Philippines; other major suppliers are Hawaii, Sri Lanka, Fiji and the Maldives.

There is as yet no evidence that any marine fish are threatened with biological extinction through the aquarium trade. Many of the popular species are abundant on reefs, and areas where they are collected

*Above: butterflyfish, like these* Chaetodon semilarvatus, *are particularly popular aquarium fish, but they rarely survive for very long as live corals are an essential part of their diet.*

*Opposite: red-toothed triggerfish (Odonus niger) – a spectacular fish much sought after by aquarists, but which will be too large as an adult to survive in most tanks.*

*Right: collecting aquarium fish with sodium cyanide is a method that is still used in a number of countries although it is widely outlawed; responsible aquarium fish dealers try to discourage it as fish caught in this way rarely survive long and rapidly bring their suppliers into disrepute.*

are usually repopulated fairly quickly. Fortunately, many rare species occur in localities too remote for collection to be commercially viable, although there has been some over-collection of high-value species that are easy to catch such as butterflyfish in Sri Lanka, the Philippines and Taiwan.

One of the main problems with the aquarium fish trade, however, is the damage done to the reef where the use of sodium cyanide is the preferred method of catching the fish. Sodium cyanide has been used in the Philippines since the 1960s for collecting aquarium fish and its impact has been particularly well documented. Sodium cyanide damages the liver, kidneys and reproductive organs of the fish, up to eighty per cent of which suffer a delayed death several weeks or months later. On the reef, numerous other plants and animals are affected and in areas where it is used extensively, it may kill up to eighty per cent of the corals.

The method is simple: sodium cyanide tablets are crushed and dissolved in seawater in plastic bottles. Collectors take these underwater and squirt the solution into cracks and crevices on the reef, quickly stupefying the fish that have fled there. They can then easily be scooped up by hand or with a net. About 2,500 fishermen in the Philippines collect fish in this way, using as much as 150 tonnes of sodium cyanide annually. Like dynamiting, the practice is not without a human cost, since cyanide is quickly absorbed by the skin and can cause lesions. The long-term health risk from diving in clouds of dissolved sodium cyanide every day is not yet known.

Quite apart from the harmful effects on the reef and reef animals of collection, the aquarium trade also involves a high degree of wastage through poor handling during collection and transport. Seventy per cent of all reef fish imported into the UK are dead within a year from stress and disease, and ten per cent die in transit before even reaching their destinations. Many species are captured which cannot survive outside the reef environment. Over half of all butterflyfish die within two months; cleaner wrasse also die quickly, both probably from starvation. The butterflyfish feed almost exclusively on live coral polyps, and cleanerfish need plenty of other fish in a tank in order to 'make a living' by cleaning them.

A fast-growing sector of the aquarium trade caters to the demand for 'mini-reefs' or live corals, not only from individual collectors, but also for commercial and public aquaria, despite the fact that live corals are notoriously difficult to maintain in tanks, and that extremely realistic artificial corals are now available. Imports of live coral into the USA grew from around 900 pieces in 1984 to about 40,000 pieces in 1988; the main suppliers are Haiti, Indonesia and other countries in Asia. Partly because individual colonies are so hard to keep alive, there has been a recent trend in the US to collect 'live rock' – large chunks of reef substrate with corals and other invertebrates still attached – which is more likely to survive and helps to keep the aquarium clean through the filtering activities of the numerous animals that encrust and live in the rock. Aquarists tend to aim for about 3.5 kilogrammes of rock for every gallon of water, and as a result large areas of reef in Florida have been stripped. Export of live rock is now banned in Florida state waters, and attempts are being made to ban it in federal waters as well as in other states.

## Management of the Marine Curio and Aquarium Trade

All too often, management of reef species for the curio trade and aquarium trade is overlooked by fishery departments and

government agencies, which frequently do not fully appreciate the high economic value of some of the species involved. There is also a scarcity of information on the levels of exploitation and the problems that may arise from heavy over-collection. Many of the techniques adopted for the management of food fisheries should be applied in this context, so that there can

*Above: a heap of discarded queen conch shells in the Bahamas – the method of removing the meat (by making a hole in the shell) has rendered them worthless as marine curios.*

*Opposite: collection of brain corals for the curio trade may be particularly damaging as their slow growth rates mean that reef recovery after their removal will be very gradual. This picture of a live brain coral with its polyps extended for feeding and a passing blenny among them is a very different sight to that of the dead skeleton marketed as a curio.*

*Left: giant clam shells stacked up in the Philippines awaiting export to the United States.*

be integrated management of all species that are taken, for whatever purpose. In several cases, valuable species are involved in both the food and the curio trades, and both issues need to be considered together. The queen conch, for example, is valued for both its meat and shell, but the traditional method of removing the meat involves making a hole in the shell, rendering it less attractive as a curio. In order to sell the shells, the meat is therefore often wasted.

Exports of reef species that are not food products, such as certain shells, pearls and corals, can make a significant contribution to the income of coastal people in developing countries and if appropriately managed, their collection could have less impact on the reef than exploitation of food species. Pearls, for instance, have a high unit value, so pearl oysters might be

a better resource to exploit than fish, which play key roles in the tight recycling system of the reef.

Potentially, the shellcraft industry could have less impact on mollusc populations than the ornamental shell trade because broken and worn shells can be used. It also creates employment and earns more for the people involved, as higher prices can be charged for skilled jewellery and craftwork than for unworked shells. By contrast, the ornamental shell trade creates few jobs, as whole shells are simply collected and exported. Similarly, jewellery and craftwork from black coral and other reef products is best made and sold locally to tourists so that the producer can retain a greater share of the profit. If an export market is developed, it should be based on worked products produced by local artisans rather than on the raw materials.

In Fiji, the Fisheries Division has issued a set of guidelines for the exploitation of non-food reef species. These have never been passed as legislation but seem to be working well, perhaps because they were developed in collaboration with local people. Collecting of reef corals is spread throughout the islands and exploratory surveys are carried out before any new areas are harvested. Maximum exports may not exceed 100,000 pieces of coral a year. Follow-up surveys have shown that less than a twentieth of available coral is taken. Aquarium fish can be caught only on certain reefs by licensed collectors using fine mesh scoops or barrier nets. Careful handling of fish and selection of more suitable species reduces wastage and, as a result, the pressure on wild stocks. Mortalities among exported aquarium fish from Fiji are estimated to be as low as 0.5%. Collectors of reef products have to obtain permission from traditional reef owners and respect their regulations, and all harvests are monitored.

In the Philippines, training courses have been set up to demonstrate alternative and less damaging ways of catching aquarium fish. In conjunction with the Haribon Foundation, a Filipino conservation organisation based in Manila, the IMA (International Marinelife Alliance) has now provided retraining for nearly 300 collectors, some of whom are now themselves running other training courses. First developed in 1984 by the IMA, the 'Netsman' method is simple. The collectors swim down to the reef armed only with a fine mesh barrier net, a little scoop net and a collecting bag. Once the barrier net is erected, selected fish are driven gently towards it, where they are quickly plucked off with the scoop net and put into the collecting bag. Each fish is individually selected and carefully caught – a far cry from the indiscriminate spraying of reefs with sodium cyanide. Collectors spend about three days on land learning about the proper handling and care of fish, diver safety, and basic principles of reef ecology and conservation. They then spend seven to ten days learning how to put this into practice underwater.

The Netsman project encountered considerable opposition soon after it began from the Philippine exporters who had been making almost as much profit from the sale of the sodium cyanide to the collectors as they did from the sale of fish overseas. Collectors and trainers alike received death threats, and for a while the courses were abandoned. But a change in government, combined with growing environmental awareness in the country and concern expressed by certain parts of the international aquarium industry, has allowed courses to start up again. The project has the cooperation of the Bureau of Fisheries and Aquatic Resources: one course has been run in conjunction with a major Manila exporter who wanted specifically to be able to market 'environmentally friendly' fish.

There is still a long way to go to retrain the country's estimated 1500 collectors, many of whom are scattered through remote islands; raising the necessary funding to run the courses has been one of the main hurdles. IMA is hoping to extend the Netsman Project to other countries. A training course has already been held in Costa Rica, even though cyanide is not used there; the intention is to get the country's fledgling aquarium fish industry off to the right start.

The aquarium fish industry might also be less damaging if collectors received a fair wage and could count on being regularly employed; this might persuade them not to take the more highly priced and vulnerable species, which could ultimately disappear if overexploited.

## Fishery Reserves

The part that reserves could play in the management of marine curio and other non-food species has yet to be fully investigated. Potentially they could both protect breeding populations of easily over-exploited sedentary reef species that take a long time to mature, and provide advantageous conditions for species in which spawning is more successful if the density of individuals is high. Sanctuaries for *Trochus* have been set up in Belau, the Federated States of Micronesia and the Cook Islands, and there is a *Trochus* reserve in French Polynesia divided into three areas, each of which is used in rotation, one year in three. As with any marine reserve, however, poaching is difficult to control, and the animals themselves have an unfortunate habit of wandering off and becoming dispersed outside the breeding ground. Ideally, reserves for species like these need to be developed in the context of a broad fishery and coastal zone management plan.

## Quotas and Size Limits

Quotas and size limits are subject to many of the same problems as those for food species. Size limits have been declared for *Trochus*, pearl oysters and green snail in many Pacific countries, but have often been randomly set. Belau has a minimum size limit at capture for *Trochus* of 7.6 cm (measured across the base of the shell), Vanuatu stipulates 9 cm and Guam 10.2 cm (4" in the regulations). In many cases it may be better to have a maximum size limit for these species, as large, old animals are often the most fertile and their shells – which tend to be heavily eroded by worms – of lower value. In New Caledonia, for example, *Trochus* may only be taken between the size limits of 9 cm and 12 cm. Animals mature at 7 cm so many young breeding stock are left, as well as the large, old, fertile animals.

Size limits could also be worked out for black and reef corals. Minimum size limits of 1.2 metres in height or 2.5 cm in stem diameter have been set in Hawaii for black coral colonies but, even so, in some areas where coral has been heavily collected in the past, stocks have yet to recover, despite the fact that collecting levels are now much lower. For reef corals, size limits have been calculated for some species but have never been put into practice; given the extreme pressure on reef corals from other sources the collection of ornamental corals should be discouraged.

Quotas for collecting aquarium fish have recently been introduced in Florida. Collectors may take a maximum of 75 angelfish per day or 150 per vessel (whichever is less) and a maximum of 75 butterflyfish per vessel. However, as with many such regulations, the figures used are totally arbitrary, since there is no data to indicate how many butterflyfish or angelfish can be removed without upsetting the balance of reef life, and these quotas are probably far too high.

## Farming and Restocking Depleted Reefs

The benefits and problems associated with mariculture of reef species have already been mentioned, and these apply in general to farming reef species for non-food uses. The high value of mother-of-pearl species makes their farming a particularly attractive proposition. *Trochus* is relatively easy to rear as the larvae feed off stored yolk reserves (so do not have to be artificially fed) and the larval stage (often the most difficult to manage) is brief. Newly settled juveniles feed on plankton and small algae and can easily

be grown in tanks. Green snail have been cultured in Japan, but the technique has not yet been applied with much success elsewhere.

For several decades pearl oysters have been cultured for their pearls, but not for their shells. The production of cultured pearls from the gold- or silver-lipped pearl oyster *(Pinctada maxima)* started in Japan in 1898 and is now carried out in several countries in Asia, and in Australia. Cultured pearls are produced by inserting a 'graft' or small piece of shell into the body of a pearl oyster. This forms a nucleus around which the layers of mother-of-pearl are laid down, until a pearl is formed. The technique was introduced from Japan to the Tuamotus in French Polynesia and to the northern Cook Islands in the 1960s and 1970s, and is used with the black-lipped pearl oyster *(Pinctada margaritifera).* The black pearl, known as the Queen of Pearls because of its rarity in the wild, is

highly sought after, and mariculture of the black-lipped pearl oyster in French Polynesia has turned it into the country's most valuable marine resource, with annual exports amounting to US$34 million. In the Cook Islands, annual pearl production is worth about US$11 million, or more than double the value of all other exports put together: the largest pearl produced in the Cook Islands in 1989 sold for US$9,000.

The spat or young larvae of pearl oysters are collected from the wild and then reared on rafts in atoll lagoons. At present, depleted natural stocks of mature pearl oysters into which grafts can be inserted is limiting the expansion of pearl farming. However, pearl oysters can now be made to spawn in tanks (the practice is already well established in Japan for the gold-lipped pearl oyster) and it is hoped that eventually it may be possible to produce enough larvae in this way to make the

*Grey angelfish* (Pomacanthus arcuatus) *– a popular aquarium fish that is now subject to quota restrictions when collected for the trade in Florida.*

whole process independent of wild stocks.

As with food species, cultured mother-of-pearl species can be transplanted on to new reefs or used to replenish reefs where populations have been depleted. This has been particularly successful with *Trochus,* which was first transplanted from Belau to Chuuk in the late 1920s; from there it has been introduced to a number of other islands and atolls in Micronesia. A similar series of introductions has taken place from New Caledonia to French Polynesia, and in many of these countries *Trochus* has now become an important resource. In 1939, nearly 7,000 *Trochus* were taken from Chuuk and released at four sites in Pohnpei. Since then, the species has spread all round the barrier reef, and there is now a sustainable yield of one tonne a year (with seven sanctuary sites), earning the country about $500,000 a year from exports. Despite the apparent success of ventures such as this, a wary eye needs to be kept on the potential dangers of disease and parasites that can be introduced through this method, or unwanted competition with native species, which could seriously disturb the balance of the reef's ecology. Wherever introductions are made, quarantine procedures need to be in place.

## Regulating Trade

One of the main methods currently used to control international trade in wildlife is the Convention on International Trade in Endangered Species of Wild Fauna and Flora (CITES), which now involves well over 100 countries and is enforced through national legislation. Its listings divide into two main categories: Appendix I deals with the most threatened species and prohibits all trade in them, and Appendix II caters for those species in which some trade is permissible, but where commercial transactions have to be carefully monitored by a process of stringent checking of records for each consignment. To date, comparatively few marine species are covered by CITES. Of reef species, all marine turtles are listed in Appendix I, which means that no trade involving them or products made from them should take place in any of the countries that are party to the convention. Appendix II lists all reef corals, black corals and giant clams, meaning that permits are required for any trade in these carried out by countries that are party to the convention.

Over a hundred countries in the world have reefs, and although only twenty or so of these have domestic legislation in place so far to restrict or ban collection for export of reef corals and shells, many more are likely to follow. There is a growing awareness among exporting countries of the need to protect their resources from the seemingly insatiable demands of foreign importers. In some places laws have been enacted that are even stricter than the CITES regulations, banning, for example, any exports of reef corals even though these are currently listed on Appendix II.

Enforcement of CITES regulations can prove difficult. Coral smuggling from the Philippines, where exports were banned in 1977, has been a long-standing problem. Members of the UK-based Marine Conservation Society, carrying out a survey of the curio trade in the UK in the late 1980s, discovered that a major chain of department stores was selling corals from the Philippines, despite the fact that CITES permits should not be issued for corals from this country. Further enquiries revealed that the coral had probably been exported under false permits. The store responded immediately by withdrawing from sale all 700 marine curio items that it had in stock. Fears that the illegal trade in coral continues were confirmed in 1991 when a random search of a Russian freighter at a UK port by Customs officials resulted in the seizure of two tons of coral originating from the Philippines; a follow-up raid on a warehouse in Lincolnshire revealed a further fifteen tonnes of Philippine coral. In the UK, guidelines for importers and retailers of marine curios have been produced by the Marine Conservation Society: consumers elsewhere should press for similar action.

Attempts are being made to manage aquarium fish collecting through trade channels. Some American importers refuse to handle fish that have not been collected in a responsible way without damage to the habitat or use of poisons, or to deal in species that are unlikely to survive in captivity. In the UK, the Marine Conservation Society is developing a scheme of 'green labelling' whereby fish would be identified according to such criteria. Consumers need to put pressure on retailers to adhere to guidelines such as these. Better monitoring of catches is required, as well as better transport and handling operations to reduce mortality rates. Trade should be stopped in those species which are difficult to maintain in captivity, such as some butterflyfish, and particularly corals (for which perfectly acceptable artificial substitutes are available).

*Mushroom corals* (Fungia *spp.) are frequently taken as marine curios and are now among the corals listed on CITES. They are unusual in that they do not grow attached to the reef like most other hard corals, which makes them easy to collect from the calm waters of the lagoon or in pools on the reef where they are usually found. They grow singly rather than in colonies; each mushroom, so-called because it resembles the gills on the underside of a mushroom, is one enormous polyp.*

# CHAPTER SIX

# REEFS & TOURISM

*Passengers who have been ferried to shore for a snorkelling trip from their cruise boat, M.S. Seaward, on Grand Cayman in the Cayman Islands.*

In the stillness of the early tropical morning, the 42,000 ton MS Seaward noses her way gently into Georgetown harbour on her weekly visit to Grand Cayman Island. As her huge anchor splashes noisily into the sea, many of the 1,500 passengers on board are planning their day's activities.

Some passengers, usually at least a hundred or more, decide to go snorkelling and see for themselves the coral reefs for which the Cayman Islands are famous. A fleet of small boats ferries them to shore and, after a short walk around the harbour, they don snorkelling gear and plunge in where the water is shallow enough for them to be able to see the coral. 'Instructors will guide you on underwater tours through opulent coral reefs and shoals of rainbow coloured fish', promises the cruise-line brochure.

Meanwhile, a few hundred yards away, the Seaward's anchor lies in twenty metres of water. The heavy chain has draped itself across a patch of reef. Although it is a calm day and there is no current, the chain tightens and shifts from side to side as the vessels swings at anchor. As the chain moves, it crushes the coral beneath it, carving out a channel up to two metres wide. Further away from the anchor itself the chain makes bigger swings, toppling giant boulder corals eight metres in circumference and sending them crashing down the reef. Clouds of crushed coral fragments settle over a wide area, up to an inch deep. Several corals have been gouged out of the reef and lie upside down with gaping holes beside them; other corals have been scalped, the living tissues scraped clean off their top surfaces to expose the chalky-white skeleton beneath. Just under the ship, where movement is greatest, the chain has sliced off a section of reef wall as easily as a knife going through butter.

As dusk falls, the Seaward weighs anchor and prepares to move on to her next port of call. While the chain is winched in, clouds of sediment are stirred up on the reef below, drifting through the water and settling on untouched reefs beyond

*The remains of a brain coral, unceremoniously chopped in pieces by an anchor, in Saba Marine Park, the Netherlands Antilles.*

Coconut palms on the lagoon beach, Abaiang, Kiribati, in the Pacific – a scene which must be close to many people's vision of a perfect tropical beach. At present, few tourists visit Kiribati, but scenes like this may soon disappear as the pressure to develop resorts increases.

Opposite: the reefs around Florida draw many thousands of visitors to the Caribbean each year, and at least half of them venture underwater snorkelling or diving to enjoy the sight of beautiful reef creatures like this gorgonian (Pseudopterogorgia).

the area already devastated. On board, passengers are comparing notes on their day's snorkelling. Tomorrow will bring another island, another reef – and another anchorage for the MS Seaward.

Around thirty cruise ships visit Grand Cayman on a regular basis and their anchors and chains have reduced most of the reefs in Georgetown harbour to nothing but rubble. In 1985, on Spott's Reef on the south side of Grand Cayman, where cruise ships sometimes anchor in bad weather, one ship in a single day destroyed an area of untouched reef the size of five tennis courts. Eighteen months later there was still no sign of new coral growth.

## The Growth in Tourism

Tourism has probably already overtaken oil as the largest single industry in the world and, if not, is set to do so. It plays a crucial role in the economies of many host nations in both developed and developing countries. For developing countries, in particular small island nations and those with striking natural attractions such as reefs, tourism represents one of the few ways in which people living there can hope to achieve an improvement in their standard of living.

In many cases, it is already the most important source of foreign exchange. Around 100 million tourists visit the Caribbean annually, most of them from the United States, contributing between forty and seventy per cent of the gross national product of some countries in the region. In the Turks and Caicos, for example, tourism (including associated construction) contributes sixty per cent to the gross national product compared with ten per cent from fishing and thirty per cent from offshore finance. In the Indian and Pacific Oceans, tourism is an important contributor to the economies of island countries such as the Seychelles, the Maldives, Mauritius, French Polynesia and Fiji, and on the islands of Guam and the Northern Marianas, tourism has accounted for ninety per cent of economic growth in recent years, with the number of visitors topping 66,000 in a single month in 1990.

The swaying palms, sandy beaches, small islands and coral reefs of tropical coastlines are a great attraction for modern travellers. Marine tourism in Australia is currently worth around US$800 million a year. Tourism to the Great Barrier Reef has been growing by thirty per cent a year since the introduction in 1983 of high-speed catamarans capable of carrying hundreds of passengers on day trips out to the reef. There are now a dozen or more 'Big Cats' ferrying people out to fixed pontoons on the reef from where they can dive, snorkel, or transfer to semi-submersibles which allow non-swimmers to sightsee underwater. Reef tourism is estimated to be worth US$1.6 billion to Florida's economy, with over two million people a year visiting John Pennekamp Coral Reef State Park and Key Largo National Marine Sanctuary alone.

Divers from the United States spend an estimated US$286 million a year in the Caribbean and Hawaii, and around 600,000 take an overseas dive trip annually. In Hawaii the income from scuba diving is currently valued at around US$20 million a year. In the Cayman Islands foreign visitors grew from a mere 3,000 per annum in the 1960s to over 500,000 by the late 1980s, and half of them went snorkelling or diving on the islands' reefs. In the Indian Ocean, the rich diversity of marine life and the sparkling coral beaches in the atolls of the Maldives annually draw over 160,000 visitors, and the number of resorts has grown from just two in 1972 to over sixty in 1992.

In many developing countries the economic advantages of tourism are not as great as they may appear at first glance. The structure of the tourist industry is such that foreign tour operators often own the hotels, the charter airlines and the travel agencies, and so profits are mostly exported from the host country rather than going to local people. In some cases, less than a quarter of the price paid for a holiday filters down to the country to which the visitors go. On top of this, foreign exchange often has to be used to import the luxury goods, food and drink expected by tourists and so the poorer countries tend to get even less income from tourism. Whilst profits go overseas, the problems of low wages, inadequate housing, poor diets, alcoholism,

crime and environmental degradation remain behind. In Bonaire, gross revenue from activities associated with dive-based tourism is estimated to be US$21 million, or about half the gross domestic product of the island. Unfortunately a large proportion of earnings leave the country – half of the hotels and dive operations are foreign-owned and almost a quarter of the work force is foreign workers. Nevertheless, it has been calculated that without diving tourism, Bonaire would lose the mainstay of its economy.

People who go on holiday often remain isolated in tourist areas, cut off from local problems to which, all too often, they are unwitting contributors. It is true that tourism creates jobs, but local people are mostly offered menial, low-paid employment. Tourist development pushes up land prices and the cost of living, forcing local people out of their homes. On Samui Island in Thailand, where much of the tourism started off based in local communities, visitor numbers increased rapidly to nearly half a million a year as increasingly large resorts were set up by outsiders: suddenly the land had begun to command high prices, and islanders felt unable to resist selling it. Sometimes villagers are compulsorily moved to make way for resorts, or their villages are overwhelmed by pollution, noise, roads and concrete monstrosities.

In Hawaii, hotels have been built on ancient burial sites on the coast, and more than twenty golf courses are under construction or being planned, robbing native Hawaiians of free access to the shoreline where traditionally they came to cast their nets and commune with their Omakuhas, or nature spirit guides. The mega-resorts which now despoil island coastlines are disparagingly referred to as 'the new plantations' by local Hawaiians. For them tourism has brought not freedom but economic dependence and the loss of the sacred coastal grounds that are so fundamental to their cultural traditions.

The indigenous culture of a country is often debased and exploited for the tourists' benefit, reduced to the status of an after-dinner floor show, with performances or dances demanded on days or in seasons which are not traditionally appropriate. Western values corrupt and destroy community morals, leading to prostitution, delinquency and child beggars. Expensive infrastructure such as airports, hotels and roads drains resources from investment in badly needed services such as health and education.

## Tourism-related Pollution and Habitat Destruction

The impact of tourism on the environment is all too often equally devastating. The tourist industry invariably markets tropical holidays with images of paradise and unspoiled nature, but uncontrolled and badly planned tourist developments may make the reality quite different. In the last two decades the increase in tourism to developing countries in the tropics has led to an explosive growth in the development of beach hotels, resorts, golf courses, marinas and associated infrastructure such as roads, shopping complexes and airports along the coast. This is causing the progressive destruction of coastal habitats, threatening some of the most productive ecosystems on the planet.

With tourism comes the inexorable building of airports. Sometimes these are built on reef flats if there is nowhere else to put them, which is what happened with the international airport at Hulule, adjacent to the capital of Male in the Maldives. Leaving aside the sacrifice of the sites on which runways are built, their construction also produces large quantities of silt that is likely to kill corals nearby.

Badly built coastal roads are easily eroded by rain, adding to siltation and reef damage. Coral rock has traditionally been used for housing on inhabited islands but it is now increasingly being taken in huge amounts for building tourist hotels, which means that much more coral mining is being carried out. Mangrove swamps are dredged to make way for ports and marinas, destroying breeding habitats which are often an important part of the reef ecosystem and damaging reefs from silt stirred up by dredging. Seagrass beds are dredged for sand to use in construction, again causing siltation as well as loss of another habitat linked with reefs. Jetties and docks are built over corals often affecting currents and the circulation of water around reefs, which can disturb both the character of the coast itself and the patterns of life on the reef. Hotels often lack proper sewage treatment facilities, creating serious pollution on nearby reefs, a problem that is exacerbated by the dive boats, yachts and cruise ships which have no holding tanks and in many cases dump sewage directly on the reef.

Golf courses are being built in ever increasing numbers in Asia, the Pacific and the Caribbean to cater for both residents and tourists, requiring vast amounts of irrigation, fertilisers and pesticides. In addition to causing environmental damage on land

*Where building for the tourist industry takes place on any scale, mangroves are frequently the first victim – ripped out and dredged to be replaced by coastal developments. Although the relatively murky waters in which mangroves thrive are rarely visited by divers, the poor visibility makes them a perfect nursery for many marine animals, which as juveniles would be only too vulnerable to the attentions of predators in the crystal clear waters on the reef.*

*Opposite: a packed beach at Waikiki, Oahu, Hawaii. Famous as a beach resort since the beginning of the century (the first beach hotel was built here in 1901), development of Waikiki has altered the shoreline, causing erosion and changes in the currents; wave patterns have changed radically since Hawaiian royalty first surfed here over a century ago, and most of the beaches now have to be replenished with sand brought in from elsewhere.*

*A boat anchor in the process of wreaking havoc in a thicket of Acropora coral off the east coast of Malaysia.*

through habitat destruction, subsequent erosion and wastage of water, they can present a hazard for reefs if their drainage with all the silt and chemicals it will carry leads out on to reefs, which is often the case on small islands.

Tourism has fuelled the demand for marine curios, which are sold in souvenir shops and on beach stalls, and has stimulated interest in corals and shells in countries far from reefs where they are now sold as stylish decorative objects in their own right. Corals, shells, dried pufferfish and other reef artefacts are often used to decorate hotel rooms, foyers and restaurants (one of the most infamous examples is the Cowrie Grill in the Manila Hotel in the Philippines, whose walls are covered with several thousand cowries and other shells).

Pressure on reef fisheries has increased greatly with the huge appetite of the tourist industry for high-value items such as lobster, grouper and snapper. The considerable prices commanded by these and other popular species have turned them into luxury foods, now often beyond the pockets of local people.

The boom in coastal tourism has also been accompanied by a similar growth in marine-oriented activities such as scuba diving, snorkelling, sailing, cruising and sport fishing, all of which can potentially damage the reef environment.

In over half the countries of the world with reefs, some form of damage has been caused by tourism to the reef habitat. Unless efforts are made to prevent further damage taking place, the situation will become worse as tourism continues to grow, leaving a trail of destruction in its wake.

## Anchor Damage

Cruise ships inflict the most severe anchor damage, with their heavy anchor chains crushing corals and stirring up clouds of sediment which settle on the reef and suffocate the polyps, but every day of the year thousands of smaller vessels of all kinds, from yachts to glass-bottom boats, send their anchors crashing down on reefs.

In the US Virgin Islands 30,000 boats a year anchor in the National Park, and about half of these were causing some damage to the reefs or seagrass beds until the recent installation of mooring buoys. Some of the most heavily used reefs in the world are in Florida, where nearly two million people a year descend on the John Pennekamp Coral Reef State Park and Key Largo National Marine Sanctuary. The five most accessible reefs can attract up to 6,000 people on busy summer weekends, and extensive areas of coral have been destroyed at popular anchorages, such as the Dry Tortugas.

Dive boats often anchor directly on reefs for the convenience of their clients. This problem is compounded by the fact that they tend to pay repeated visits to the same reefs. Large live-aboard dive boats are becoming more popular, meeting the demand from experienced divers for long journeys to unexplored reefs. To live up to promises of 'pristine reefs', they have to venture further and further into remote seas, but all too often the coral reefs are no longer pristine once the dive boats have visited. Tubbataha Reefs in the Philippines are a sad example of this. Lying in the middle of the Sulu Sea about 150 kilometres from Palawan, the easternmost of the Philippine Islands, these romantic reefs now attract tourism worth about US$1 million a year, having been declared a marine park in 1988. The dive boats that visit the area are booked up months in advance by divers from Japan, the USA and Europe, and, despite the isolation and the fact that diving is possible only from March to June because of the monsoons, it has become the Philippines top dive spot. In the five years since the park was established, the reefs have noticeably deteriorated and an estimated quarter of the corals have been damaged, partly due to illegal dynamiting by migrant fishermen, but largely because of the regular visits of the dive boats.

## Diver damage

Over the past ten years or so, there has been an enormous increase in the number of people taking up scuba diving, partly due to new equipment and teaching techniques which make learning much easier. Television films and documentaries about the underwater world have also encouraged this trend, and there are now hundreds of thousands of scuba divers in developed nations such as the United States, Britain, Germany and Japan, many of whom spend their holidays visiting tropical reefs.

Compared to the effects of say, pollution, the ill-advised behaviour of an individual diver on the reef may have only a minimal impact, but the cumulative effect of destruction caused by divers and snorkellers in large numbers can be considerable. Dive guides all over the world can point to once-pristine, flourishing dive sites where broken and silted corals mock the former richness of the reef.

*This photograph was taken at Tubbataha Reef in the Philippines in 1984 and shows the reef crest and slope with almost one hundred per cent hard coral cover and a high diversity of species – a richness which is now being lost in many locations across the tropics.*

## Fish feeding

Much of the fascination of reef diving lies in fish-watching. Inevitably, divers and dive guides began to feed and tame fish and other reef creatures in order to guarantee (particularly for photographers) a 'close encounter of a reef kind'.

Fish feeding is now common on many reefs visited by tourists. On the Great Barrier Reef, divers can hand feed giant potato cod weighing up to 110kg each. At Ras Mohammed in the Red Sea, divers used to carry down a boiled egg or two for the massive Napoleon wrasse which live there until this was banned. Feeding tame moray eels is now so common that it is no longer considered special – in Bonaire, one divemaster has had to resort to feeding five morays at once to attract any interest. Elsewhere, dive guides feed jewfish, Nassau groupers and barracuda.

In the Maldives and the Bahamas, shark-feeding for divers has been taking place for many years. On Bora Bora in French Polynesia, wild sharks are fed in just a few metres of water in the shallow lagoon so that snorkellers can watch. The Cayman Islands has Stingray City, where over 20 tame southern sting rays come to be handfed; this has become a major attraction, with as many as 150 divers and snorkellers visiting the site every day to interact with the playful rays. In addition to spectacular displays such as these, there are numerous locations all over the world where smaller fish have become accustomed to being handfed by divers and snorkellers.

Although fish-feeding may initially lead to an increase in the numbers of fish, in the long term it distorts populations of some fish at the expense of others. It may also create a dependence on hand-outs, and fish become vulnerable to being caught by fishermen once tamed. Much of what is fed to them has little or no nutritional value, and a diet of bread, frozen peas, potato chips, biscuits, cake, eggs, canned cheese, and the remains of picnic lunches – all of which are fed to fish somewhere or other – may do more harm than good. In Hanauma Bay, visitors are now forbidden by law to feed the fish with anything except specially-formulated pellets or fish sticks (standard aquarium fish food) which have the right balance of nutrients and fibre for the health of the fish.

One consequence of fish-feeding is occasional attacks on divers by creatures expecting to be fed. In the Red Sea, Napoleon wrasse have been known to follow divers for long periods, sometimes making an unprovoked

attack in the search for food. Moray eels have also 'attacked' divers and had to be killed because they were becoming a menace. One diver recalls being followed and circled by sharks in the Maldives, with the sharks eventually forcing the divers to retreat into the shelter of the lagoon: only later were they told that their chosen dive site was a regular shark-feeding location.

The only way to be sure that fish-feeding causes no harm is not to do it – until it can be proved to have no ill effects, the practice should be discontinued. In any case, many divers would rather see reef life in its natural state than be mobbed by the more aggressive fish that have adapted to an artificial diet.

*Above: diver photographing grey reef sharks (Carcharhinus sp.) attracted with bait in the Coral Sea, Australia, and (right) another diver feeding sergeant majors (Abudefduf saxatilis) and butterflyfish in Bali. Fish-feeding has now been banned in many tourist areas due to concerns for fish health and diver safety.*

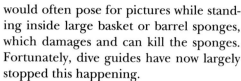

The Red Sea is one of the world's top diving locations and the rapid development of the Sinai coastline in Egypt in the late 1980s saw a massive increase in the number of divers visiting the region. Research at three of the four most popular sites in the Ras Muhammed area (where over 75,000 dives are made annually) has shown that there are more broken corals, loose coral fragments and partially dead corals than at neighbouring sites where diving happens less frequently; some divers have even reported seeing damage along a 'diver's highway' at depths of between ten and twenty metres.

In the US Virgin Islands, visitors to the Trunk Bay Beach underwater trail in the National Park increased from 20,000 a year in 1966 to over 170,000 a year in 1988. In spite of supervision by park wardens, the reef has deteriorated noticeably through coral breakage and the illegal collection of souvenirs.

Divers can easily damage coral by standing on it, bumping into it, kicking it accidentally with their fins, allowing their depth and pressure gauges to drag along the reef beneath them, or by holding on to it to steady themselves in a current or to look at marine life. A study in Florida found that on average divers touch coral seven times in every half hour underwater, most frequently with their fins (the researchers also discovered that male divers caused more damage than female divers because they tend to be more energetic

and adventurous and to touch the reef more). Even light pressure on the living tissue of a coral colony can damage the mucus that protects it from infection and dirt. Underwater photographers, especially, are notorious for crashing into fragile corals whilst manoeuvring for a good shot. Until recently divers in the Caribbean

would often pose for pictures while standing inside large basket or barrel sponges, which damages and can kill the sponges. Fortunately, dive guides have now largely stopped this happening.

Snorkellers and divers stir up sediment and disturb reef creatures; snorkellers in particular create considerable turbidity when they tread water. Divers swimming through caves affect marine life because their exhaled air forms large bubbles which remain in the caves and kill delicate animals or plants on the roof that are then stranded out of the water. Even people trying to be careful can unwittingly inflict damage, particularly when in large groups, with divers bumping into one another and crowding in together on a particular part of the reef to look at something special.

Shore diving often involves divers trekking across the reef flat, laden with tanks and equipment, and snorkellers may have to walk across the reef flat or lagoon to reach the reef. Some resorts also offer guided reef walks at low tide for those unable or unwilling to take to the water. There is as yet no conclusive evidence

*Careless behaviour by visitors to reefs or sheer pressure of numbers can cause considerable damage. The result of thousands of people taking day trips to the small marine reserve at El Garafon, Mexico (top) is that the reef there is largely dead – irreparably harmed by physical contact with people; above, a brain coral (Colcophyllia natans) in the Turks and Caicos Islands bears clear signs of damage, probably from being sat or stood on.*

*Opposite, top: reef walkers with guide, Heron Island, Queensland, Australia; by tracing the same path on each occasion, detrimental effects can be minimised. Opposite, bottom: a magnificent barrel sponge of the sort that used to suffer the indignity of divers clambering inside to pose for photographs. Luckily, most divers are now aware that this sort of careless behaviour is nothing short of vandalism.*

*Left: bryozoans, sponges and algae encrusting the underside of a coral ledge on the Great Barrier Reef – these animals, which must be totally emerged in water to survive, could die if trapped by bubbles of air from scuba equipment.*

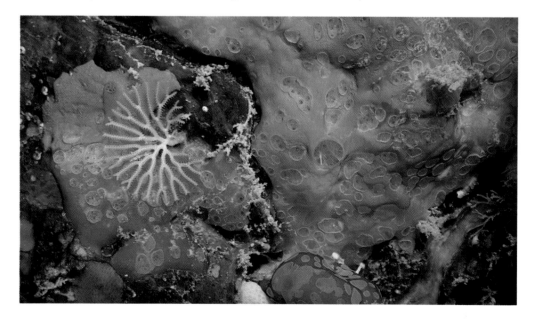

that reef-walking causes damage. At one site on the Great Barrier Reef, live coral cover declined from forty-one per cent to seven per cent after eighteen crossings by reef walkers, but another study where guided reef walks have been taking place for forty years has shown almost no change on the reef flat.

## Preventing Tourist Damage

'Ecotourism' is now being widely promoted as the solution to many of the ills spawned by the tourist industry. If properly managed, environmentally sound tourism can ensure that natural resources are protected and provide economic benefits for the local community, by giving them a sustainable livelihood. But too often, the term 'ecotourism' is applied to rather more indefensible styles of holiday and is guilty of 'greenwashing' – covering up undesirable activities with a gloss of superficial environmental platitudes. Nature-based or wildlife tourism is frequently referred to as ecotourism, on the assumption that just looking at nature is in itself environmentally friendly. This can be far from the truth – and some forms of ecotourism may even do more harm than good both to the environment and to the indigenous culture. Expeditions to wilderness areas, for instance, can disrupt wildlife, leave litter, erode footpaths and so on. Indeed, much tourism in the Caribbean this century has been 'nature' tourism in that it has been

centred on beaches and reefs, but this has been far from uniformly beneficial.

A great deal of the damage currently being caused to reefs and other coastal ecosystems by tourism can be attributed to large-scale developments. Arguably, large tourist resorts limit the spread of environmental disturbance by concentrating many people in a relatively small area. But the reality at the moment is that because of the absence of careful planning of coastal zones and of proper environmental controls on developments, huge problems are often caused to coral reefs and other natural habitats that are vulnerable to the inevitable side effects of large-scale construction. Sustainable tourism is more likely to be achieved by building small-scale resorts, designed to fit in both with the landscape and with local styles of building, and catering to guests who are prepared to pay for a relatively unspoiled natural environment.

Given the right framework, it should be possible for tourism to grow and yet create a net benefit both for the reef environment and for coastal peoples. The tourism industry at all levels must take steps to prevent the progressive destruction of coastal ecosystems for which it is responsible. This is, after all, in the interests of those whose business depends on there being a beautiful natural attraction for people to visit. Some shoreline hotels, for example on Bora Bora in French Polynesia, have taken the initiative in establishing marine reserves on adjacent reefs in advance of legislation. Tourist hotels must also be willing to install or finance mooring buoy

schemes and to prevent coastal pollution from sewage discharges by using biological waste treatment systems. Initiatives to provide interpretative materials are also important. A Visitors' Code produced by the Marine Conservation Society, for example, is being distributed by an international hotel chain in its resorts in the Seychelles and Djibouti, and by dive tour operators in the UK. Preventing tourism damage to reefs will require a combination of approaches, the focus depending on the particular situation.

## Community Control

If sustainable forms of tourism are to be put into practice successfully, much greater attention needs to be paid to involving the local community in tourist developments and their management. As with fisheries, local people have to be able to see clearly that they can benefit from taking steps themselves to protect their natural resources.

In the Philippines, the Philippine Tourism Association (PTA) has been developing the concept of 'backyard' tourism. On Balicasag Island, for example, it has set up a small beach hotel catering for divers. Villagers are employed in the resort and are involved in running it; the profits are directed to marine conservation, in particular to the maintenance of a marine park. Divers are charged extra to dive in the sanctuary area of the park, where fishing is prohibited. The additional employment created by the resort and the creation of the sanctuary area have reduced fishing pressure on

the reefs and led to a noticeable increase in fish abundance and diversity. The tourists who come there tend to show a lively interest in the reefs and park, and buy food and souvenirs in the village, and the contact local people have with their visitors has helped to reinforce their commitment to protecting the reefs.

Similar tourist arrangements exist on several islands elsewhere. On Pohnpei, in the Federated States of Micronesia, the village of Enipein Pah established the Enipein Pah Marine Park Corporation in 1988 to promote tourism. Using a grant from the US Job Training Partnership, the villagers built canoes to take tourists out on day trips to the mangroves and reefs and constructed a visitor centre; work is underway to promote the enterprise and attract more visitors.

On the island of Koh Samui in Thailand, community involvement in tourism management is being increased through activities such as a Coral Festival to raise awareness on reef issues, and on the other side of the Kra isthmus, a management plan is being implemented in the Koh Phi Phi National Park to increase community involvement in marine conservation. The park contains several islands, the best known of which are the twin islands of Phi Phi Don and Phi Phi Ley. Phi Phi Ley is uninhabited,

*Yacht moored at Koh Phi Phi, Thailand, where tourism has grown rapidly in recent years as people have sought to escape over-development on nearby Phuket Island.*

but Phi Phi Don has been settled for several generations by sea gypsies and a few Muslim families who have traditionally relied on subsistence fishing.

Starting from a modest trickle of visitors in the early 1980s, tourism to the two islands has now become a floodtide, threatening to swamp the local community. Most of the locals have abandoned fishing activities during the tourist season and instead have modified their small fishing boats to carry tourists around the islands. The tourist boom has led to a seven-fold increase in land prices, causing local people to sell their property to outside holiday operators: this in turn has led to cultural conflicts with the villagers who still live there. Sadly, the new owners appear to be less concerned about environmental degradation than the residents, and development has now started to encroach on forest reserves.

A series of consultations with community leaders and tourism operators confirmed that local people were already aware that the coral reefs, beaches and nearshore waters needed to be protected from environmental degradation to preserve a viable tourist industry. Strengthening understanding of environmental problems and allowing the people living there to act is an integral part of the park management plan, and a liaison committee has been set up to increase community participation. The preferential employment of local people in businesses associated with tourism is being encouraged; zoning has been introduced to minimise conflicts, and mooring buoys installed at twenty key reef sites. Entrance fees for tourists have been introduced to support the cost of the park plan.

In several cases in Fiji, tourist developers have leased islands from local communities to develop them as resorts. The development is carried out in close collaboration with the communities who approve the plans and set the conditions of the lease. At Namenalala, in the Koro Sea, where a resort comprises only five per cent of the land, the developer was required to establish a reserve to protect the main part of the island and adjacent reefs. The local communities had been concerned about illegal removal of turtle eggs, giant clams and fish and saw the resort development as the best way of protecting their island and traditional fishing grounds. They also suggested that they should fish only outside the reserve area and, in addition, that they would act as fishing wardens. A similar arrangement exists at Tai (renamed Beachcomber by the resort) and Luvuka (renamed Treasure) Islands in Nadi Bay, where the local people are employed in the resort and hire out boats to the tourists.

In many countries, village-based tourism is being developed. Visitors stay either in people's homes or in low-impact, small-scale resorts (preferably constructed from local materials in vernacular styles), which encourages interaction between guests and hosts and generally permits a greater share of the profits to be kept in the local community. Elsewhere, this kind of tourism may not be appropriate for cultural reasons: while local people may be employed in tourism they may wish to maintain more of a distance between themselves and the influences of tourism.

In the Maldives, for instance, tourist resorts have been built on separate islands from the villages, not only because of lack

*Nature-based tourism – mangrove tour in Enipein Marine Park, Pohnpei, Micronesia.*

of space but also because of the possible effects of Western values on the Maldivians' Islamic lifestyle. The islands in the atolls have all been zoned for different exclusive activities: some are given over entirely to tourism, while others with existing villages are for local use only; some islands are being developed for industrial and commercial use, and a few pristine and untouched islands are to be kept as such. As well as minimising social disruption, this system is potentially beneficial for reefs as different pressures are distributed across them rather than being concentrated in any one place.

## Marine Parks

One way of controlling and managing tourism in coastal areas is through marine parks and reserves. Some protected areas are strict nature reserves with limited access, but many others encourage carefully managed tourism and play a role in promoting education and public awareness about reefs with visitor or interpretation centres and underwater trails.

It is perhaps surprising to discover that, in some areas of the Great Barrier Reef Marine Park, spear-fishing and even commercial fishing are permitted. This is a result of a decision to create a system of

zoning designed to cater for a multiplicity of uses, so avoiding or reducing the conflicts that might otherwise arise between people wishing to use the reefs for different purposes, and ensuring an overall, controlled and sustainable pattern of exploitation. Around 35 of the 2,900 ribbon reefs are used by tourists; though this is a relatively small number, the fact that these are the most accessible reefs, and therefore suffer the heaviest use from other activities such as fishing, mariculture and yachting, makes it necessary to take steps to protect them. Zoning was originally introduced to deal with problems of over-fishing, but with the huge growth in visitors to the reef over the last decade tourism has recently been brought into the plan. Some areas have been designated as completely off-limits for tourism; on others, by contrast, structures like jetties and pontoons may be constructed; and on more vulnerable reefs only mooring buoys can be installed.

Much smaller marine parks can also be effectively zoned for tourism. In 1987, a marine park was set up in the Netherlands Antilles, around Saba, which is a small extinct volcano that rises directly from the seabed. The park encircles the entire island and its fringing reef, extending from the high water mark down to a depth of about 60 metres. Areas within the park have been designated as a general recreational zone, an area for both diving and fishing and an all-purpose zone. It is hoped that the park will eventually become financially self-sufficient; within two years of being established, it was already generating enough income to cover half its costs (the remainder being met by a local government subsidy). Visitor fees are the main source of income, with divers and snorkellers (of which there were nearly 3,500 in 1990) contributing a dollar each and tour operators paying a monthly fee; there are also plans to charge yachts to anchor there. Souvenir sales are another significant source of income, and overseas visitors are encouraged to join the 'Friends of Saba Marine Park' through which they can make tax-deductible donations back home. All proceeds go towards park maintenance.

Clearly marine parks are capable of generating considerable revenue from tourism (through entry fees, sponsorship, donations, and concessions from dive operators or shops) and of becoming profitable. In Bonaire, also in the Netherlands Antilles, 18,000 divers a year visit the marine park. A survey conducted in 1990/91 found that over ninety per cent of the divers visiting the park would be willing to pay a fee that would be used for park management, and sixteen per cent would be prepared to pay a fee as high as US$50. As of January 1992, a fee of US$10 per visitor has been introduced and will comfortably cover the annual running costs of US$150,000 for the park. In the British Virgin Islands, scuba diving at just one site, the Wreck of the Rhone Marine Park, generates US$1 million per annum. In the US Virgin Islands, the National Park and Biosphere Reserve generates over US$23 million a year with annual costs of only about US$2 million.

In Belize, the Hol Chan Marine Reserve was set up in 1987 near the popular tourist island of Ambergris Caye. Before the establishment of the reserve the reef was suffering from over-fishing, anchor-damage from boats and the attentions of souvenir hunters. Visitors are now charged a fee, and the proceeds are ploughed

back into the reserve to pay for, among other things, installation of mooring buoys, regular patrols by wardens and the establishment of a visitor centre. Reserve staff also run educational programmes for tourist guides, fishermen and local schools.

The snag about marine parks is that they often have a honeypot effect. The promise of unspoiled reefs can draw more visitors than a park can cope with and the marine environment then becomes damaged through over-use. Controlling how many people come to a park can be very difficult. Access to off-shore reefs can be restricted by controlling the number of divers or boats who are allowed to visit them, but this assumes that there are adequate enforcing measures such as wardens and patrol boats. With fringing reefs close to shore the situation can be even more difficult, as visitors may arrive on foot or by car.

Molokini Crater in Hawaii is a dramatic, half-sunken volcano with extensive shallow reefs mid-channel between the Hawaiian islands of Maui and Kahoolawe. Its designation as a Marine Life Conservation District contributed a considerable amount to its promotion as a dive site, and soon it became the most heavily used site in Hawaii. From just a handful of dive boats frequenting Molokini in the early 1980s, numbers have now risen to between thirty and thirty-five a day, disgorging hundreds of snorkellers and divers into the water. One boat operator claims that you can now actually see a 'bath-tub ring' of suntan oil around the crater wall because of the sheer numbers of people swimming there. Tame fish compete for hand-outs, damaged coral is common, rare shells have disappeared, and manta rays have deserted the cleaning station (where they habitually came to allow cleaner fish to remove parasites from them).

On Oahu in Hawaii, Hanauma Bay also suffered from the honeypot effect. It was designated a Marine Life Conservation District in 1967, which drew attention to its beautiful reefs. By the late 1980s, visitors to this tiny bay a short distance from Waikiki Beach often topped 10,000 a day in peak season and the shallow areas are now largely devoid of living coral. In an attempt to give the reefs a chance to recover, regulations have been introduced to prevent coaches from off-loading their passengers in the car park, ban commercial snorkelling tours and close the park completely once a week so that staff can clean up and carry out maintenance. Restricting numbers, and similar measures, may have to become much more widespread in marine parks in order to avoid defeating the whole purpose of setting them up. Damage can be minimised by channelling visitors into the less sensitive areas. In the US Virgin Islands National Park, tourists are encouraged to visit beaches where the fringing reefs are mainly made up of the more robust corals, so that if they go snorkelling they are less likely to damage fragile species. Land-based aquariums and marine life centres can relieve the pressure to a certain extent, but they still tend to encourage people to visit the reef itself.

Much of the damage caused by tourists is accidental; if people understand how a reef functions and how vulnerable it is, they are more likely to try to avoid contributing to the damage. On the Great Barrier Reef, guided snorkelling tours are hugely in demand, and the Great Barrier Reef Marine Park Authority distributes a variety of information materials to resorts, tour operators and the media, including a quarterly video news programme. Underwater trails have been set up in several places including Green Island in Australia, Grand Cayman, Buck Island in the US Virgin Islands and Eilat in the Red Sea. These are difficult to keep in good condition and manage so as not to cause reef damage, but several parks run them successfully; visitors can snorkel or swim with scuba gear and identify marine flora and fauna from waterproof information boards set into the seabed.

## Preventing Diver Damage

In recent years, there has been a significant change in attitude among the majority of divers, which has led to a move away from exploitative activities such as spearfishing and souvenir hunting towards more benign pursuits such as underwater photography or simply observing and marvelling at the behaviour of creatures on the reef. Coupled with the general growth in environmental awareness, this has led to many more divers being conscious of reef conservation issues and of the damage they could unwittingly inflict on the marine world. Most divers nowadays are highly motivated to try and prevent reef damage, since it is ultimately the untouched beauty of the reef which provides one of the principal attractions of tropical diving.

The diving industry, including dive guides, professional instructors and boat operators, has an important role to play, not least in its own interest, in maintaining reefs in good condition. A survey by a leading US diving magazine found that the most important criterion for choosing a holiday destination was the quality of the diving, which far outweighed other factors including price: divers are willing to pay extra for healthy reefs and abundant fish life.

Local dive guides increasingly see that their future prosperity depends on thriving reefs and some of them have been in the forefront of practical measures to help prevent damage by individual divers. Dive guides and instructors are a crucial link in diver education, since they provide the first glimpse of the underwater world to students and act as their first role models. Their sense of responsibility to the underwater environment will be reflected in the attitudes of the divers they train, and their importance in teaching new divers to be caring and responsible underwater cannot be overestimated.

The world's largest diver training organisation is the Professional Association of Dive Instructors (PADI), whose 1,400 dive centres worldwide introduce more than 400,000 people a year to scuba diving. In

*Opposite: two scenes from Saba Marine Park in the Netherlands Antilles, in parts of the reef where recreational activities are permitted; top, a reef crest, often referred to as a 'drop-off' by divers – one of the most productive zones on the reef. Bottom: a glorious scene with pillar coral* (Dendrogyra cylindrus), *yellow goatfish* (Mulloidichthys martinicus), *and a community of sponges.*

*Right: Hanauma Bay, Oahu, Hawaii. The remains of a partially sunken volcanic crater, Hanauma Bay is Hawaii's most popular snorkelling and diving location. However, the sheer quantity of visitors is cause for considerable concern and the authorities have had to take steps to limit the damage caused by tourism to the reefs and creatures living in them by restricting visitor numbers.*

recognition of the influence that instructors have on diving behaviour, PADI has launched Project AWARE, a ten-year programme to stress what divers can do to help protect the underwater environment. Through educational materials, practical projects (such as joining up with local pressure groups campaigning on marine issues) and by offering courses on the marine environment and supporting environmental legislation, PADI aims to turn the sport diving community into an active force for conservation.

One way of helping to reduce diver damage is to provide 'green codes' so that divers themselves can learn how to modify their behaviour and reduce their impact; in the United States, PADI has published a booklet on 'Ten Ways a Diver Can Protect the Underwater Environment', which is being distributed through their members.

Similarly, in Britain the Marine Conservation Society has produced a Code for Visitors as part of their 'Let Coral Reefs Live' campaign, with copies being sent out (with the cooperation of tour operators) to every diver booking a tropical holiday. And in French Polynesia, Greenpeace has published a brochure on Dos and Don'ts for divers and 'boaties' in Maohi, French and English.

One of the most effective ways in which dive professionals can help minimise reef damage is by training snorkellers and divers how to control their buoyancy and fins so that they avoid hitting or touching the reef. Too many novices are let loose on reefs before their training is complete and before they have learnt sufficiently good buoyancy control. Instead, divers should be matched to dive sites according to their ability; the inexperienced should

*Divers are becoming increasingly aware of the need to protect reefs, in the knowledge that scenes like this cease to exist when reefs become unhealthy.*

*Opposite: a snorkeller holds on to a coral colony to pose for pictures. Unfortunately, the touch of her gloved hand will destroy the living coral polyps.*

be kept off fragile sites and, conversely, divers who can demonstrate good control underwater can be rewarded with dives on better reefs.

Because divers wearing gloves touch corals and reefs significantly more often than those with bare hands, many dive centres have adopted a 'no gloves' policy. In the Cayman Islands, gloves are not permitted on the better-quality dive sites around Little Cayman and Cayman Brac, and a similar policy has been adopted by some dive boats on the island of Cozumel in Mexico. Many conservationists argue that the reef should never be touched, but initial 'hands-on' experience (under supervision) can provide an invaluable introduction to reef life. In Australia, marine biologists operate interpretative snorkelling tours for clients on the Big Cats (high-speed catamarans) and encourage people to pick up and touch the reef creatures that are not harmed by handling, but where there is no such guidance, it is better not to touch anything at all.

The characteristics of a reef have an important bearing on the amount of diver pressure it can withstand. A reef that has delicate branching corals will be more susceptible to damage than one consisting mostly of massive corals. Shallow reefs are particularly likely to be affected by divers, snorkellers and boats.

Dive operators are beginning to realise that the intensive marketing of particular sites is a mistake, since everybody then wants to dive there and they soon become spoiled. In the Cayman Islands, famous locations such as Bloody Bay Wall on Little Cayman and Tarpon Alley on Grand Cayman have become so over-exposed that, as a matter of policy, some operators now refuse divers' requests to visit them. In the competitive atmosphere of the Cayman Islands dive industry, which is oriented heavily towards customer's desires, this is a brave decision, and one applauded by Greenpeace. If divers are spread out among different sites the impact on particular reefs can be reduced. In Grand Cayman, for instance, about eighty per cent of all diving takes place on reefs on the west side of the island, where there are around thirty dive operators are based near the hotels and resorts. These reefs are under intense pressure from around 150,000 dives per annum. If larger,

faster boats were available to take divers to the relatively un-dived reefs which surround the rest of the island, the pressure would be reduced, but such a move would need to be well-controlled or it would simply increase the total number of divers on all reefs, causing problems for even wider areas of reef.

Concentrating divers and snorkellers in one place can have some advantage if the right reefs are selected. On the Great Barrier Reef, the high-speed catamarans which carry hundreds of people out to the reefs every day, have to moor at permanent pontoons installed in areas where the reef is just deep enough to be safe from much accidental damage. On the outward journey, passengers are briefed on reef conservation. Even with hundreds of people entering the water, the potential impact is less than it would be from numerous individuals arriving in their own boats, and anchoring, littering, collecting or fishing over wide areas of reef. Where diving is often shore-based, as in the Maldives, there should be clearly marked access points to minimise damage from trampling on the reef flat. Reef walks should be carefully controlled by wardens or rangers.

## Tourists and Monitoring

Sport divers can be an enormous help in conserving reefs just by recording what they see and reporting damage to the relevant authorities. They can also participate more directly in reef conservation through organisations such as Earthwatch, a non-profit-making organisation that sends volunteers on paying holidays to work on scientific expeditions. Earthwatch has contributed to several projects involving reefs, including mapping reefs in Bonaire, assisting a giant-clam breeding programme in Tonga, and studying reefs in Fiji. In the UK, divers can participate in Coral Cay Conservation, a non-profit organisation which is helping the Government of Belize establish the coastal zone management plan for the Barrier Reef. Already 84 volunteers have participated in assessing the impact of tourism and fishing on South Water Cay, a small coral island in the southern half of the Barrier Reef which will probably be made a marine reserve. Further expeditions, also under the guidance of marine scientists, are planned to continue through until 1996.

In Trinidad and Tobago, local divers set up the Crusoe Reef Society in 1986 to campaign for management and protection of Buccoo Reef on the western tip of Tobago, at present the country's only marine reserve. In recent years, they have been joined by students from Glasgow University in Scotland who have helped them carry out various projects to devise better ways of managing the growing number of tourists.

Individual divers going on holiday anywhere in the world can take with them check sheets provided by the Reefwatch programme (run by the Tropical Marine Research Unit at the University of York in England) and collect information which is then collated and analysed at TMRU and used to supply data on reef health to a variety of organisations and projects. Volunteer divers can also contribute to some of the long-term monitoring projects that are being set up to follow the health of reefs, the most successful of which use straightforward techniques so that people with minimal training or qualifications can take part.

Instructors and dive guides are in an excellent position to help monitor reefs as

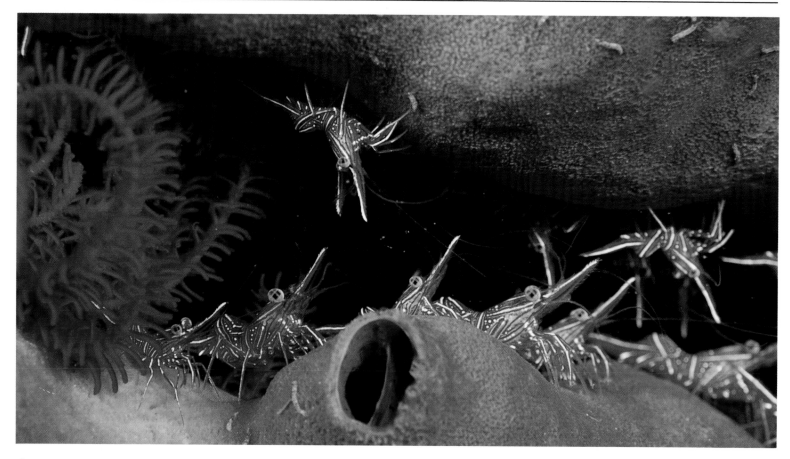

they spend a large proportion of their time around them. In Singapore, where there are many local diving clubs, the 'Reef Conservation Project Committee' was set up in 1988 by the Singapore Yacht Club, Singapore Institute of Biology and Singapore Underwater Federation. This will help to collect information on the health of the remaining coral reefs of Singapore, where many have now disappeared. By 1988, thirteen instructors had been trained to survey reefs and were in turn to train others.

In St Lucia dive instructors have been closely involved in planning and constructing the equipment for a monitoring programme on reefs near Soufriere on the south-west coast of the island. Sediment traps have been installed on the reefs which dive leaders can easily collect and replace at regular intervals whilst guiding clients. The sediment is sent to a laboratory for analysis so that gradually a picture will be built up of how much is settling on the reefs. A record of the number of dives made on particular sites is kept so that some indication of diver pressure can be obtained, and photographs are taken at

regular intervals so that any changes can be noted. Frames to hold the camera have been permanently set up at each site to make sure that exactly the same area is photographed each time and no specialist knowledge at all is needed to operate the camera which is set up ready to function and is simply attached to the frame.

In Hawaii, there is a possibility of this idea being taken a step further: reefs will be monitored by volunteer divers using underwater video cameras. These can be attached to a permanent framework at each monitoring site so that regardless of who is using them exactly the same area of reef is filmed each time. Such a project, with the film being analysed later by marine biologists, would make data collection highly cost-effective.

In the Maldives, dive operators in the resorts are being encouraged to take part in an 'Adopt-a-Coral' scheme, whereby they select one or two healthy coral colonies within snorkelling distance of the resort, give them a name (one current adoptee is called 'Greenpeace') and help to monitor them on behalf of the Marine

*Divers in the south-west Pacific have a good chance of catching sight of these captivating creatures, hinge-beak shrimps (Rhynchocinetes uritai), which are common throughout the region. But no-one knows how far the increasing problems that beset their habitat, coral reefs, will affect these and thousands of other animals.*

*Opposite: Greenpeace divers in American Samoa drilling before laying concrete foundations for mooring buoys. Dive boats frequently cause enormous damage to coral reefs by anchoring on them. One way to stop this is to install permanent mooring buoys.*

Research Section of the Ministry of Fisheries and Agriculture. Fourteen resorts have so far joined the scheme.

In Florida, pressure groups such as Greenpeace, Project Reefkeeper and Reef Relief joined forces with local diving organisations and other scientific and environmental groups to form the Coral Reef Coalition with the intention of increasing protection of the Florida Reef Tract. Members of the various groups have actively campaigned against development that threatens reefs, lobbied government, participated in public hearings and organised petitions. The establishment of the Florida National Marine Sanctuary in 1991 was largely due to their efforts.

## Mooring Buoys

In the early 1980s, the American reef biologist John Halas designed a simple mooring buoy for installing on reefs. It has since proved to be one of the most effective ways of preventing damage from boat anchors, particularly at heavily visited reefs, and is now in use (with various modifications) all over the world. One or two holes are drilled into the seabed and a steel eyebolt, to which the buoy is attached, is cemented into each. Most of the better-managed Caribbean marine parks and reserves, such as the US Virgin Islands Marine Park and Biosphere Reserve, Saba Marine Park and the Caymans, as well as popular dive sites in many other parts of the world, like Hawaii and the Great Barrier Reef, have installed them. Some Caribbean countries have initiated 'Adopt-a-Buoy' programmes in which visiting divers name buoys and dive sites in exchange for contributing to the cost of installing moorings. The installation of mooring buoys solves only one of the many problems affecting reefs, but it is a practical step that can easily be taken, provided the labour and materials are available.

Greenpeace has assisted with mooring-buoy installation in several locations. In 1990, the crew of the Rainbow Warrior, along with local activists from Reef Relief and staff of the National Marine Sanctuary Programme conducted a week-long project to install around thirty buoys at Key West reef in Florida. In the same year, the Rainbow Warrior crew helped the local environmental group, Le Vaomatua, in American Samoa and staff of the US National Marine Sanctuary Program to install buoys in Fagatele Bay National Marine Sanctuary (this was aimed primarily at encouraging local fishermen, rather than dive boats, not to drop anchor on the reefs, since few dive boats visit here). In 1991 the crew of the Moby Dick and local activists carried out work on Sombrero Key in Florida Keys Marine Sanctuary, repairing some of the twenty-five existing buoys and installing eight new ones.

Mooring buoys are not always desirable or necessary, particularly where divers are 'drift diving' (following the currents as they swim) and boats need to follow them. In the Maldives, dive boat operators are being encouraged to operate a 'no anchoring' policy, which is easily achieved if there is a good boatman in charge. Where permanent moorings cannot be installed, suitable sites should be clearly marked, as should areas where anchoring is prohibited. Damage from dive boats can be significantly reduced if divers place their anchors by hand on the seabed and then recover them in the same way after the dive. In the US Virgin Islands, permissible anchoring areas have been designated, and marker buoys have been installed to prevent groundings and prohibit anchoring in sensitive areas.

In places, where no deep-water anchorage is available for cruise ships, permanent moorings are again the solution to anchor damage by cruise ships, but such an enterprise can be tackled only at national level because of the high financial cost. In the Cayman Islands, the Government has committed itself in principle to building permanent moorings, although the programme has been delayed because of cost and the thorny problem of legal liability, should something happen to the vessel whilst moored. In the US Virgin Islands, discussions are being held with cruise-ship companies to find ways of minimising anchor damage, either by anchoring cruise ships outside the marine park, or through some system of controlled anchoring.

Cruise ships that specialise in visiting remote areas where it would be impossible to install permanent mooring or docking facilities pose a much greater problem. In these circumstances, the cruise company must be held responsible for preventing damage, and this will happen only through consumer pressure.

# CHAPTER SEVEN

# HOPE FOR THE FUTURE

There is now no doubt that the world needs to take positive action to secure a healthy future for coral reefs. In the past, many of the measures that have been taken at the behest of outsiders or governments to preserve natural habitats under threat have tended to disregard the needs, intentions or desires of the people living near them. It has now become abundantly clear that if schemes for protection of the environment do not at the very least enlist the support of local people, they stand scant chance of success. Wherever possible the local community should actually initiate and control such schemes themselves.

It is inevitable that there will be development in areas that are linked either closely or distantly with coral reefs. The challenge is to select viable ways in which it can be pursued without causing harm to the environment. Increasingly Greenpeace and other reef conservationists are seeking to draw on the wisdom and experience of those who for generations have lived in close contact with the reefs, often developing impressive systems of managing their resources.

The origins of traditional methods of organising access to reefs and the use of their resources remain, for the most part, shrouded in mystery, for this is a huge, complex and little-documented subject. What is known is that most community-based management systems have grown up in long-established societies, notably among the ancient peoples of the Pacific. In more recently settled places, such as many Caribbean islands, where the existing population has mainly arrived over the last 150 years, fishing seems primarily to be an individual rather than a community-based pursuit. Sometimes traditional regulations have evolved for broadly social and political reasons, as in Papua New Guinea, although the result has often been to conserve marine resources. Elsewhere, traditional systems exist that seem to be more clearly aimed at husbanding the resources of reefs and safeguarding

their future. Where the land has offered only very limited scope for agriculture, as on Pacific atolls, it has made good sense to organise the harvest from the reefs in a manner designed to allow the community to benefit from it in perpetuity.

Traditional knowledge of reefs and of the methods used to manage them is disappearing fast. Changing lifestyles and the imposition of legislation typical of Europe and North America that designates the ocean and its resources as common property rather than as the responsibility of communities living nearby have also had their effect. It is vitally important to ensure that the wealth of expertise that still remains in living memory is not lost.

## Sharing Reef Resources

Until relatively recently demands on the marine environment were far less intense and wide-ranging than they now are; most exploitation was for subsistence purposes and populations were small. Often, coastal communities developed complex and sophisticated ways in which to look after their reefs so that they and succeeding generations could benefit from the reefs' bounty. Many Pacific islanders regulated their resources through tenure systems or traditional rights, often handed down through families and lineages, although in some societies they could be transferred or purchased. Control was usually in the hands of the community leaders, religious leaders, fisheries experts or village councils, although on some islands the chiefs had absolute power and controlled the reefs on behalf of the community.

In the Cook Islands, the focus of traditional management (more developed on the atolls than on the more fertile higher islands) was the *rahuii* or *raui'i*, used specifically as a method of conserving reef resources. A chief of a tribe or head of clan could place a *rahui* (often indicated by a sign such as a coconut leaf tied around a

*Opposite: fishing boat off the coast of Fiji – indigenous Fijians have strongly maintained their traditional rights to reefs and coastal areas throughout the twentieth century; often seen as a hindrance to modern development, these traditional rights can in fact help in the process of sustainable management of the sea's resources.*

*The coconut crab (Birgus latro) is the largest terrestrial invertebrate in the world, measuring up to a metre from leg tip to leg tip and weighing up to three kilogrammes. Its size, combined with its delicious flavour, has meant that it has been hunted almost to extinction on many islands in the Indian and Pacific Oceans. Where there are traditional controls on its collection, as in the Cook Islands, it may stand a better chance of survival.*

tree on a path leading to the area involved) on lands, lagoon areas or particular species to ban their exploitation at certain times. Coconut crabs, for example, are a staple food on some atolls, but highly vulnerable to over-exploitation because they are so easy to catch, and are frequently put under a *rahui*. On several atolls, the system is still vigorously maintained, and on some of these its precepts are actually enshrined in modern law. On Pukapuka, each of the three villages has rights to its own area of land, lagoon and reef, and on other atolls, including Manihiki, the *rahui* system is used in the management of pearl and *Trochus* fisheries and farms. Traditionally the threat of punishment or fear of the supernatural was enough to enforce the prohibition; nowadays a *rahui* is more likely to be administered by an Island Council committee and enforced by people appointed

to patrol the lagoons. *Fa'a-Samoa* (the Samoan way of life), which also incorporated a traditional management system in Western Samoa and American Samoa, probably had similar origins. Ownership of reefs was vested in the village chiefs in order to safeguard them; many Samoans still live according to these precepts.

In the Pacific, traditional systems of resource management now enjoy official recognition in many countries, either under national constitutions or within national legislation. An early example of official sanction of this kind is Fiji, where extended social units called *yavusas,* made up of family groups called *mataqilis,* have traditional rights to fish over reefs from mean high water mark to the outer edge of the reef. In 1881, Sir Arthur Gordon, the Governor of what was then a British colony, took the unusual step of pledging that all reefs and

shellfish beds should be assigned to indigenous Fijians for subsistence fishing and harvesting, under the auspices of a Native Lands and Fisheries Commission. Since then, traditional rights to the reefs have been generally respected and have played an important part in marine resource management. If any development or exploitation is planned, traditional rights owners have to be consulted and must give their approval before the plan can go ahead; in the event of any subsequent negative effect on the fishery, compensation is likely to be payable.

In Papua New Guinea, over ninety per cent of the land and reefs is still under traditional ownership, the rights to which are guaranteed under the country's constitution. This has presented a promising opportunity to weld together existing structures and modern conservation ideas:

Wildlife Management Areas have been set up by local communities, which define the boundaries, draw up regulations and take responsibility for their enforcement, in the knowledge that they can request assistance from the Department of Environment and Conservation if necessary. So far, most Wildlife Management Areas have been set up on land, but a few have been established to protect turtles and dugongs, and there are plans for others which will include reefs.

In American Samoa, the National Parks Service, which under US Federal law has to buy land in order to turn it into a park, has recently had to adopt a more imaginative approach in the setting up of the American Samoa National Park to cope with a traditional Samoan law according to which it is forbidden to sell land. The problem has been solved by a collaborative effort between the Parks Service and Samoan leaders, which involves the villagers leasing their lands and reefs within the boundaries of the park to the Service, on condition that no cultural sites are disturbed, no roads are built into forests and no hotels are constructed. The villagers have retained their rights to the reefs, provided that only traditional fishing methods are used. As the Samoan chiefs explained, their management practices were based on 2,000 years of experience and they were not happy using a system developed by a country that in their opinion was scarcely more than 200 years old.

Traditional rights to the 700 square kilometres of reefs, mangroves and seagrass beds of Marovo Lagoon in the Solomon Islands are divided among the several clans that make up the population of 8,000. These rights are now being invoked both to regulate fishing practices and to control other activities. Dive tour operators are now obliged to ask for permission and pay fees for entering reef areas; foreign yachts are prohibited from anchoring; foreign fishing boats can be expelled; and giant clam mariculture operations are sited on reefs according to traditional ownership patterns. The community has taken a very strong role in all aspects of management, adapting traditional practices to new issues as they arise.

## Zoning

Nowadays competitive human demands on reefs and their resources are much more widespread than they have ever been. Changes in the nature of reef exploitation, the speed of development and the growing number of people needing to live off the reefs have sharply focused these conflicts. Problems of this sort can be greatly alleviated by assigning different uses to different parts of the reef, much as traditional reef owners in the Pacific managed their resources – a strategy which is now called zoning.

Zoning systems vary greatly in scale and complexity. The Great Barrier Reef Marine Park, a vast area of 350,000 square kilometres, has now been zoned in a process that stretched from the mid 1970s to 1988 – a lengthy but crucially important stage because it allowed extensive public participation and collaboration with all the communities that use the area in the forming of policy. Originally, the system was designed to cope with the problems of overfishing; now tourism, which has grown hugely in scale and importance, is incorporated into the plan too. Some reefs are essentially all-purpose and can be used for a variety of activities, others are open only for fishing or recreation, others again are designated for reef research only and still others enjoy total protection. At the other end of the scale, community-managed marine parks in the Philippines are often composed of only two zones: one where fishing is strictly prohibited and a second where it is permitted if non-damaging methods are used.

Sometimes certain parts of reefs are nominated for special protection – in the context of fisheries, these might be breeding areas for certain species or sites of spawning aggregations. Where tourism is important, special consideration might be given to particularly attractive reef formations and richly diverse communities of plants and animals – the 'coral gardens' that are visited by large number of tourists in glass-bottomed boats in resort areas. Areas with a high diversity of species or populations of rare or endemic animals or plants might be judged especially worthy of protection, as might reefs whose position in relation to ocean currents means that larvae or food

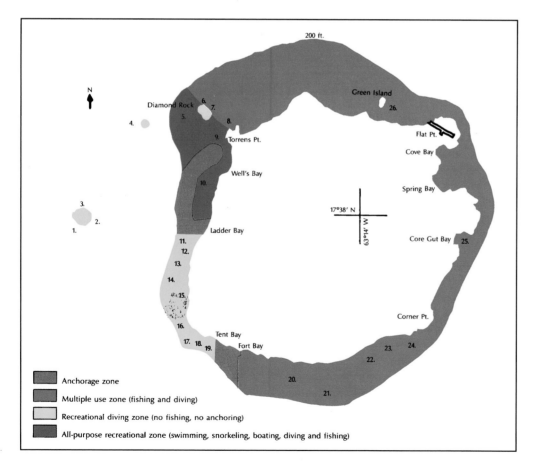

Anchorage zone

Multiple use zone (fishing and diving)

Recreational diving zone (no fishing, no anchoring)

All-purpose recreational zone (swimming, snorkeling, boating, diving and fishing)

*Right: a scene in the beautiful and largely unspoilt Chagos Archipelago, recommended as a World Heritage Site; the reefs and atolls cover a large area and are relatively unknown because of their inaccessibility.*

*Opposite: plan of Saba Marine Park showing how it has been zoned for different purposes. The numbers indicate dive sites.*

*Below: some particularly pretty areas of reef thrive just below the surface of the water, like this colony of coral in the Marshall Islands, and are a magnet for tourists who can sometimes view them from boats, without even having to dive. Access to profuse but easily damaged coral life like this needs to be carefully organised so that the reef survives unscathed.*

are transported to other reefs downstream from them.

A problem in making considered judgements as to the relative value of different areas is lack of information about them. In Japan, for instance, it was realised only in the late 1980s that despite the northerly location of the reefs, the range of coral species is extraordinarily rich and diverse. Projects are now underway in several places that put together information from museums, publications and other sources and amalgamate the data on maps, providing a good basis for planning which areas of coast should be given priority protection.

Earlier this century, when there were relatively few wide-ranging sources of damage to reefs, so many virtually untouched reefs remained in the world that their existence was pretty much taken for granted. Now undamaged, untouched reefs are extremely rare, only surviving, in general, where they are very remote and therefore difficult to get to; when they are home to a particularly rich range of reef animals or to rare or endemic species, it is especially important for them to remain undisturbed. They also provide important reference points for judging the health of other less unspoilt reefs.

The Chagos Archipelago, which lies in the centre of the Indian Ocean, is extremely remote. There have been occasional visitors to the five atolls since they were first exploited in the sixteenth century by the Portuguese, and a small amount of colonisation has occurred from time to time. But since the early 1970s, the only resident human population has been the service personnel at the military base on the atoll of Diego Garcia. Diego Garcia itself has suffered grievously from the activities of the military, mainly as a result of construction; but in making the archipelago more difficult to visit than it would otherwise have been, their presence has at least brought a level of protection to the reefs around all the other atolls, which are among the most pristine in the world. They have never been affected by modern development, pollution or siltation, for example, and have the highest number of coral and mollusc species of any reef in the Indian Ocean, including at least one endemic coral (*Ctenella chagius*), as well as being home to large and undisturbed populations of many species that are exploited elsewhere: giant clams, black corals, spiny lobsters, fish, turtles and seabirds.

This situation, however, may not exist in the long term, and international recognition for areas like the Chagos Archipelago is essential to any attempt to ensure their survival. One way of doing this is through the World Heritage Convention, which is overseen by UNESCO. Countries that are party to the Convention (of which there are 120) undertake to provide protection for places that have been designated World Heritage Sites because they are unique and outstanding examples of the world's natural heritage. Financial support for this protection is available through a special fund. So far few reefs have been listed, mainly because of lack of information, but those that have achieved World Heritage Site status include Sian Ka'an, the Great Barrier Reef, Henderson Island in the eastern Pacific, the Galapagos, and the Sierra Nevada de Santa Marta on the Caribbean coast of Colombia. The Chagos Archipelago, Belize's Barrier Reef and Belau have all been nominated but the procedure for acceptance is lengthy. Listing does not in itself guarantee protection, but it provides an incentive for appropriate management, and plays a crucial role in convincing governments of the importance of an area. Where human communities are dependent on these outstandingly precious natural sites,

a wide range of approaches will need to be discussed by all those involved in order to develop a strategy that will take account of the requirements of local people as well as maintaining the unique characteristics of the natural environment.

Until fairly recently, the most usual way for a marine habitat to be protected was for a government to declare it a marine park or reserve. The rather rigid schemes of some early conservationists, which depended primarily on excluding local people from protected areas, also inevitably alienated them. In the face of the increasing demands being made on both land and sea, it is clearer than ever before that people must be part of the equation for conservation to work. Direct management of resources by local people obviously provides a much better incentive for long-term commitment to making any scheme work. Community involvement makes enforcement easier. People respond to peer pressure, and funds are not needed for expensive patrol boats to stop illegal fishing or the use of damaging fishing methods if local people are already keeping an eye out for infractions of this sort.

Montego Bay Marine Park in Jamaica had long been a classic example of a 'paper park': established in 1974 but ignored by users of the area as well as enforcement agencies, until the local community became involved. In 1990, funding was made available to start a new intitiative, this time extending the park to cover a larger area that included mangroves and seagrass beds

as well as reefs, and zoning it to include fishing and non-fishing areas, and sites for recreation. Public education and participation were seen as the first priority. A Local Advisory Committee composed of representatives of the fishery cooperatives, the tourist industry, the marine police, local government and other interested parties was set up. Fund-raising was also carried out on a local basis, and an intensive awareness campaign mounted, using all outlets from television and newspapers to schools and churches; even local taxi drivers sported marine park stickers on their cabs. Local people, now trained as park rangers, will work with the local fishermen and the tourists to help them understand and benefit from the park area.

Obviously, if there is little or no resident population in an area of reef designated as a marine park, there is a risk that inappropriate and exploitative use may be made of the reef simply because there is no-one there to blow the whistle or protest. In circumstances of this sort, governments must be prepared to intervene. One such example is Tubbataha Reef, which lies in the middle of the Sulu Sea about 150 kilometres from Palawan, the easternmost of the Philippines islands. Home to some 300 species of coral and nearly 400 species of fish (including six shark species), the two islets are regularly visited by hawksbill and green turtles, and have enormous seabird colonies including about 1500 nesting brown boobies. In 1988, the area was declared a marine park;

*Turtles, like this green turtle (Chelonia mydas), have been over-exploited all over the tropics, and it is only in remote locations like Chagos that they enjoy freedom from human predators.*

*Opposite: another potential World Heritage Site is the Belize Barrier Reef, where this impressive cluster of tube sponges was photographed; the longest barrier reef in the Caribbean, and the second largest in the world, it is still relatively unscathed.*

tourism interests were rapidly mobilised and a verbal battle between the opposing parties occupied column inches in the nation's papers for weeks. Not for the first time in the Philippines, conservationists were made aware of the unpopularity of their views in some quarters. Then in late 1989, President Aquino herself approved the removal of the farm. A naval cruiser, loaded with some forty civilian observers and journalists, sailed from Palawan. The buildings were burnt, the remains removed, and the last eight staff of the seaweed farm taken off. The park is now managed with the assistance of the Tubbataha Foundation, a consortium of conservationists and dive operators, and the only uses to which the area is put are diving by tourists and fishing by Cayancillo Islanders.

## Biosphere reserves

One initiative that has originated outside local communities is the Man and the Biosphere Programme, sponsored by the United Nations Educational, Scientific and Cultural Organization (UNESCO). This promotes the idea of environmental protection whilst laying emphasis on safeguarding the interests of local people living within a protected area via the concept of the 'biosphere reserve'. Reserves have been set up whose aim is to provide 'demonstration sites of harmonious, long-lasting relationships between man and the natural environment'. Each biosphere reserve is zoned, with a core area of minimal human disturbance, a buffer zone where activities such as research, traditional land or marine use, recreation, tourism and education are allowed, and a transition area outside the reserve in which its work can be applied directly to the needs of the local communities.

Sian Ka'an, on the Yucatan peninsula, was established in 1986 as Mexico's first biosphere reserve. It is a huge expanse (528,000 ha) of rainforest, mangroves, bays of crystal blue waters dotted with green, jewel-like islands, sweeping white sandy beaches, and vibrant coral reefs. Its Mayan name means 'birth of the sky', and it provides a classic example of what is meant by the biosphere, the thin skin of life on the planet. It consists of roughly one third

fishermen from the nearby Cayancillo Islands sometimes come to the reefs and the atolls are regularly visited by dive boats in the holiday season, but there was no resident population to make sure that the regulations of the park were not breached. Early in 1989, visiting divers found to their horror that a seaweed farm was being built on the reefs.

Seaweed farming is a major industry in the Philippines and can be a sound alternative to extractive industries which damage reefs. By the late 1980s, there was still plenty of scope of the world market for expansion, but the Philippines was running out of space to put the farms. For Benson Dakay, the wealthy head of a multi-million dollar seaweed-exporting firm, Tubbataha Reef

seemed ideal, and permission was obtained to set up a farm within the park. By the time that divers visiting the area saw what was happening, houses had been constructed on stilts on the shallow reef flat and seaweed lines had been set up. Isolated on their 'desert island', the impoverished Filipino families who had been brought in to service the farm would be hard-pressed not to take turtle and bird eggs, and there would be a strong temptation to use dynamite fishing as in their home villages; as for rubbish, sewage and other waste, there would be no alternative to dumping on the reef.

There was widespread outrage when it emerged that some 6,000 families were to be installed here. Public opinion and diving

forest, one third marsh and mangrove, and one third reefs, lagoons and bays. Its reef is part of the barrier reef system that runs from the top of the Yucatan peninsula down through Belize. Its mangrove-covered coral cays and mangroves are nesting sites for roseate spoonbills (*Platea ajaja*), magnificent frigatebirds (*Fregata magnificens*) and other seabirds.

This wildlife paradise is also home to about 1000 people, mainly of Mayan descent, who live as fishermen, hunters and farmers, with the majority working as lobster fishermen. The two main bays (Bahia de la Ascencion and Espiritu Santo) are the most important spiny lobster nursery area in Mexico, and the reef provides abundant shelter for the adults. A private support group, the Amigos de Sian Ka'an, has been set up to work with the Mexican government to implement the biosphere reserve principles. At present the area is under no immediate threat, but tourism development is spreading southwards down the Quintana Roo coastline towards Sian Ka'an at an alarming rate. Top priorities include development of a programme of sustainable ecotourism before uncontrolled mass tourism reaches Sian Ka'an, and more sustainable management of the lobster fishery.

Another biosphere reserve with reefs is the US Virgin Islands National Park, which was established in 1956 and subsequently declared a Biosphere Reserve in 1976 (although it was not formally set up until 1983). The Virgin Islands Resource Management Cooperative was set up to oversee management of the reserve, with representatives of private institutions and government agencies in it. This helped to provide training in research and management to local people, some of whom have been involved with reef projects in the reserve. Traditional fishing with hook-and-line and pots for fish, lobster and conch is permitted provided certain regulations and quotas are observed. Initially the fishermen had felt excluded from the reserve in favour of tourists, and this led to confrontations with park staff. In 1988 the 'Friends of the Virgin Islands National Park' was set up specifically to encourage communication between local people and park staff and biologists.

## Coastal Zone Management

Despite the obvious success of some marine parks that have been set up in an enlightened manner by or with local communities, schemes of this kind can never be the whole solution to the range of problems confronting coral reefs. For a start, a marine park will inevitably be very different from a terrestrial one, because it is simply not feasible to try to protect marine environments by erecting fences or barriers. Ultimately, though, the reason why marine parks alone cannot protect reefs is that the real sabotage often originates in land-based activities, sometimes far away from the habitats that ultimately suffer.

The Great Barrier Reef Marine Park is one of the most complex and well-funded marine park systems in the world, but the reef is nevertheless potentially threatened by increased quantities of sewage and fertilisers entering coastal waters. Florida has some of the longest-established marine parks in the world (Fort Jefferson National Monument was set up in 1935 and John Pennekamp Coral Reefs State Park in 1961) and yet the 320 kilometres of reef along the Florida coast appear to be at serious risk. In 1986, researchers calculated

that the average rate of decline in coral cover was four per cent a year: in 1991, parts of the reef were losing live corals at the rate of ten per cent a year.

Once again, there are ancient precedents for coping with modern problems. Managing the sea, the coast and its hinterland as one unit has been a familiar concept to some Pacific islanders for centuries. In Hawaii a system has existed which was effectively an early form of environmental planning. The land tenure system operated on a 'ridge to reef' basis, so that village groups or *konohiki* were themselves responsible for managing their land and watershed to prevent damage to the reefs. The islands were divided like a pie into wedge-shaped sections called *ahupua'a* which ran from the peaks to the shoreline and then on out to the edge of the reef. Each *ahupua'a*, allocated by the island chiefs, guaranteed access to the coastline for its inhabitants and could fulfil most of their needs, providing forest products on the mountain slopes, crops and fruits on the more gentle slopes, and fishing on the reef. An elaborate *kapu'o* or taboo system reinforced the conservation value of the *ahupua'a*: fishing was often prohibited in the spawning season and in some cases only the chiefs could eat certain species. A similar system evolved on the high volcanic islands of the Cook Islands, with a tribe's ownership rights covering areas running from the tops of valleys to the outer edge of the reef.

Management of the entire coastal sytem and its watershed as an integrated unit, as in the Hawaiian *ahupua'a*, is now called coastal zone management. Plans are being set up in many countries to integrate management of tourism and fisheries with the protection of vital habitats and threatened species, to reduce conflict between different uses of the coast, to prevent pollution from land-based sources and from shipping, and to prevent coastal erosion. Incorporated in the plans, there have to be negotiated agreements relating to alternative sources of income for those deprived of their livelihood by new regulations. Likely possibilities would involve diversification of fisheries, development of mariculture, artificial reefs or small-scale tourism. The management plan needs to extend as far

inland as the activities which could harm the reefs.

Ideally, a coastal zone management plan covers the entire coastal zone of a country and is devised before reefs have become too heavily damaged. Needless to say, there are few nations where this has been possible. An exception is Oman, where perhaps uniquely the reefs are as yet subject to low human pressure and the government has made environmental management a high priority and has the financial resources to implement plans. Following a countrywide survey of the reefs, the entire coastline has been placed under a management plan, and some areas have been designated for a range of uses such as fishing and recreation, while others have been set aside as marine parks. Few countries will be able to tackle coastal zone management in such an all-embracing way but the principles can be adopted on a smaller scale.

Belize is responsible for the world's second largest barrier reef, described by Darwin in what may be something of an understatement as 'the most remarkable reef in the West Indies'. The fact that it is a small country is helpful in the development of a national coastal zone management plan. This is currently in preparation as a co-operative effort between conservation organisations, government departments and local community action groups. The country's small

*Opposite, top: successful marine parks and coastal management programmes involve terrestrial habitats as much as the oceans themselves. These roseate spoonbills (*Platea ajaja*) nest in coastal vegetation, such as mangroves. Protection of reefs involves the protection and management of all the associated habitats and wildlife.*

*Opposite, bottom: despite the marine parks along its coastline, many of Florida's reefs are showing signs of severe stress, with corals succumbing to a variety of ills, of which this unhealthy sea fan coated with algae in Florida Keys is an example. Often the direct cause of the problem is difficult or impossible to discern, but the explanation almost certainly lies in a combination of human impacts on the environment, many of them stemming from land-based activities.*

*Below: French grunts (*Haemulon flavolineatum*) and goatfish (*Pseudopeneus sp.*), like these in John Pennekamp Coral Reefs State Park, often take shelter on the reef in schools during the day and move to seagrass beds at night to feed on other fish and invertebrates. The dependence of species like these on a variety of habitats necessitates a very broad approach to management of the coast and sea.*

population (180,000) and its slow rate of development have meant that until recently the barrier reef, and its associated patch and ring reefs, mangroves and brackish lagoons, have been relatively untouched by human activities. By 1989, though, the country was receiving as many tourists each year as there are residents, and most of the visitors stay on the coast where three quarters of the country's 188 hotels are located. Fisheries production has increased, with the harvest of conch, lobster, shrimps, reef fish and other species worth US$8.8 million in 1989. Shipping and tanker traffic has grown, and more and more land is being put to the cultivation of citrus fruits and bananas, with the attendant dangers of soil run-off and pollution from fertilisers and herbicides. The coastal zone management plan includes a major educational initiative (for schools, government departments, developers and tour operators) to ensure that everyone is involved and understands the reasons for the plan. It takes into account existing marine parks and reserves (such as Hol Chan Reserve and Half Moon Caye Natural Monument), provides for a number of new reserves, requires the seasonal closure of fisheries in spawning areas such as Glover's Reef, and includes an oil spill contingency plan.

In larger countries, it may be easier to initiate coastal zone management at the regional level first, where action can be taken by individual communities, without the long delays that may be involved in negotiations at government level. This approach

is being taken in Papua New Guinea, where a coastal zone management plan has been drawn up for an area on the south coast, running east from Port Moresby along much of the length of the Papua barrier reef. The Hiri people, who live here, have been collaborating with the Department of Environment and Conservation, with assistance from Greenpeace. The first action was to set up the Hiri East Coastal Zone Management Area Committee, which is made up of Hiri District council members and representatives of other interested parties. The Council members report back to the villagers to obtain feedback on proposed plans. In 1991, a team of biologists surveyed the locality to prepare a map that will be used in setting the boundaries for the coastal zone management area. They also trained a number of Papua New Guineans in basic techniques to allow them to carry out surveys and monitoring.

Coastal zone management plans are on the drawing board or already operating in a number of sites in several south-east Asian countries. The Association of Southeast Asian Nations (or ASEAN countries) – Thailand, Singapore, Brunei, Malaysia, Indonesia and the Philippines – have each developed a pilot coastal zone management programme for one site, under a cooperative programme with financial support from US-AID. It is hoped that the fishermen of Bolinao in the Lingayen Gulf (Philippines) will, along with other similar fishermen, benefit from this project aimed at finding alternatives to dynamiting and

over-exploitation of the reefs through community-managed mariculture and coastal planning. The ASEAN programme has also led to the preparation of guidelines for coastal zone management that can be used as a model in other countries. Thailand and Indonesia have taken an additional step in preparing national coral reef strategies which will use reefs as a flagship to increase public and government support for the concept of coastal zone management.

On small islands, where the entire land area and surrounding reefs together make up the coastal zone, an overall approach is essential. Kosrae, in the Federated States of Micronesia in the Pacific, has a population of just under 7,000 people, grouped into five coastal communities. The economy is still mostly a subsistence one, with about 250 species of fish caught for food from the largely pristine fringing reef, seagrass beds and mangroves that girdle the island. Development has so far been limited to the building of an airport, docks, harbours and a causeway linking the small island of Lele with the main island. Although

these activities had only a temporarily deleterious impact on reefs, it was enough to alert the islanders to the dangers of further unplanned development. A coastal zone management plan is now being developed with the close involvement of the island's inhabitants, as they will all be affected by it. An atlas which maps all the principal coastal resources of the island is being used to identify zones for particular activities, and, with the help of various environmental groups, the intention is to establish marine-protected areas able both to support and to benefit from small-scale nature-based tourism. The state legislature has recently passed a law establishing a land-use plan and an approval procedure, with the aim of ensuring that any economic or social development carried out is environmentally sustainable.

## Direct Action

Even in areas where there is no strong tradition of communal management, the local community can mobilise itself or be enabled to take action if its core asset, the natural environment, is threatened. Shiraho, on the island of Ishigaki in southern Japan, is a peaceful traditional village, with many inhabitants still making a living by fishing and gathering shellfish, lobsters, sea urchins, seaweed and other products on the nearby reef (altogether, up to thirty-eight

reef species are harvested). Little did anyone realise what passionate determination lay beneath the surface of this quiet community until the Japanese government decided to build a second airport on the island to increase tourism. In the early 1980s, without bothering to consult the villagers of Shiraho, the government approved a US$125 million plan to construct the airport virtually on top of much of the reef. Once these intentions became public, several action groups sprang up. The villagers feared for their traditional way of life, and conservationists were deeply disturbed at the prospect of losing a unique habitat. About ninety per cent of the reefs around Japan's main subtropical island, Okinawa, are badly degraded by pollution, sedimentation and crown-of-thorns starfish outbreaks, and most of the other accessible reefs in Japan are similarly damaged. Shiraho reef is one of the last remaining undamaged reefs in the country. It is home to more than 130 species of coral, among them unique huge colonies of blue coral, found here in one of the largest surviving concentrations in the northern hemisphere. The irony of a facility for tourism destroying the main attraction for visitors to the island was not lost on the protesters.

Not everyone declared opposition to the plan: Japanese reef scientists were reluctant to become involved for fear of losing their jobs; the local fishermen's cooperative agreed to

relinquish their fishing rights in exchange for 500 million yen, about the value of only one year's catch, which resulted in some of the fishermen filing lawsuits against the cooperative. Events rapidly took a bitter turn, and in September 1984 the leader of the fishermen's protest group, aged over sixty, was arrested with two others, one of whom was badly beaten up by police.

Fortunately, the issue was taken up by Friends of the Earth Japan, the World Wildlife Fund in Japan and a number of international conservation organisations including Greenpeace. Shiraho became a *cause célèbre*, even drawing 1,200 people to a benefit poetry reading attended by Allan Ginsberg and other literary luminaries in San Francisco. The combination of local campaigning, the involvement of the international scientific community and international media attention finally began to sway some Japanese politicians and national newspapers. The first change of heart was a proposal to relocate the airport four kilometres from the original site. This had little impact on the protesters' arguments and the battle continued. In 1991, nearly a decade after the issue had first arisen, local politicians who had campaigned against the airport were voted into office, and the proposals have (at least temporarily) been shelved. The Shiraho community will no doubt need to remain vigilant, and action is still required

*Opposite, top: Half Moon Caye on Lighthouse Reef in Belize, an outstandingly beautiful and unspoilt example of a coral cay ecosystem, declared a Natural Monument in 1982; bottom: in many countries where there is little or no effective fisheries management, the good-sized tasty reef fish have now been over-fished and catches are increasingly dominated by small, low-value species. This basket of tiny rabbit fish is now a typical catch on the depleted reefs of the Philippines. Right: Kosrae airport, whose construction prompted the islanders here to take stock of the effects of development on the reefs. Many island nations, formerly accessible only by boat and small plane, are now building international airports capable of receiving jumbo jets and hundreds of tourists. Atoll islands are usually too small, and high volcanic islands rarely have enough flat land for a runway, so land is invariably reclaimed, as here.*

to prevent damage to the reefs from the existing threats of pollution and soil run-off, but for the moment, at least, an important victory has been won.

Not all community action happens in such dramatic circumstances. In Thailand, it has led to the organisation of Marine Awareness weeks. In Guam, young people are now running their own 'Kids for Coral' campaign; in the little-known and beautiful Andaman Islands, local people have produced their own booklets on saving the reefs; in Cozumel, a cartoon called 'Pepe the Polyp' is being used to put across the conservation message.

It is now clear that there are ways to allow environmentally sound development on land and sea without threatening the health or survival of coral reefs. But short-sighted, short-term exploitation must cease and considered long-term solutions must follow. The extraordinarily complex web of relationships within the reef habitat and between reefs and other ecosystems, like mangroves and seagrass beds, taken together with the needs and aspirations of

human populations living near them and depending on them, mean that no single management strategy can ever be sufficient. There is no substitute for integrated schemes of management that take account of all the known ecological requirements and different uses of the reef. Sometimes these may be relatively simple to work out, where there are a few, easily identifiable threats to the environment and only slight human demands on it. In other cases, competing interests and the cumulative effect of a variety of stresses on the reef, as, for example, on the Great Barrier Reef, may call for enormously complex responses. Community management now seems to be the key. Even where there are no local traditions of this kind, the concept can be introduced and once the system is seen to work, readily accepted. With adequate technical guidance, development can be constructive and sustainable for the benefit of all. Any outside agencies, including national governments, that wish to see this kind of policy implemented must be prepared to accept the gradual pace that tends to characterise community decision-making. If properly considered, a jointly approved course of action is far more likely to work in the long-term than an imposed solution.

Driven by short-term considerations and vested interests, government and industry more often than not lack the vision to take the necessary steps to protect valuable ecosystems such as coral reefs. Politicians need constantly to be reminded of the importance of these resources. In many parts of the world, local communities are now starting to make their voices heard in the battle to save the reefs; Greenpeace welcomes the efforts of all those whose aim is the protection of this exquisitely beautiful but desperately vulnerable part of the world's natural heritage.

*Top: the first step in preparing a coastal zone management plan is to map and compile a full inventory of all the ecosystems involved. Here, volunteers working with the organisation Coral Cay Conservation help to survey a reef at Ambergris Caye in Belize.*

*Right: divers in the Red Sea enjoying the impressive sight of a humpheaded wrasse* (Cheilinus undulatus) *cruising down the reef in an underwater landscape as fascinating and mysterious as anything to be found on land and just as worthy of respect and protection.*

# HOW YOU CAN HELP

Until recently, not many people realised just how fragile coral reefs and the animals living in and around them can be, and only a few were ever lucky enough to see them. But now the numbers are growing, and, happily, an awareness of how careful visitors to coral reefs must be is also increasing. Here are some tips to help you make your visit to a reef an environmentally friendly one.

## Divers and snorkellers

1. Try to avoid letting your body, diving equipment or camera touch living marine organisms. A careless swipe of the fins or clumsy manoeuvring next to the reef can damage or disturb corals and other animals and plants on the reef.

2. Be particularly careful to control your fins: their size and the force of kicking can damage large areas of reef. Keep your fins away from the reef at all times and try not to use deep fin strokes next to the reef, as the surges of water you produce may damage delicate organisms (remember how large you are by comparison with many of the reef creatures around you). If you feel you are out of control and about to collide with the reef, don't steady yourself with your fins against the reef; instead use your fingertips on a part of the reef that is already dead or covered in algae. Do the same if a current unbalances you.

3. Avoid kicking up the sand. Quite apart from spoiling visibility, this creates a cloud of sand that will eventually settle over the reef and may smother corals. Snorkellers in particular should be careful when they are treading water in shallow reef areas.

4. Never stand on corals, however robust some of them (such as giant brain coral or mountainous star corals) may seem. The living polyps on their surface are easily damaged by the slightest touch. Never sit, stand or kneel inside giant basket or barrel sponges. If you need to adjust your diving equipment or mask or for some other reason have to sit or stand temporarily, choose a sandy area well away from the reef.

5. The friendliness and curiosity of many reef creatures as they approach divers and snorkellers may tempt you to touch or stroke them or even to hitch rides as they go past. But these actions can cause stress and interrupt mating or feeding behaviour. Don't move marine organisms around to photograph or play with them, particularly if they are sessile species (which are permanently attached to the substrate).

6. Fish-feeding may seem like a harmless and enjoyable activity but it can disturb normal feeding patterns and provoke aggressive behaviour. It may also cause stress by introducing food that is not part of the normal diet and may be unhealthy for the fish.

7. Take all litter away from the beach or from your boat and pick up any refuse you see on the reef for proper disposal or recycling on land.

8. If you visit a marine park or reserve on a regular basis, or go to one on holiday, find out about the regulations and make sure you observe them.

9. Join your local or national beach clean-up campaign.

## Scuba divers

Scuba divers need to take special care because of the extra equipment they carry. Here are some points to keep in mind.

1. Good buoyancy control is vital to preventing damage: a significant amount of harm is caused by divers sinking too rapidly or crashing into corals while trying to adjust their buoyancy. Make sure you are correctly weighted and learn to achieve neutral buoyancy by relaxing and slowing down your breathing pattern. (A simple test will tell you whether you have the correct weights: when fully kitted up, float upright – say, beside the dive boat – and take a half breath. You should settle at a position where the water is at eye level.)

2. If you haven't dived for a while, your skills may be rusty – especially in buoyancy control. Before diving in the fragile reef environment, spend some time with an instructor or divemaster polishing up your skills in a location where you won't cause damage. Better still, take a refresher course.

3. Make sure that your depth and pressure gauges (and spare regulator if you have an octopus rig) don't drag along the bottom. Keep them secured and close to your body

4. Take great care in underwater caverns and caves. Avoid crowding into the cave and don't spend too long there. Air bubbles collect in pockets on the roof of the cave, and the delicate creatures living there can 'drown in air'.

5. Avoid spear-fishing. This is now prohibited in many countries and your equipment may in any case be confiscated by Customs. Leave spear-fishing to local fishermen, who will have a better understanding of which fish and how many of them can be taken from the reef without endangering populations. If you are living on a boat and relying on spear-fishing for food, make sure that you are familiar with all local fish and game regulations and obtain proper licensing where necessary. Only take creatures that you are going to eat, and respect the rights of local fishermen. Avoid spear-fishing in areas where other divers are simply enjoying or photographing the reef.

6. Divers are in a unique position to help monitor the health of reefs and other coastal ecosystems. If you see pollution on the reefs, large diseased patches on corals or signs of other disturbances, report them to the relevant local authorities. Before you go on a diving holiday, consider taking part in one of several monitoring schemes currently being organised by reef conservation organisations, or, better yet, volunteer for a dive

trip which will actively contribute to reef conservation.

## Boat users

1. Always use mooring buoys if possible, rather than just throwing an anchor over the side. If none are available, anchor carefully in sand or patches of dead coral rubble. Keep your anchor chain as short as possible to prevent it dragging on reef areas. When hauling in, motor towards the anchor to prevent dragging.

2. If you are booking a trip on a commercial dive boat, ask questions in advance about the company's environmental policies, particularly on anchoring and the discharge of sewage. Make it clear that you think that taking measures to prevent damage is important.

3. Mind the reef! Grounding is bad for both your boat and the reef. Navigation in reef waters needs special care.

Even if you are not lucky enough to visit a reef, there are important ways in which you can contribute to the efforts to keep them healthy.

1. Learn more about reefs and marine life in general and the problems facing these environments.

2. Get involved in looking after the reefs by joining Greenpeace or your local environmental group.

3. Join letter-writing campaigns on issues such as global warming, ozone depletion, pollution and other environmental concerns and urge politicians to take appropriate action. Repeated lobbying can be a very effective tool. Individuals must play their role in influencing governments to take the necessary steps to prevent future harm being done to reefs through wilful or ignorant human misuse of the environment.

4. Do not buy tropical marine fish or other live reef animals, including corals, to keep in an aquarium unless you are certain that the species are being collected and marketed in a sustainable way.

5. Find out about the species listed in Appendix 1 of CITES (the Convention on International Trade in Endangered Species, referred to in Chapter 7) and never buy any curios or other products made from these animals and plants. Trade in species listed in Appendix 2, such as corals and giant clams, is strictly controlled in many countries, but it is difficult for the individual to check on whether or not specimens have been legally exported and imported, so it is best to avoid buying these too. Always refuse curios that are labelled as rare; if the description is at all accurate, the animals should not have been collected in the first place.

Finally, watch out for news and information on the state of one of the planet's richest and most threatened habitats, and find out as much as you can about what is happening. Frequently, once the information is available, what should be done becomes plain. It is up to all of us to safeguard the health of coral reefs by making sure that they are given the protection they deserve.

## Greenpeace Offices

Greenpeace Australia, Studio 14, 37 Nicholson Street, Balmain, NSW 2041, AUSTRALIA  Tel: 2 555 7044

Greenpeace Ireland, 44 Upper Mount Street, Dublin 2, EIRE Tel: 1 619836

Greenpeace New Zealand, Private Bag, Wellesley Street, Auckland, NEW ZEALAND Tel: 9 3776128

Greenpeace UK, Canonbury Villas, London N1 2P,  UK  Tel: 071 354 5100

Greenpeace USA, 1436 U Street NW, Washington, DC 20009, USA

Greenpeace International, Keizersgracht 176, 1016 DW Amsterdam, THE NETHERLANDS  Tel: 20 523 6555

## Other Organisations

No comprehensive dirctory of the organisations concerned with coral reef conservation yet exists, though one is currently in preparation. Here are the addresses of some of the many organisations working to protect the reefs.

Australian Coral Reef Society,  c/o Hon. Sec., Dr T. Done, Australian Institute of Marine Sciences, PMB No. 3, Townsville MSO, Townsville, Queensland 4810, AUSTRALIA

CEDAM International, Fox Road, Croton-on-Hudson, NY 10520, USA

Centre for Marine Conservation, 1725 DeSales Street, N.W., Washington 20036, USA  Tel: 202 429 5609

Coral Cay Conservation Ltd, The Sutton Business Centre, Restmor Way, Wallington, Surrey SM6 7AH, UK Tel: 081 669 0011

Cousteau Society, 870 Greenbrier Circle, Suite 402, Chesapeake, Virginia 23320, USA  Tel: 804 523 9335

Crusoe Society, P.O. Box 890, Port of Spain, TRINIDAD AND TOBAGO  Tel: 1 809 622 2081

Earthwatch, 680 Mount Auburn Street, P.O. Box 403, Watertown, MA 02272-9104, USA  Tel: 617 926 8200

Earthwatch Europe, 57 Woodstock Road, Oxford OX2 6HU, UK Tel: 0865 311600

Environmental Defense Fund, 257 Park Avenue South, New York, NY 10010, USA  Tel: 212  505 2100

Environmental Solutions International, 6 Farmer Street, London W8 7S, UK  Tel: 071 727 6526

Friends of Saba Marine Park/Saba Conservation Foundation, The Bottom, Saba, NETHERLANDS ANTILLES

Global Coral Reef Alliance, 324 North Bedford Road, Chappaqua, New York, NY 10514, USA Tel: 914 236 8788

Great Barrier Reef Marine Park Authority, Townsville, Queensland 4811, AUSTRALIA Tel: 077 81 8811

Intercoast Network, Coastal Resources Center, University of Rhode Island, Narragansett Bay Campus, Narragansett, RI 02882 USA Tel: 401 792 6224

International Marinelife Alliance US, 415 Ivory Court, Greenmeadows Avenue, Quezon City, PHILIPPINES 1100 Tel: 632 721 4392

International Society for Reef Studies, c/0 Membership Scretary, Kansas Geological Survey, Campus West, 1930 Constant Avenue, University of Kansas, Lawrence KS 66045, USA Tel: 913 864 3062

Marine Conservation Group, Malayan Nature Society, c/o Newman Biomarine Pte Ltd, 60B Martin Road, 07-01/02 CMDC, SINGAPORE 092

Marine Conservation Society, 9 Gloucester Road, Ross-on-Wye, Herefordshire HR9 5BU, UK Tel: 0989 66017

The Nature Conservancy, Pacific Regional Office, 1116 Smith Street, # 201 Honolulu, Hawaii 96817, USA Tel: 808 537 4508

Ocean Voice International, Inc., 2883 Otterson Drive, Ottawa, Ontario K1V 7B2, CANADA Tel: 613 990 8819

Project Reefkeeper, 16345 West Dixie Highway, Suite 1121, Miami, Florida 33160, USA Tel: 305 294 3100

Reef Relief, P.O. Box 430, Key West, Florida 33041-0430, USA Tel: 305 294 3100

Reefwatch, Tropical Marine Research Unit, Dept of Biology, University of York, York YO1 5DD, UK Tel: 0904 416611

Singapore Underwater Federation, c/o Dept of Zoology, National University of Singapore, 10 Kent Ridge Crescent, SINGAPORE 0511

Society for Andaman and Nicobar Ecology (SANE), c/o Tarangs, Middle Point, Port Blair, Andamans INDIA.

Wildlife Conservation International, Zoological Park, Bronx, NY 10460, USA Tel: 212 220 5100

Worldwide Fund for Nature, Panda House, Weyside Park, Godalming, Surrey GU 1XR, UK Tel: 0483 426 444

Worldwide Fund for Nature, Avenue du Mont Blanc, CH-1196 Gland, SWITZERLAND Tel: 22 364 9503

WWF-US, 1250 24th Street N.W., Washington, D.C. 20007, USA Tel: 202 293 4800

WWF-Australia, Level 17, St Martins Tower, 31 Market Street, GPO Box 528, Sydney, New South Wales 2001, AUSTRALIA

Tubbataha Foundation, 2172 Pasong Tamo Street, Makati, Metro Manila, PHILIPPINES

WWF-Hong Kong, The French Mission, 1 Battery Path, Central, HONG KONG

WWF-Indonesia Programme, Jl. Pela 3, Candaria Utara, Kebayoran Baru, P.O. Box 29 JKSKM, Jakarta Selatan 12001, INDONESIA Tel: 021 7203095

WWF-Japan, Nihonseimei Akabanebashi, Bldg 7F, 3-1-14 Shiba, Minato-ku, Tokyo 105, JAPAN

WWF-Malaysia, P.O. Box 10769, 50721 Kuala Lumpur, MALAYSIA

If you have information about organisations engaged in coral reef conservation that are not listed here, please send it to Greenpeace at 139 Townsend Street, San Francisco, CA 94107-1922, USA

## Further Reading

There is currently very little literature generally available on the subject of reef conservation, but if you would like to learn more about the biology of coral reefs and their inhabitants, the following titles may be helpful:

*Reader's Digest Book of the Great Barrier Reef*, Reader's Digest Services, Sydney, Australia, 1984

Sheppard, Dr Charles R.C., *A Natural History of the Coral Reef*, Blandford Books, London, UK, 1983

Stafford-Deitsch, Jeremy, *Reef: A Safari through the Coral World*, Headline, London, UK; Sierra Club, San Francisco, USA, 1991

Wells, Susan M. (ed.), *Coral Reefs of the World*, 3 vols, United Nations Environment Programme/International Union for Conservation of Nature and Natural Resources, Cambridge, UK, 1988.

Wood, Dr Elizabeth M. *Corals of the World: Biology and Field Guide*, T.F.H. Publications Inc., Ltd, Neptune City, New Jersey, US; Redhill, Surrey, UK, 1983.